# The Sinful Knights

# The Sinful Knights

*A Study of Middle English Penitential Romance*

ANDREA HOPKINS

CLARENDON PRESS · OXFORD
1990

Oxford University Press, Walton Street, Oxford OX2 6DP
Oxford New York Toronto
Delhi Bombay Calcutta Madras Karachi
Petaling Jaya Singapore Hong Kong Tokyo
Nairobi Dar es Salaam Cape Town
Melbourne Auckland
and associated companies in
Berlin Ibadan

Oxford is a trade mark of Oxford University Press

Published in the United States
by Oxford University Press, New York

British Library Cataloguing in Publication Data
Hopkins, Andrea
The sinful knights: a study of middle English
penitential romance.
1. Poetry in English, 1066–1400. Romances. Critical
studies I. Title
821.109
ISBN 0-19-811762-0

Library of Congress Cataloging in Publication Data
Hopkins, Andrea.
The sinful knights: a study of Middle English penitential romance
Andrea Hopkins.
p. cm.
Revision of the author's thesis.
Includes bibliographical references.
1. Romances, English—History and criticism. 2. Christian poetry,
English (Middle)—History and criticism. 3. Knights and knighthood
in literature. 4. Repentance in literature. 5. Penance in
literature. 6. Sin in literature. I. Title.
PR365.H57 1990
821'.1080382—dc20 90–6898
ISBN 0-19-811762-0

Typeset by Eta Services (Typesetters) Ltd, Beccles, Suffolk
Printed in Great Britain by
Courier International Ltd,
Tiptree, Essex

*For my mother and father
and for Rhys*

# Preface

THIS book is a detailed study of a small group of Middle English romances which concern themselves with the sin, repentance, and atonement of their heroes. Despite being few in number they form a coherent and distinctive group and have never previously been studied in association with each other. The main point to emerge from the study is that in this closely related group of texts, the kind of penance experienced by the heroes and its treatment by the authors reflects archaic traditions and views at variance with the contemporary teaching and practice of the Church, and that this surprising departure is largely determined by the nature of the kind of literature to which the poems belong—romance.

The four poems—*Guy of Warwick*, *Sir Ysumbras*, *Sir Gowther*, and *Roberd of Cisyle*—have suffered adverse reactions from scholars and critics over the years. The main reason for this is the widely held view that religious subjects are somehow inappropriate for romance, and that therefore poems which are clearly religious and didactic are not really romances but something else. This is a controversy with which every student of medieval romance must come to grips. This book explores the question of whether the writers of these four poems consciously exploited the literary conventions of a certain kind of 'romance' in order to teach their moral lessons, and if they did, how they went about it. It is therefore important to discuss the question of generic terms and definitions, and to reach some understanding of what a romance is, and the extent to which our poems are entitled to be considered as romances.

The statement that other idealisms than those of love and war were proper subjects for romance has important implications; detailed examination of the penitential romances illuminates other more important and frequently studied texts, particularly *Sir Gawain and the Green Knight*.

A.H.

# Acknowledgements

I would like to thank Denis Horgan and Douglas Gray for all their help and advice during the preparation of the thesis upon which this book is based, and subsequently while I was turning the thesis into a book. My thanks, too, to all my friends and colleagues who have given me support and encouragement, and especially to Rhys Lewis.

# Contents

NOTE ON REFERENCES                             x

1. Introduction                                 1

2. Penance: A Brief History                    32

3. *Guy of Warwick*                            70

4. *Sir Ysumbras*                             119

5. *Sir Gowther*                              144

6. *Roberd of Cisyle*                         179

7. Conclusion                                 196

APPENDIX A                                    200

APPENDIX B                                    219

APPENDIX C                                    223

BIBLIOGRAPHY                                  226

INDEX                                         243

# Note on References

FOR ease and speed in reading I have translated all quotations from their original Latin, and given other people's translations of quotations originally written in Greek. All references to Latin texts of the Church Fathers are to Abbé Migne's *Patrologiae cursus completus series latinus*, and will be signified by *PL* followed by the volume and column number of the text referred to. One or two Latin texts are to be found in the *Patrologiae cursus completus series graecus*, and these will be signified by *PG* followed by the volume and column number of the text referred to.

All references to Councils are to Giovanni Domenico Mansi, *Sacrorum conciliorum*, 1–13 (Florence, 1759–67); 14 (Venice, 1769) and will be signified by Mansi followed by the volume and column number.

Quotations from the Bible are taken from the Vulgate.

The following standard abbreviations are used throughout the book:

| | |
|---|---|
| *AUMLA* | *Journal of the Australasian Universities Modern Language and Literature Association* |
| EETS | Early English Text Society |
| ES | extra series |
| *JEGP* | *Journal of English and Germanic Philology* |
| NS | new series |
| OS | old series |
| *PMLA* | *Publications of the Modern Language Association of America* |
| SATF | Société des Anciens Textes Français |

# I

# Introduction

## i. The Idea of Romance

If anyone were asked, today, to say what they thought was the meaning of the word 'romance', they would probably reply that it meant the intimate, passionate relationship between a woman and a man. After a little thought, they might add that it summed up the essence of that inexpressible yearning which sometimes overtakes us for life to be simpler and more beautiful, our feelings to be more sincere and profound, our motives to be clearer and more admirable, our actions more significant and satisfying. In general terms, the first of these two ideas is probably the most dominant in modern consciousness, but the second—that of escape from the confusing and belittling humdrum of modern life—is really the more important concept. Love is only a subsection of the second idea; for love is just one of many ways of heightening experience, of adding glamour and intensity to life. These two dominant semantic impulses, love and wish-fulfilment, have collected a large group of associated meanings and usages, from *OED* I.1, 'the vernacular language of France, as opposed to Latin', to 5b, 'a love affair', or 6, 'an extravagant fiction'.

In terms of literature, 'romance' also has many meanings. In a modern bookshop the shelves labelled 'romance' are full of love stories, enlivened perhaps by a foreign setting or even a dangerous adventure; the designation 'romance' is used to distinguish these books from other perceived types of popular fiction, such as horror, crime, or science fiction. At the same time it is clear to anyone who has read medieval romances that their true modern equivalent is not a Mills and Boon novelette, but the *Star Wars* films.

John Stevens has listed some of the many kinds of romances:

The romantic *genres* [comprise] various types of medieval romance; the

I

Italianate Elizabethan romance; the heroic play of the Restoration period; the Gothic novel; the horror film; science fiction.[1]

To this list we could add early Greek romance, the last plays of Shakespeare, the works of the Romantic poets, as well as the more and less reputable productions of the modern romantic novelist. In terms of form and content and style these works are all quite different—how can they all be romances? Clearly 'romance' cannot be defined in terms of a literary genre—the field is too broad, and the definition would have to encompass too many different sub-species. No definition in terms of form will yield satisfactory results. Instead, 'romance' expresses something more profound—a way of looking at life, a particular perspective on human experience. It can then be seen to be a 'mode', which is so fundamental as to have been present more or less throughout the history of literary expression, and which re-emerges in different ages in new forms.

It is often said that romance deals with 'experience liberated' from the prosaic fetters of verisimilitude. Although there may be realistic elements in a romance, it is generally speaking a non-realistic fiction, and its action takes place in a privileged world somewhere between the folk-tale, the fairy story, and the novel. Romances tell stories which typically examine the conduct of their characters in relation to an ideal, and very often in doing so acknowledge the imperfections of contemporary reality. They are characteristically preoccupied with particular idealisms: most often 'the idealised sexual relationship we call romantic love' and 'the idealised integrity which we call honour'.[2]

Medieval romances, in common with other products of the romance mode, deal with the deepest human concerns—the growth to maturity, the testing of virtue by adventure, courage, fear, sorrow, anger, loyalty, love. They do not attempt an original or consistently realistic representation of experience, but evoke universally recognizable truths by the constant recombination of familiar motifs and language. They have been aptly described as 'poised between the mythic and the mimetic'.[3] R. W. Southern, in the final chapter of his great study *The Making of the Middle Ages*,

---

[1] John Stevens, *Medieval Romance: Themes and Approaches* (London, 1973), p. 16.
[2] Stevens, *Medieval Romance*, p. 21.
[3] W. R. J. Barron, *English Medieval Romance* (London, 1987), p. 6.

discusses the romances of Chrétien de Troyes. Chrétien's knights, he says, are engaged in a quest for 'adventures of the heart':

> Since he is writing stories and not a treatise, he does not aim at any systematic doctrine; yet a systematic treatise could be written from his stories. It would distinguish three stages in the quest. The first is the life of the court, where men and women entertain each other . . . without any serious wounds being given or received. Then there is the stage of lonely peril, grief and exertion in which the heart feels the wounds of love without attaining assured possession of its object. Beyond this there is a third stage, always in the future, in which the heart and its object are perfectly joined in an unbreakable union. It was with the second stage that Chrétien's stories were chiefly concerned: the stage of journeying, seeking and suffering.[4]

If references to love as the object of the quest and the placing of the third 'stage' in the future were omitted, this statement would become profoundly descriptive of romance in general, and medieval romance in particular. The object of the quest is not necessarily 'love' and in a sense is not relevant, so long as it is not ignoble. It is the period of exile, of suffering and isolation, which the hero must undergo in striving to attain his goal, to embody the ideal, which strikes the crucial note and expresses the essence of the romance spirit. W. R. J. Barron agrees:

> At the heart of the romance mode in all its manifestations certain values remain constant . . . they find expression through the same conventional motifs: the mysterious challenge or summons to a mission; the lonely journey through hostile territory; the first sight of the beloved; the single combat against overwhelming odds or a monstrous opponent. The conventions may be variously disguised, particularly in an age when the mimetic mode is dominant, but the power of their conventional nature can be felt through the trappings of realism. They may be marshalled in a variety of ways, but the essential formal medium is always adventure. However the incidents are related . . . the underlying structure is always a quest.[5]

In the light of these remarks, it is easy to see how very much of a romance the *Star Wars* trilogy is: its heroes and heroine are engaged in a quest to restore freedom to their world and to rid it of unjust, oppressive tyrants. In addition, the young untried hero

---

[4] R. W. Southern, *The Making of the Middle Ages* (London, 1953), p. 245.
[5] Barron, *English Medieval Romance*, pp. 4, 5.

Luke Skywalker receives a mysterious summons to leave the obscurity of his uncle's farm and attain the high wisdom and skill of a Jedi Knight. To do this he must prove himself by many difficult tests, including lonely journeys through hostile territories and single combats against opponents of superhuman strength. His dedication to the Jedi ideal, his abhorrence of the cruelty and injustice perpetrated by the evil Empire, and, above all, his love and loyalty to his friends, sustain him; but he and the Rebel Alliance are not successful until all three protagonists have suffered loss, sorrow, and hardship. Finally they attain their goals and experience a happy resolution. One could take the analogy even further and compare the films with a certain type of medieval romance. The *Star Wars* films are very popular, and also very long. The warrior élite call themselves 'Knights', there are many monstrous beasts, and there is much use of magic.

The time has come, having established an idea of the nature of the romance mode, to examine its manifestations first in the Middle Ages, and then in thirteenth- and fourteenth-century England.

The confusing multiplicity of possible applications for the word 'romance' has its origin in the semantic history of the word, which began its long life as a general term for the vernacular languages used in the western provinces of the Roman Empire, to distinguish them from their parent, the official Latin. *Romanz* then came to mean successively: writings translated from Latin into those vernaculars, all vernacular writings, particular kinds of vernacular writings dealing with aristocratic interests, courtly fiction, the social values expressed in such fiction, and so on. The fiction, and the values it expressed, took many forms as it was addressed to many different audiences, and the resulting latitude among what we now call Medieval Romances has caused great trouble to generations of scholars attempting to establish a formal definition of a genre of Medieval Romance. Even by the later Middle Ages the term 'romance' was not used in a precise, definitive way, as was demonstrated by Reinald Hoops in 1929.[6] Hoops made a list of twenty-four Middle English writings which refer to themselves as romances. These were: *Beues of Hamtoun, Arthour and Merlin,*

---

[6] Reinald Hoops, 'Der Begriff Romance in der mittelenglischen und fruhnen-englischen Literatur', *Anglistische Forschungen*, 68 (Heidelberg, 1929), 34–7.

*Richard Coer de Lion*, *Sir Perceval of Gales*, Minot's *Poems*, *Octovian*, *Alexander*, *Bruce*, *Myrour of Lewed Men*, *St Gregory*, *Sir Eglamour of Artois*, *Meditations on the Life and Passion of Christ*, *Laud Troy Book*, *Le Bone Florence of Rome*, *Roland and Otuel*, *Sir Gowther*, *The Sowdane of Babylone*, the *Romaunt of the Rose*, *Dyoclecyane*, *Sir Ysumbras*, *Torrent of Portyngale*, *The Romauns of Partenay*, *Partenope of Blois*, and *Lancelot of the Laik*. Only sixteen of these twenty-four works are now classified as romances,[7] and of the remaining eight, most are not only not romances, but demonstrably something else—a saint's life, an allegory, a Passion poem, a chronicle, and so on. This is not surprising; the medieval concept of fiction was itself by no means so clear-cut, or so important as the modern one. A medieval writer did not usually make up his own story material, but inherited it from another, older source which might or might not have been recording the truth; and in any case the truth could be perceived on many levels. Few medieval histories offer a record of the sober, literal truth; the truth they present is to be sought at other textual levels. We should not be surprised, then, that medieval literary genres, where they exist, should not be hard and distinctive, but a little blurred round the edges.

In view of this, it is perhaps more worthy of note that of the list cited above, sixteen works *are* still considered to be romances—an overwhelming majority. It is clear that the concept of romance as a genre, with a set of recognizable literary conventions, did exist; medieval writers knew what it was, even if they did not consistently call it romance. As pointed out by John Finlayson, Chaucer's famous parody of a metrical romance, *Sir Thopas*, offers important evidence of what a medieval reader recognized as formal characteristics of romance:

To be effective, or even exist, parody must depend on the audience's recognition of the standard elements of a convention. Chaucer's parody of the romance depends on the audience's recognition of the standard pattern of romance, 'the knight rides forth to seek adventure' and of certain ubiquitous 'characteristics', such as the love motif, the encounter with the supernatural, and the elaborate *descriptio personae*.[8]

[7] J. Burke Severs, *A Manual of Writings in Middle English, 1050–1500* (New Haven, 1967), I (Romances), 13–16.
[8] John Finlayson, 'Definitions of Middle English Romance', *Chaucer Review*, 15 (1980/1), 44–63, 168–81; quotation from p. 47.

In modern anthologies and, more significantly, in medieval compilations, it is recognized that romances are of various kinds, and they are grouped together accordingly. The groupings may be by subject-matter, as suggested by Severs[9]—'Matter of England', 'Matter of France', 'Matter of Troy', and so on—or, as suggested by Mehl, by length and tale-type.[10] Many romances are short enough to be read aloud at one sitting. A significant number, however, are very long indeed, covering not just one adventure or one series of adventures, but the hero's whole life. These romances end with the hero's death and are justifiably distinguished by Mehl from those which finish when the hero is just settling down to live happily ever after.

One of the ways in which people have attempted to pin down the definition of Medieval Romance is to contrast it with other kinds of literature, most usually with 'epic' literature.[11] More recently it has been appreciated that the term 'epic' is not itself susceptible of hard and fast definition; but a general comparison of the types of story most frequently employed in each body of poems, the nature of characterization, and the function of the narrative elements does yield some interesting and worthwhile results. Some critics have discussed this question exclusively with reference to French *chansons de geste*; others, such as Carl Schmidt and Nicolas Jacobs, have broadened the terms of reference, and suggested that 'it is in the genre of tragedy that we should seek the complementary form and illuminating antithesis to romance'.[12] In essence, the valuable distinctions which emerge from this comparison are as follows.

In medieval epic poetry, the hero is typically seen primarily as a member of his society, performing a role essentially related to the advancement or protection of that society. His system of values is

[9] Severs, *Manual, passim.*

[10] Dieter Mehl, *Middle English Romances of the Thirteenth and Fourteenth Centuries* (London, 1968).

[11] What follows are general statements on the nature of epic and romances drawn from a number of important and often-quoted critical works: Erich Auerbach, *Mimesis*, trans. Willard R. Trask (Princeton 1953), chap. 6; W. P. Ker, *Epic and Romance*, 2nd edn. (London, 1908); Dorothy Everett, 'The Characterization of the English Metrical Romances', in *Essays on Middle English Literature* (Oxford, 1955), pp. 6–10; Derek Pearsall, 'The Development of Middle English Romance', *Medieval Studies*, 27 (1965), 91–116; A. V. C. Schmidt and Nicolas Jacobs, *Medieval English Romances* (2 vols.; London, 1980), 1. 1–7, 2. 20–39; Finlayson, 'Definitions', *passim.*

[12] Schmidt and Jacobs, *Medieval English Romances*, 1. 6.

6

based on a communal bond of loyalty—to his peers, to his country, to his God, and overwhelmingly, to his lord. This loyalty finds expression in his tremendous courage and prowess in combat; combat almost always undertaken on behalf of his lord or society. The values of epic relate to war, that is, to the real function of the warrior class; the epic hero may often be found fighting to the death against overwhelming odds. He proves his superior qualities not necessarily by triumphing over his enemies, but in embracing a glorious death. Epic writing often displays an attitude towards experience of a deeply fatalistic kind, which bears comparison with classical stoicism. Key words relating to epic are 'feudal', 'military', 'heroic', 'tragic'. Epic poems in the Middle Ages inherit from their classical antecedents that sense of the hero–warrior consenting to his fate. There is no sense of going on, of profiting by experience; loyalty is inexorable, impersonal, and absolute unto death.

In romance, on the other hand, the hero is essentially solitary, and typically does not engage in combat with an enemy for the purpose of protecting his society and lord, so much as seek adventure with a view to proving himself. The ethos of romance, while obviously related to the functions of the warrior élite, is more idealized, self-contained, and absolute. The term 'vassalage', common in the *chansons de geste*, is taken over by 'corteisie'. New values, such as 'refinement of the laws of combat, courteous social intercourse and the service of women',[13] regulate the hero's attitude and behaviour.

The adventures encountered by the romance hero are designed to 'call forth the very essence of the knight's ideal manhood'.[14] If the hero is to embody the values of chivalry properly, however, he must successfully overcome his opponent in the end. When he does triumph, he may fall short of perfection in some subtle way; or, as often happens, he may at first fail to achieve his goal and then learn from his mistakes.

Further, while the epic world is one of military comradeship in which there is small place for women and for love, in romance, love (i.e. the proper practice of love as codified by Andreas Capellanus) is an important motivation. The knight who wants to prove himself is often proving himself worthy of his lady's love. The

[13] Auerbach, *Mimesis*, p. 134.
[14] Auerbach, *Mimesis*, p. 135.

knight is as a consequence of this solitary; he seeks to be the Best, and is in competition with other knights. He does not usually experience the great comradeships of the epic warrior-hero.

This is to state the extremes. There are of course epic poems in which the heroes do not get killed in the end, and romances in which the hero has close friends and fights to save his society. Besides, there are as many difficulties in creating a rigid definition of epic as a genre, as there are in doing the same thing for romance. It is often hard to distinguish where the one ends and the other begins; but in most cases it is clear that the two are different and represent different ways of looking at and describing experience.

Carl Schmidt and Nicolas Jacobs open the introduction to their anthology of Middle English romances with the bold and positive statement: 'The medieval English romances are stories told in verse which deal with the adventures of noble men and women *and which end happily*' (my italics).[15] It is their contention that romance is a fundamentally comic literary genre, as opposed to epic, which is a tragic one:

If the structure of a romance is comic, it is comedy in Dante's sense, and the hero generally has to go through a purgatory of 'loneliness and pain' before reaching the heaven of true (earthly) happiness . . . The suffering in a romance normally tests the temper of the hero's spirit, the capacity to face and overcome his weaknesses.[16]

As a statement about the nature of romance, this is exciting and illuminating. Schmidt and Jacobs rightly point out that because of the inherent tendency of romance heroes to be tested in some way to see if they truly exemplify the chivalric ideal, romance has an innate quality of 'flexibility': for 'whilst perfection can be lost, shame can be redeemed . . . It is because the evil in the hero's soul is capable of being purged that his story inevitably ends happily.'[17] This remark, which attempts to state something central to the concept of romance generally in terms of Christian morality, merits further exploration. It is obviously applicable to a great number of romance poems, particularly to the shorter examples. However, there are a significant number of poems which have always been called romances, but which do not end happily, and several whose endings are deeply ambivalent.

[15] Schmidt and Jacobs, *Medieval English Romances*, 1. 1.
[16] Schmidt and Jacobs, *Medieval English Romances*, 1. 6.
[17] Schmidt and Jacobs, *Medieval English Romances*, 1. 6.

Schmidt and Jacobs support their definition of romance with a detailed discussion of the stanzaic *Morte Arthur*, which according to them is a romance, and the alliterative *Morte Arthure*, which is not. Most commentators agree that the alliterative *Morte* is less 'romance-like' because of its close kinship to epic poetry. Its structure is tragic, its ethos communal, feudal, military. The stanzaic *Morte*, as Schmidt and Jacobs point out, can be said to end happily, though 'the happiness won by its hero and heroine is . . . singular; renunciation of erotic fulfilment in recognition of their responsibility for evil'.[18] The happiness achieved by the hero of *Guy of Warwick* at the end of his story is of a similar, unworldly nature, but is equally capable of being recognized as a good, as representing fulfilment of a deeply personal nature to the character, though not constituting happiness in the conventional, material sense.

However, this cannot be said to be the case with all the versions of the fall of the Round Table. There is no such sense of redemption and consolation at the end of Malory's *Morte Darthur*, for example, in which, though it tells substantially the same sequence of events as the stanzaic *Morte*,[19] the painful sense of waste and loss at the ruin of the Fellowship is too bitter to be sweetened by the saintly end of Lancelot. Thus the statement that romances are necessarily comic and must end in redemption and not in despair leads to some fine hair-splitting over the treatment accorded to the various versions of the *Mort Artu*. A group of poems so important and so central to the tradition cannot be excluded from the body of romance; therefore each author's handling of his material must be subjected to the most sensitive scrutiny, for certainly the story itself is inclined to be tragic rather than comic, as are the stories of Sir Tristram, Alexander, Roland, and the Siege of Troy, all of which have been the subjects of medieval romances.

On the other hand, the statement that romances are fundamentally comic is clearly true of a great number of other romances, particularly shorter poems, which are not based on classical stories or epic poems, and which do not end in the death of the hero. Indeed,

---

[18] Schmidt and Jacobs, *Medieval English Romances*, I. 6.

[19] That Malory made use of a version of this Middle English romance, sometimes preferring it where it differs from his main source the *Mort Artu*, is shown by Eugene Vinaver's analysis in *The Works of Sir Thomas Malory*, 2nd edn. (3 vols.; Oxford, 1967), 3. 1615–25, 1628–63.

it is apparent from many of these shorter poems that an author could go to great lengths to compel his story to end happily, making free use of miraculous events and improbable coincidences, as for example in *Sir Ysumbras*, where the hero not only regains his lost wife and family, but with divine aid conquers an entire pagan country, ending up even richer and more powerful than he was at the start of the poem.

Rather than rejecting the useful statement that romance is a comic form, or denying that poems which do not end happily are romances, or trying to argue that some poems which are not apparently comic in structure or treatment are so really, it seems sensible to propose that there are two kinds of romances, and that these can generally be distinguished from each other by the nature of the material on which they are based, or the treatment of that material. One kind tends to be tragic, is usually long, and is based on material from either pagan, classical stories or from more recent Dark Age history and epic. The other kind is comic, usually short, and is based on later material.[20] Both should be classed as romances because they are concerned with adventure and chivalry, the operation of knightly qualities, and both exhibit the characteristic style and narrative techniques of romance; but in one, learning and progress and change take place, while in the other, destiny is fulfilled. These statements are offered as general guidelines rather than hard and fast rules, for of course there are exceptions; for example, *Sir Orfeo*, a poem based on a tragic classical story which has been radically altered to make a short, comic romance.

At any rate, it can be said that one kind of romance is modern in attitude, and the other antique. It is possible to relate the 'modern' romance to the developments in the intellectual climate which took place during the twelfth century (at the same time as the emergence of romance in France as the dominant literary mode), which found perhaps their most influential and important expression in the writings of St Bernard of Clairvaux. Along with a more personal, intimate view of the individual's relationship with his Creator, and of God's concern and involvement with the individual's salvation, went a new awareness that fate was not inexorable, that great hardship and suffering undertaken in co-operation with divine grace could and should be rewarded.

[20] There are of course exceptions, such as *Apollonius of Tyre* or *Floris and Blancheflur*, which are comic and based on ancient Greek romances.

Stories such as the miracles of the Virgin became popular, in which the crucial intervention of divine grace would save the deserving; stories of all kinds would demonstrate the actions of a just and caring God. In classical stories, a man's fault leads to his downfall. There is no redemption; death is inevitable and almost a relief. For the Christian, however, the whole point of faith is that sins *can* be forgiven, men's characters *can* be reformed, and the most damning faults can be redeemed. The great pre-Christian tragedy was the irredeemable loss of Paradise; but the succeeding generations overturned this with a promise of infinite potential for regaining it. God saves. There can always be a happy ending; providing that it is earned. In the case of romances which are based on tragic, classical stories or doom-laden epics, the absence of modern Christian 'comic' motivation is inherited from the material. Few romance authors were prepared to do such violence to their material as the creator of *Sir Orfeo*.

However, it is with the kind of romance which we have characterized as 'modern' and 'comic' that this book is concerned. For this comic romance there is a great archetypal story. Derek Pearsall points out that 'the central tradition of Middle English romance is embodied from 1340 onwards in a series of romances with a marked unity of plot material'.[21] The six poems which he names (*Octavian*, *Athelston*, *Sir Ysumbras*, *Sir Eglamour*, *Torrent of Portygale*, *Sir Triamour*) are remarkably similar in some respects, but there are many more besides which proceed by testing the virtue of their hero in a story of 'trial, constancy and reward'.

Middle English romances bear close resemblances to, and are often translations of, Anglo-Norman romances, and a recent study has demonstrated that these developed in England in a distinct and individual way, owing less to the great mainstream tradition of the French romances than to the emergent sense of nationality in England during the thirteenth century.[22] It has often been noticed that these 'insular romances' are markedly more pious than their Continental counterparts, because they have incorporated story motifs and Christian ideals of behaviour from saints' lives and other devotional literature. We shall now move on to consider the claim made by many scholars that 'exemplary romances' such as

[21] Pearsall, 'Development of Romance', p. 92.
[22] Susan Crane, *Insular Romance* (London, 1986).

*Guy of Warwick*, *Sir Ysumbras*, *Sir Gowther*, and *Roberd of Cisyle* ought to be considered as a separate genre from less obviously pious romances, and assessed as a hybrid of romance and hagiography which is generically distinct from either.

## ii. 'Secular Hagiography'?

In recent years scholars have felt an increasing dissatisfaction with the critical terminology available for classifying and discussing the large group of poems known as Middle English Romances, and in particular have expressed a desire to consider religious poems as a separate group. Many religious romances, it has been pointed out, have a strong affinity with saints' lives, and some commentators have felt that they 'occupy a position exactly in the middle between these two genres'.[23] Dieter Mehl calls such poems 'homiletic romances'. Hanspeter Schelp calls them 'exemplary romances', Maldwyn Mills 'edifying romances', Fr. Delehaye *'romans hagiographiques'*, and Ojars Kratins suggests the term 'secular hagiography', making an eloquent plea for more accurate and descriptive terminology:

... labelling the work with one or the other term becomes a matter of making a statement about the area of meaning of the work and about the techniques with which this meaning is conveyed. In medieval studies, the latitude in application of the term *romance*, and its consequent diminishing usefulness for descriptive purposes might have been felt more keenly if it were not for the assumption that the tracing of the sources of a given work has contributed the most significant part to its understanding ... The few writers who have ventured to deal with the whole body of the so-called romances and to make judgements on their respective merits have ignored the possibility that, without finer and more specific terminological distinctions, they may be mistaken about some of the ugly ducklings.[24]

[23] Mehl, *Romances*, p. 121.

[24] Ojars Kratins, 'The Middle English *Amis and Amiloun*: Chivalric Romance or Secular Hagiography?', *PMLA* 81 (1966), 347–54; quotation from p. 347. See also Mehl, chap. 5, 'Homiletic Romances' (Mehl includes in this category *The King of Tars*, *Emaré*, *Le Bone Florence of Rome*, *Athelston*, *The Sege of Melayne*, and *Chevalere Assigne*, but not *Guy of Warwick*, which he classifies as a 'Novel in Verse'); Hanspeter Schelp, *Exemplarische Romanzen im Mittelenglischen* (Gottingen, 1967) (Schelp covers *Guy of Warwick*, *Sir Ysumbras*, *Sir Gowther*, *Roberd of Cisyle*, *Havelok the Dane*, *Sir Cleges*, *Emaré*, *Le Bone Florence of Rome*, *Alexander*, *Morte Arthure*, *Siege of Thebes*, and the Troy romances); Maldwyn Mills,

The same points are made by other scholars, most of whom feel that the terms of reference for these religious, didactic poems ought to be different from those used to discuss other romances, because 'by lumping romances and secular legends together we can get only a distorted view of what a romance is . . . and we set up a standard against which the didactic works inevitably seem "inferior"'.[25] The critical discourse on medieval romances has for fifty years been bedevilled by the problem of definition. In the evolving struggle to define 'Middle English Romance' as a generic term, many have felt that religious romances cloud the question, obscure the sought-after vision, and are too different from proper 'romance' to be taken into account.

In view of the fact that so many Middle English romances are distinctly religious and didactic, it is interesting that it is so difficult to escape from the idea that romances were written for the sole purpose of entertainment of a more or less refined sort. It is assumed that their stories of knights and ladies, love and adventure, necessarily relate to chivalry in a limited, secular way. This is perhaps a consequence of seeing romances as the secular flip-side of medieval literature, so that sophisticated, courtly romances are perceived as the aristocratic, secular equivalent of complex, intellectually demanding devotional literature, and popular romances full of fabulous beasts and marvellous events are perceived as the secular equivalent of saints' lives, sermon exempla, and miracles of the Virgin.

An interesting aspect of most critical discussions of romance has been the way in which scholars, while complaining of the confusion caused by the word and pleading for more accurate and distinctive terminology, have frustrated their own ends. The argument generally proceeds in this way: it is acknowledged that romances should not be judged by one fixed standard, because

Six Middle English Romances (London, 1973), p. vii; Fr. Hippolyte Delehaye, The Legends of the Saints, trans. V. M. Crawford, ed. R. J. Schoeck (London, 1961), p. 4.

[25] Diana T. Childress, 'Between Romance and Legend: "Secular Hagiography" in Middle English Literature', Philological Quarterly, 57 (1978), 311–22. See also Kathryn Hume, 'Structure and Perspective: Romance and Hagiographic Features in the Amicus and Amelius Story', JEGP, 69 (1970), 89–107; Margaret Hurley, 'Saints' Lives and Romance Again: Secularization of Structure and Motif', Genre, 8 (1975), 60–73; Laurel Braswell, 'Sir Isumbras and the Legend of St Eustace', Medieval Studies, 27 (1965), 128–51; J. A. W. Bennett, Middle English Literature, ed. and compl. D. Gray (Oxford, 1986), chap. 5, 'Romances', pp. 121–201; Lee C. Ramsey, Chivalric Romances: Popular Literature in Medieval England (Bloomington, 1983), pp. 45–68, 216–23.

those which differ widely in style or length or subject-matter will be found wanting. There are in fact different kinds of romance, and each must be appreciated in its own way. But there must be, it is felt, a sense in which these different kinds of romances are all romances. At this point the writer suggests his own definition of romance, and is compelled to exclude a more or less sizeable portion of the works currently so called because they do not fit the proposed definition. This would be quite acceptable, save that no two scholars exclude the same poems. It is probably fair to say, however, that the one group of poems most often attacked by critics for not being proper romances is the homiletic/didactic/edifying group.

A case in point is the long article by John Finlayson called 'Definitions of Middle English Romance', one of the most thorough and provocative exercises of the kind.[26] Finlayson shows admirable clarity and logic when discussing the confusions created by his predecessors in trying to establish a definition, and promises a different approach:

> if we take certain 'characterising' elements, not as rigid essentials, but rather as indicators of the precise nature of the particular artifact, then it becomes evident that within the basic genre there are specific types ... Romance is not a monolithic genre, but in its more sophisticated practitioners a mode which we can often characterise by isolation of elements such as the concept of the hero, the treatment of the marvellous, of time, of place, the nature and function of adventure, and the episodic nature of the structure.[27]

In practice, this means that poems based on French *chansons de geste* cannot be included within the boundaries of Professor Finlayson's genre, on the grounds that they are not romantic but epic;[28] he also dismisses religious poems because they 'speciously employ *romance* elements in a way which has got nothing to do with the essence of *romance*'.[29] It must be observed at this point that this definition, which was not going to characterize romance by rigid essentials, has with little effort discarded about half the current canon.

Professor Finlayson's uneasiness about religious poems is

---

[26] Finlayson, 'Definitions', pp. 44–63, 168–81.
[27] Finlayson, 'Definitions', p. 170.
[28] Finlayson, 'Definitions', pp. 51–6.
[29] Finlayson, 'Definitions', p. 174.

echoed by others. It is really a return to the old assumption that Medieval Romance constitutes a genre perfectly represented by the *roman courtois* and that works which vary from that norm are deviant; if they are not as a consequence to be stigmatized as inferior, they must be classified as something else, or they will suffer by comparison. A person whose idea of a dog was a Great Dane would not think very much of a Chihuahua. Even if he was sensitive to the merits of the Chihuahua he might claim, influenced in spite of himself by the admirers of Great Danes, that the Chihuahua was not a dog at all, but a cross between a dog and a cat, or even a cat which had aped some of the characteristics of a dog, and that it was necessary to acknowledge this distinction before being able to appreciate the Chihuahua's qualities. Just so with religious romances. Most frequently they are supposed to be a cross between a saint's life and a romance, or an exemplum and a romance. Finlayson sees religious romances as impostors. He distinguishes between two types of religious romance: one in which the world of chivalry is taken up and imaginatively used to explore religious questions—he cites the Grail romances as examples—and another in which a religious exemplum is cursorily rewritten with the hero as a knight and one or two of the stylistic features of a romance in order to cash in on romance's popularity. This kind, which 'violate, rather than adapt' the romance mode, are for the most part the homiletic romances:

Clearly the impulse which generates the Grail romances is generally the same as that of the homiletic romances, but the results are very different: in one religious truth is reached *through* the quest, through the imaginative world of romance; in the other, certain events have a romance dress imposed on them, and the truths proposed are equally imposed. That is, certain characteristics of romance are added to a story which is told primarily for its moral significance.[30]

Finlayson is here justly discriminating against bad writing; the distinction he makes is, as he has already pointed out, 'one of quality and not of kind'.[31] It is clearly a valid critical procedure to judge an individual author's success or failure to transmute base, 'unromantic' material into the gold of true romance. Some 'homiletic romances' are more successful than others. *Guy of Warwick*, for

[30] Finlayson, 'Definitions', p. 175.
[31] Finlayson, 'Definitions', p. 175.

example, which is loosely based on a saint's life (among other things), reaches a religious truth through the quest and makes very thorough imaginative use of the world of romance. *Sir Ysumbras*, which is closely based on a saint's life, is artistically successful in achieving the same goals. On the other hand, *Roberd of Cisyle* is a less thoroughly and consistently worked example of the technique, and this is reflected as much in its classification in medieval manuscripts as in modern critical debate.[32]

But Professor Finlayson can't have it both ways. If the impulse which generates the Grail romances is generally the same as that of the homiletic romances, then he cannot also claim that a story which is told primarily for its moral significance cannot be successfully made into a romance. If he is saying that the Grail romances are bona fide romances because they are told not for their moral significance, but for some other, more acceptable reason, then he is making a distinction of kind and not of quality.

Finlayson himself cites the poem *Amis and Amiloun* as an example of the literary usurpation of the homiletic romances. He does not wish to call this poem a romance because, he says, the romance elements which are present in it 'are in no way central to the "Truth" which is proposed':

Amiloun's victory may demonstrate his prowess, but it is completely irrelevant to any concept of his character; he is neither proving nor examining himself or any chivalric ethic in his martial feat, but is merely providing a way out of a complicated physical problem . . . while the author reproduces the stereotyped elements of *romance*, their function and meaning are absent . . . it is trial by ordeal, not adventure, and its end is the granting of grace, not the achievement of self-knowledge . . . A miraculous story, in other words, does not become a *romance* simply by calling the characters knights and describing an individual combat.[33]

Indeed not. For Professor Finlayson, and for others, romance typically offers an extended exposition of, and sometimes a critique of, the ideal of chivalry as embodied in the hero of the poem. This is the 'function' he refers to in his article. The ideal itself may vary from one poem to another in infinitesimal or in obvious ways, but it is essential that the ideal should be there, and that the characters are presented as acting in relation to it. In *Amis and Amiloun*, he is accordingly disturbed by the chivalric persona

[32] See Appendix B, below.
[33] Finlayson, 'Definitions', p. 176.

16

of the poem's hero: 'The knightliness of Amiloun is not the subject, and it is in no way relevant to the conclusion.'[34] He sees the poem as having a hagiographic structure and functioning solely as an exemplum; the disasters which overtake the hero he interprets as being 'partly as a punishment for transgression, partly as a test of faith'.

*Amis and Amiloun* has not been included in the group of romances which are the main subject of this book, because in my opinion, its heroes do not sin and therefore perform no penance.[35] Professor Finlayson and I agree that the poem's plot structure is of the 'virtue tested and rewarded' type. The afflictions which befall the heroes are clearly intended to be regarded as a test; and if they are a test of anything, it is of the strength of Amiloun's love for his friend, and vice versa. In other words, the particular aspect of the heroic character under scrutiny in the poem is the quality of friendship, the love and loyalty between knights—a legitimate subject for a romance. From the earliest extant version of the story[36] it is the extraordinary nature of the trust and love shown to each other by the friends which is the main point of the narrative. It is seen as overwhelmingly their first priority, the most important thing in their lives.

Chivalrous attitudes and behaviour are central to the action and meaning of the poem. Amis would not be in the position of having to uphold the wrong side in a duel if he had not felt obliged to protect Belisaunt's honour, and much is made of the fact that he places a naked sword between himself and Amiloun's wife each night as he takes his friend's place in bed. Nor is the individual combat—present in the story from its earliest telling—the only romance element in the poem.[37] The friendship between the two

---

[34] Finlayson, 'Definitions', p. 176.

[35] See Kathryn Hume, '*Amis and Amiloun* and the Aesthetics of Middle English Romance', *Studies in Philology*, 70 (1973), 19–41 and Saul N. Brody, *Disease of the Soul* (London, 1974), pp. 165, 166 for agreement with Finlayson's assessment; however, Kratins, op. cit. and Susan Crane, 'Insular Tradition in the Story of *Amis and Amiloun*', *Neophilologus*, 67 (1983), 611–22 show that this reading is based on a misunderstanding of the poem.

[36] Part of a Latin epistle in verse by Radulphus Tortarius, addressed to his friend Bernard, eulogizing friendship. A translation of this poem appears in Appendix A of Mac-Edward Leach's edition of *Amis and Amiloun*, EETS, os, 203 (London, 1937). Leach gives the date of the epistle as *c*.1090.

[37] On the contrary, the importance attached to the account of the single combat appears to decrease in the successive romance versions of the story. In Radulphus's poem the single combat occupies about one-third of the whole. In *Amis e Amilun* it takes up 84 out of 1,250 lines; in *Amis and Amiloun* 72 out of 2,508.

knights is given a more 'knightly' tone than in other versions of the tale by constructing around it an edifice of formal, ritual oath-taking such as a knight must make in the dubbing ceremony, and which is echoed and alluded to throughout the poem. To say that Amiloun's victory over the envious steward does nothing more than demonstrate his prowess and is otherwise irrelevant to his character shows insensitivity to the poem's structure and lesson. The point of the judicial combat in *Amis and Amiloun*, as in no other version of the story, is that Amiloun undertakes it to save his friend's life, and the lives of Belisaunt and her mother, at enormous personal risk to himself—not so much risk, in fact, as absolute certainty that as a direct result of the deed he will be visited with appalling suffering. Nevertheless he continues, disregarding his own danger.

If the chivalric nature of the central character must bear a crucial relation to the meaning of the poem, then *Amis and Amiloun* can be properly classified as a romance. The lesson of the poem is specifically concerned with what constitutes proper knightly behaviour. Just as Chrétien's knights struggle to place in a true perspective their desire for prowess and their desire to please their ladies, and as the Grail romances show that purely secular chivalry is not enough, so *Amis and Amiloun* makes the statement—perfectly allowable, even if you don't happen to agree with it—that fidelity to your sworn friend and your sworn oath is *the* most important knightly quality; this is the virtue which is tested, found true, and ultimately rewarded.

Finlayson's most important objection relates to the structure of the poem. He finds it unsatisfactory that it proceeds on a trial by ordeal, not adventure, and that 'its end is the granting of grace, not the achievement of self-knowledge'. It is of course rather in the nature of the 'virtue tested and rewarded' type of story that the hero does not undergo a great learning process; his character is simply confirmed as being virtuous. *Amis and Amiloun* is of course far from being alone in employing this type of plot.[38] But it is by no means a simple poem. Its construction is a very finely balanced pattern of imaged acts, events, characters, and motifs designed to explore the consequences of conflicting loyalties, of the choices made by the characters under the pressure of these loyalties, and less obviously, of different ways of interpreting events—Amiloun's

[38] See n. 11, above.

wife's way, which is (ultimately) wrong, and Amis's wife's way, which is right. The whole poem appears morally perverse until this paradox is perceived, presenting as it does one hero who tricks an ordeal, and another who murders his children. This paradox—of seeming wrong and being right—is one familiar in saints' lives, particularly the famous Life of Saint Alexis, but its subtleties are not unknown in the world of romance.

It is unusual for a romance to display so prominently a narrative strategy more characteristic of hagiography, but this feature alone should not disqualify the poem from being a romance. It does not, in fact, make a very satisfactory saint's life, as acknowledged by Leach.[39] The background and framework of moral reference is entirely secular; the story exists as a paradigm of perfect friendship between two good men, divinely tested and divinely approved. But Amis and Amiloun strive to be at one with each other, not with God.

No scholar of medieval romance would wish to assert, or to seem to assert, that chivalry, being the main subject of most medieval romances, ought not to include a religious dimension. A recent study has argued that although real medieval knighthood constantly eluded the Church's attempts to subdue and regulate it by relating its existence to largely ecclesiastical ends and by taking over its ceremonies, yet it was impossible for an individual knight to see himself and his function in entirely secular terms.[40] Piety and devotion are constantly encountered and referred to as essential qualities for a knight, as for any other member of medieval society; and this is reflected in romances. Yet there is frequent critical resistance to the idea that poems which have a strong religious motivation should be regarded as romances. A knight-hero can be pious, humble, and god-fearing as well as unbeatable in tournament and terrifying in battle; but if we encounter him in a story which demonstrates the necessity of these qualities to a knight, rather than the usual ones of courtesy, generosity, and so on, then it is not a romance—unless it happens to be the Grail story, in which case it is. This is a view with which the present study does not concur; we shall proceed on the premiss that a religious poem displaying features characteristic of romance is not a saint's life, or

---

[39] See Leach's introduction to his edition, pp. xix–xxvi.
[40] See Maurice Keen, *Chivalry* (New Haven and London, 1984), pp. 44–82.

a sermon exemplum, or a homily, or a religious treatise, but a religious romance.

## iii. The Penitential Romances

The four poems we are about to explore are religious romances. They all exhibit the 'comic' romance story pattern. An initial period of stability and prosperity is ended, usually by a moment of critical revelation, and the hero is suddenly cut off from all he has known and everyone he loves, and embarks on a period of 'journeying, seeking, and suffering' in solitude, in order to achieve something. In many Middle English romances this questing is brought to a successful conclusion in ways which suggest the operation of an active divine or poetic justice in rewarding the virtues of the protagonist. Our four poems display a significant variation of this sequence; instead of the hero's virtue being tested, found true, and rewarded, his sin is repented of, atoned for, and forgiven.

This story is worked out in each poem in very different ways; but in spite of their considerable individual differences, our four poems show some striking similarities. They share a distinctive common conception of the sinner/hero, of the way in which he becomes aware of his sin, and the ways in which he decides to atone for it. Particularly striking is the fact that all the heroes are unaware that they are sinning at the time they commit their sins. In the cases of Guy, Ysumbras, and Roberd, this ignorance corresponds closely to the Bernardine concept of the habitual sinner, who has become impervious to any sense of guilt because he is so hardened to the nature of his sins that he no longer sees them as such. In *Sir Gowther* the proposition of ignorance is carried to an extreme: Gowther is predisposed to evil because he is the son of a devil, and is psychopathically oblivious to the notion of right and wrong.

The way in which the heroes become aware of their sin is also analogous. It is sudden, it is traumatic, it is the result of an external stimulus. This is an element of these poems which clearly owes something to the influence of saints' lives and stories of conversion. This is plain in *Sir Ysumbras*, which borrows its scene of supernatural revelation of Ysumbras's sin directly from the scene of St Eustace's conversion to Christianity. In the case of *Sir Gowther*, it is the shock of being informed of his diabolical origin which leads to Gowther's recognition of his sin and the beginning of his repentance; the sight of the night sky ablaze with stars has a similar effect on *Guy of Warwick*.

In all cases, the result of this moment of critical revelation is a sudden and profound change of heart. The proud and callous sinner becomes the humble and heart-broken penitent. For Gowther, Ysumbras, and Guy, the penance they then undertake involves a long journey away from home, a penitential pilgrimage. In all cases it involves a loss of worldly privilege, even a loss of identity, albeit temporary and superficial. All four heroes spend time at a court incognito; in the cases of Guy, Ysumbras, and Roberd, it is their own court. When Guy and Ysumbras do this, their own wives do not recognize them; while Roberd's brothers the Pope and the Emperor of Germany fail to recognize him.

The way in which penance is undertaken by the heroes is also remarkable in that it bears little resemblance to the procedures of the Church which would have been familiar to readers of romances in the thirteenth, fourteenth, and fifteenth centuries. Even in the heightened and dramatic world of romance, a hero sometimes encounters an aged hermit in the forest to whom he makes a formal confession; but in these poems there is conspicuously little recourse to the offices of the Church (Gowther being, of course, the exception). Guy, indeed, deliberately rejects the possibility of conventional restitution by confession to a priest and penance consisting of the endowment of a religious foundation, suggested by his wife as a fitting atonement for his sins, in favour of a self-imposed life of poverty and hardship, apparently without any confession at all. Ysumbras is given a penance by a divine messenger in the form of a bird, while Roberd of Cisyle receives some very active divine intervention from an angel.

The penances themselves are shockingly harsh. Each hero is reduced to poverty and his fine clothes replaced by rags. Ysumbras, Gowther, and Roberd nearly perish of starvation. Gowther and Roberd may eat only what they can snatch from dogs. Guy's penance is performed until his death. Ysumbras's endures for fourteen years. Roberd's lasts 'þre ʒer and more' (l. 119). (No period is mentioned in *Sir Gowther*.)

The forgiveness of the heroes, which does not take place until *after* their penances have been performed, is marked by miracles after the manner of saints' legends. In *Sir Gowther* the mute princess speaks to reveal God's forgiveness of Gowther's sins. In *Sir Ysumbras* an angel appears and gives the hero bread and wine in his extremity, telling him that God has forgiven him. In *Roberd of Cisyle* the angel exchanges places with Roberd once more, and disappears back to heaven. In *Guy of Warwick* angels bear Guy's soul to heaven on his death, and his sanctity is indicated by the sweet odour that comes from his body.

The elements which the four poems have in common settle themselves into distinct narrative patterns which can be found on a smaller scale in other romances. These patterns may be roughly divided into two groups. In the first, the characteristic sequence is as follows: the sinner commits his sin, in a state of ignorance. He is made aware of his sin by means of some external agency, and the revelation has a profound effect on him. He gives up his former way of life at once and prepares to perform a harsh penance. This penance may be imposed on him, possibly by the Pope. It usually involves a long journey away from home and a period of residence in either his own court, or someone else's court, incognito, and in great hardship and poverty. After due time, his sins are forgiven and he may return to the world; but his character has been profoundly altered and he does not resume his former way of life. This sequence of events is similar to that portrayed in Hartmann von Aue's *Gregorius*. It occurs in *Guy of Warwick*, *Sir Gowther*, *Sir Ysumbras*, and, on a smaller scale, in *Valentine and Orson* and *The Romauns of Partenay*.

The second pattern resembles the story of Hartmann von Aue's *Der Arme Heinrich*. In this type, the sinner has blinded himself to his sinfulness, and God strikes him with punishment while he is still unrepentant. After enduring the punishment, the influence of some external event causes his internal revelation, and this is swiftly followed by his heartfelt repentance. He is then forgiven and his former position restored, but he is a changed and chastened man. This is what happens in *Roberd of Cisyle* and, it has been argued, in *Sir Gawain and the Green Knight*.[41]

Because these patterns emerge so distinctly in the four romances

---

[41] See John Burrow, *A Reading of Sir Gawain and the Green Knight* (London, 1965), pp. 104–12, 127–59; see Appendix A, below.

which are our main subjects, I have not brought into the discussion any romances in which confession and penance appear in other narrative patterns, even if only in a minor way. Therefore I have not discussed Malory, or any other romance in which the hero confesses his sins to a solitary hermit in the forest during his quest. This pattern is in any case most uncommon in Middle English romance and, where it exists, is derived directly from the French romance tradition, and explores a rather different group of ideas.

Other poems in which sin and penitence appear as minor elements are discussed in Appendix A. One of these other poems is *Sir Gawain and the Green Knight*. Although powerful arguments have been advanced in favour of understanding the meaning of this poem in terms of the sin and repentance of its hero, and although references to confession and penance, as well as evocations of the second penitential plot pattern, clearly exist within the poem, it is not in my opinion principally concerned with the same network of religious ideas as our four penitential romances. My discussion of it in Appendix A is aimed principally at assessing the relevance of the penitential elements within it in terms of its own internal logic and structure; but comparison with the other poems suggests that it has not been composed primarily with moral instruction on penitence in mind.

## iv. Telling Stories and Teaching Lessons

There is a sense in which all literature is morally educative, in that the reader is constantly invited by authorial direction to make judgements according to the standards presented within the frame of the work. This procedure is common and operates in works of all standards; the reader must at least distinguish the hero from the villain in a pulp Western story according to the conventional, recognized values of the genre, even if it is only by the colour of his hat. Standards thus created in the fictive world by the author and for which we are invited, temporarily, to abandon our own may in some instances appear to be more aesthetic than moral, but can rarely be freed from all moral implications.

An author is concerned to present his *matière* and *sens* in a particular way; he is artistically purposeful. Even if he does not have a directly didactic moral message to convey to his reader, he wishes to create special sensations in response to his writing. For an author who is dealing with moral issues, there are two main methods of guiding his reader's judgement. One is dramatic, the other analytic. In the latter case, he can invite the reader to contemplate his characters and their behaviour objectively, and pass judgement on them from an external standpoint. The characters created to be analysed in this way are basically exemplary types, though they may be extremely complex and subtle.

There are a number of ways to employ this method. Usually the narrator is external to the action. He is remote, omniscient, the acknowledged creator of his world, and his opinions concerning it are to be relied on. The way in which he describes things to his readers forms a kind of conspiracy in evaluating the moral character of the material. This is a technique which is particularly suited to an attitude of confidence, even certainty, on the part of the author/narrator. It is very often employed in religious medieval literature of all kinds. The author can present to his reader a Good Example, wherein virtue is rewarded, as in a saint's legend, like the perennially popular stories of St Katherine or St Margaret, or a Bad Example, in which wickedness is punished, such as the story of Nebuchadnezzar told to Belshazzar by Daniel in *Cleanness*.[42] In *Ancrene Wisse* the author gives us both at once in the story of the Knight and the Lady who stand for Christ and the Sinner. The reader is shown clearly that the Knight is the ideal of love, charity, generosity, courage, and loyalty, while the Lady is a type of fickleness, ingratitude, callousness, and weakness.[43]

Not so clear-cut is the case of Chaucer's *Canterbury Tales*. Here no direct authorial guidance is given; instead the reader is presented with the opinions of a narrator who is specifically identified with the author, the creator of this fictional world, and yet whose judgements are so at odds with the reader's own response to the highly developed exemplary types which are their objects that he is compelled to decide for himself. As George Kane puts it, 'a choice is put to the audience between accepting critical direction and acquiescing in the preposterous ... Chaucer developed the art of representing human behaviour to the point where, apparently,

---

[42] *Cleanness*, ed. A. C. Cawley (London, 1962), ll. 1641–1708.
[43] *Ancrene Wisse*, ed. J. R. R. Tolkien, EETS, os, 249 (1962), pp. 198–9.

giving it the label "wicked" seemed to him an inferior artistic procedure.'[44]

The other method amounts to an exposition by demonstration and involvement rather than by example and statement. The author here induces identification between the reader and the character, and causes them to learn together throughout the course of the work. This can be done despite blatant artificiality of form or improbability of narrative. It requires the evocation of common experience so that the reader recognizes the truth of what is being presented to him. The process of learning is a gradual stripping away of false perceptions and opinions. The reader is to some extent still the observer, but he is also a vicarious participator. He is invited not merely to be an impartial judge of, but to experience with the character on the printed page. The effect is to create a sensation of recognition, aptly described by Bob Dylan in 'Tangled Up In Blue':

> She opened up a book of poems and handed it to me
> Written by an Italian poet of the 13th century
> And every one of them words rang true
> And glowed like burning coals
> Pouring off of every page
> Like it was written in my soul.[45]

It is as if he had known it already, but it is just being revealed to him in new, meaningful clarity. The reader is experiencing illumination, intellectual and emotional enlightenment; he says to himself as if with relief, 'of course—it is all clear now', and feels that he has experienced the revelation of a truth.

In his essay 'The "Irresponsibility" of Jane Austen', John Bayley speaks of this sharing with the character as 'a primal experience in literature, and one of an essentially different kind from our being invited to contemplate the character as a portrait, and to assist in the analysis of its composition'.[46] He argues that although we are able to make independent evaluations of Emma's conduct, we are not able to see the whole truth of the matter until Emma herself has learned it, and we and the author are to some extent her

[44] George Kane, *The Liberating Truth: The Concept of Integrity in Chaucer's Writings*, John Coffin Memorial Lecture (London, 1979), p. 19.

[45] Bob Dylan, 'Tangled up in Blue', from 'Blood on the Tracks'.

[46] John Bayley, 'The "Irresponsibility" of Jane Austen', in *Critical Essays on Jane Austen*, ed. B. C. Southam (London, 1968), p. 5.

accomplices in her misdeeds, and sharers in her guilt. There are plenty of warnings of Emma's wilfulness, partiality, and snobbery, but we feel complacent about them because at the same time we are finding that the Emma whom we see, objectively, to notice only what supports her own ideas and wishes is also a patient, affectionate, attentive daughter, a loyal and loving friend, and is just enough to admit her own mistakes when she has been shown what they are.

One such crucial realization takes place after the excursion to Box Hill. Professor Bayley writes:

> Good manners require that we behave towards people not as we feel about them, but as their position or predicament in life dictates ... Emma is rude to Miss Bates because she forgot (we might say that her unadmitted resentment of Jane Fairfax willed her to forget) the impoverished spinster status, and thought only of being witty at the expense of the boringly garrulous individual. The intimate impact is that Jane Austen and ourselves have often done the same kind of thing, and have afterwards (one hopes) been ashamed of it. In reading Jane Austen (as in reading Shakespeare and Tolstoy) we both do the deed and rue it.[47]

The author who wishes to make his work morally educative sets out to create this 'intimate impact' because he knows that, although his reader can learn adequately by following a rationally disclosed argument, he will learn a great deal better by finding things out for himself. This technique is admirably demonstrated by Plato's account of the mathematical experiment conducted by Socrates with the help of Meno's slave.[48] Socrates causes the slave to solve a geometrical problem by asking him questions about it. The slave eventually calculates the right answer, and it seems to him so logically perfect and right that he feels as if he had always known it really, but had just had it brought to his attention. W. C. K. Guthrie, editor of the Penguin English translation of *Meno*, comments:

> What the experiment teaches could be expressed as the fundamental difference between empirical and *a priori* knowledge, the one referring to the natural, changeable world in which we live, and the other to universal and timeless truths; and it suggests that, whereas we have to learn facts of the former kind either from our own experience of the outside world or

---

[47] Bayley, 'Jane Austen', p. 7.
[48] Plato, *Meno*, trans. W. C. K. Guthrie (London, 1956; repr. 1982), pp. 130–8.

on the authority of another, the latter type of truth does seem in some way to come up from inside of us so that we can work it out for ourselves. The date of an historical event, or the chemical formula for water, are simply things we have to be told. Not so the truths of mathematics (nor, in Plato's belief, of morals).[49]

Here a distinction must be made between the sense of recognition derived from reading a book which presents us with 'universal and timeless truths', and that recognition we experience by reading of something we all know about simply because it is part of our common cultural heritage, part of our system of knowledge and belief, attitudes and responses. Love, at its most basic, would seem to be an example of the former, whether the love of man for woman, or mother for child, or son for father, or friend for friend; some sort of strong attachment between individuals either closely related or deeply attracted exists in every kind of human society, and it is a sensation which we have all felt at some time, and which we would recognize if we found it described in the literature of any age or culture. Even the 'Courtly Love' of the medieval romance, stylized and elaborate as it may be, recognizably yields to the modern reader the physical symptoms of strong sexual attraction. Similarly, anger, fear, and, I would argue, shame are sensations universally experienced by human beings (though for a variety of reasons) and thus universally 'recognized' in literature; and to the extent that romances deal with such basic human wishes and feelings they are easily able to create 'recognition' in their readers, whether of the fourteenth or twentieth centuries.

It is for this reason not so strange as it might first appear, to claim that medieval romances characteristically employ the technique of inducing identification with the protagonist in order to make the reader learn through vicarious experience, and to compare them with the more sophisticated and more realistic medium of the novel. The world of medieval romance is full of marvels and the supernatural, peopled by wicked villains or prodigies of knightly or womanly virtue, and in it the unlikeliness of events is paralleled by their familiar, quasi-mythic nature. In addition, medieval romances are typically a formal, conventional kind of literature, relying on the continuous repeated use and rearrangement of similar characters, episodes, set descriptions, lines, and

[49] *Meno*, ed. Guthrie, p. 109.

phrases. These are all features which distance romances from reality, and techniques which rely on the evocation of the reader's knowledge of the world and sympathies with the characters should be confined to a reasonably realistic, mimetic mode of representing experience. There are, of course, realistic elements in some romances, genuine attempts to describe as well as to create the world of aristocratic pursuits and characters, the chivalric ideal and behaviour consequent on it. But romances do not attempt to present a consistent and plausible fictional version of life as experienced by medieval knights; the real power of this kind of literature to exploit the techniques I have described is derived from their appeal to universal human wishes:

They disregard mimetic truth in favour of a deeper meaning which underlies the surface events; their logic lies not in the improbable adventures which befall the hero but the resultant testing of his powers ... Details and incidents which seem implausible when they are read as accounts of material cause and effect appear perfectly plausible when seen as part of a self-consistent pattern expressing the inner stresses, desires, and aspirations to which the mind ... is subject. Such stories, though symbolic rather than mimetic in their methods of expression, are realistic in that they are concerned with fundamental and universal realities.[50]

The creators of medieval romances rely to a considerable extent on the reader having a broad familiarity with the ethos of romance—its values, its symbols, its ideology. They do not explain, they do not apologize. The reader is expected to know why a knight behaves in such a manner—pursuing a quest, testing his valour, obeying the vows of his calling, or whatever—without having to be told. In some of the more sophisticated examples of the genre, the writers play on this knowledge of their readers, through inducing the 'sharing with the character' described above, and subtly undermine and modify that knowledge. In simpler and more popular examples as well, it is clear that a similar process takes place: the authors create certain expectations, disappoint them, and reach a new level of understanding, as the reader experiences and learns with the characters. This technique is highly characteristic of romance, from *Lancelot* and *Yvain* down through *The Tempest* and *Pericles* to a modern descendant in 'Ode to a

---

[50] Barron, *English Medieval Romance*, p. 4.

Nightingale'. It is a technique which is employed conspicuously in the romances which are discussed in this book.

In order to do this, romance writers make use of a third kind of knowledge, which we possess unconsciously by having absorbed it from birth from our society and environment. It does not consist of universal and timeless truths, but is not, strictly speaking, empirical, since it operates on a much deeper level than the conscious acquisition of facts. Recognition of this kind of knowledge, when it takes place, is an experience indistinguishable from the recognition of universal and timeless truths; but because these truths are in fact relative to locality and period, 'recognition' may not occur. If the signals given in a particular work, the values of the fictional world, are very different from the ones accepted and understood in everyday life by the reader, then he is not able to understand what the author intends him to understand. No author can totally invent a world; he has to rely to a certain extent on things which he assumes his readers know and take for granted. Thus, coming from a widely different cultural background, or being far removed in time, can interfere strongly with a reader's ability to appreciate a piece of writing.

Interference of this kind does not occur to quite the extent that might be anticipated in the appreciation of medieval romances by twentieth-century readers. Much of the chivalric ethic has become a well-known, if not well-practised, part of our society's system of values. It is not uncommon for a modern person to have an understanding of chivalry quite adequate for the interpretation of medieval romances which deal exclusively with that area.

However, religious romances have been less well appreciated than those which deal with purely secular chivalry and romantic love, perhaps because, although many people are tolerably familiar with such concepts as chivalry and 'courtly love', it is not so common nowadays for a reader to be able to re-create in his mind the religious sensibility of a medieval person. In particular, the modern reader will almost certainly lack the medieval person's daily experience and knowledge of penitential doctrine, discipline, and literature. The popular penitential manuals, and the instruction in the basic articles of faith which it was the duty of every parish priest to impart to his parishioners, were the main means by which the people who read or listened to romances came to know the sacrament of penance and the theological concepts behind it. A discussion of those ideas and their development, with particular reference to those which are most strongly reflected in the romances, forms the substance of the following chapter.

It has been remarked that, just as the audience for Middle English romances was not so sophisticated or aristocratic as that for French poems, a large proportion of the surviving examples are of a more pious and homiletic nature than is generally the case with their Continental antecedents. Copies of these religious romances are often found in large manuscripts containing miscellaneous collections of writings, often predominantly religious in nature. A recent editor comments:

> The association in this manuscript [Cambridge University Library MS Ff. 2. 38] of popular devotional texts, simple verse summaries of basic doctrine, exemplary stories about the conduct of daily life, and [romances] about families and virtuous women, suggest that [it] was compiled for devotional and recreational reading in a pious household.[51]

Three of our four romances survive in an unusually large number of manuscripts and early prints, and were clearly widely known and popular.[52] Yet despite their much-vaunted pious and homiletic nature, they were condemned by writers of other religious works along with more frivolous examples of the genre.[53] This suggests that medieval readers did not generally make a distinction between religious didactic romances and other romances, and that they enjoyed the former just as much as, if not more than, the latter.

To sum up briefly: having decided that there is such a thing as Romance, Medieval Romance, and Middle English Romance, we must add the proviso that romance is not susceptible to rigid definition as a genre in modern critical terminology. However, this study proceeds on the premiss that the concept of romance was known and had meaning in the thirteenth and fourteenth centuries, whether the writers and readers of the poems concerned con-

---

[51] *Octovian*, ed. Frances McSparran, EETS, os, 289 (London, 1986), Introduction, p. 9. This MS contains *Roberd of Cisyle* and *Guy of Warwick* as well as *Octovian*, *The Erle of Toulous*, *Sir Eglamour of Artois*, *Sir Triamour*, *Le Bone Florence of Rome*, *Beues of Hamtoun*, and *Sir Degare*. A more detailed examination of the contents of the MSS in which our four romances appear can be found in Appendix B, below.

[52] *Guy of Warwick* survives in six MSS and three early prints; *Sir Ysumbras* in nine MSS and three early prints; *Roberd of Cisyle* in ten MSS.

[53] See e.g. *Cursor Mundi*, ed. R. Morris, EETS, os, 57 (repr. London, 1961), ll. 19–29.

sistently called them by that name or not. Those who have stated that religious subjects cannot be appropriately treated in romances are mistaken. Because romances were usually composed for recreational reading does not mean that religious, didactic poems are not romances. Terms such as 'didactic' and 'homiletic' are the applications of twentieth-century critical terminology, with its urge to define and distinguish.

In fact, most romances are didactic in that they teach (by example, by statement, by dramatic demonstration) what is proper chivalric behaviour, values, attitudes. In this way it can be seen that 'the figures of romance are essentially stereotypes in the service of its didactic purpose.'[54] If it is true, as some have argued, that the subject of knightliness, treated as an extended exposition of theory, is central to any literary concept of medieval romance, that is not to say that the question of religion and how it fits into the chivalric world view must therefore be excluded. There is no great divide between romances which are overtly religious in tone or content and those which are not.

However, the argument proceeds on the assumption that there is a great divide between romances, which tell stories, albeit sometimes educatively, and other forms of literature, which teach lessons, albeit entertainingly. *Ancrene Wisse*, *Handlyng Synne*, *Pricke of Conscience* were all popular—the latter two, medieval bestsellers—all showing the perennial popularity of the subject of sin and penance, diligent and scrupulous examination of one's conscience; but they are not at all like *Guy of Warwick*, which has a similar message. They are all written in the 'analytic' mode: they state the case, then use examples to support their arguments. A romance, on the other hand, tells a story and manipulates its reader, more or less subtly, into learning its lesson. A close examination of the four poems which are our main subject will show how their authors achieved this, by evoking their audience's common knowledge of knights, ladies, loves, adventures, noble deeds, and sentiments, and subverting, undermining, modifying those preconceptions to reveal a deeper truth.

[54] Barron, *English Medieval Romance*, p. 5.

# 2

# Penance: A Brief History

The penance experienced by the heroes of our four romances is a
very different thing from the penance which we can suppose to
have been a familiar part of life to the average romance-reader or
hearer. Of course, it is only to be expected that a romance hero's
penance, like his adventures and character, should be larger than
life. But it is noticeable that penance as it appears in the romances
is consistently strikingly at variance with established contempor-
ary practice in several important respects. These include the
public nature of penance, entailing a loss of social status and
change of identity for the penitent; the lack of recourse (in the
majority of cases) to the Church, and consequent emphasis on the
penitent's relationship with God; and the attitude that penance is
not a matter of spiritual routine, but a once-only, life-changing
event.

I shall show that penance in the romances bears a greater
resemblance to the 'solemn penance' meted out in the Middle
Ages only very occasionally and only to sinners whose offences had
caused public scandal,[1] than to the penance which was taught and
practised in the thirteenth and fourteenth centuries. 'Solemn
penance' was a late and specialized form of the public penance
practised in the early Church; and we shall see that many ideas,
associations, and forms prevalent during the first few centuries of
Christianity are echoed in the romances.

We may begin with a brief review of the history of penance, noting
where this idea and that procedure originated, how they pro-
gressed, and at what stages of its long evolution the penance de-
veloped by the Western Church influenced the romances. They
characteristically look backwards to a simpler, more direct, and

---

[1] H. C. Lea, *History of Auricular Confession and Indulgences* (3 vols.; London, 1896), 1.
37.

more archaic idea of the forgiveness of sin than that prevailing at the time of their composition.

It is unlikely that the authors of our four romances were learned men, who possessed detailed, first-hand knowledge of the works of successive generations of scholars and theologians; but they lived (as we do not) in a society whose views on penance had been formed by the long tradition of theological debate and corresponding changes in practice on the subject, which was one ever-present in the thoughts and daily life of the later Middle Ages. In addition, though the authors may not have been learned men, they were certainly lettered (none of the four poems is in my view likely to have been composed orally) and therefore, if not in holy orders themselves, had probably received a clerical education. A brief history of the intellectual background to the subject of these popular literary products provides a summary of the knowledge which their authors and audience took for granted.

The history of penance in the Western Church is a vast subject. From the early Church's reluctance to admit temporal remission of post-baptismal sin to the thirteenth-century Church's insistence that every sinner must confess and receive absolution at regular intervals is a period of over one thousand years. During this period there were many local variations in the forms and procedures of penance, and hotly contested arguments over its theology and meaning. When the Church's views on and understanding of the sacrament of penance had been thoroughly analysed, and had more or less crystallized, by the mid-thirteenth century, it began the long process of educating its clergy and their flocks in this as in other fundamental articles of faith. I shall divide my discussion of the development of penance into three parts. The first will look at the gradual development of the external form taken by the ceremonies associated with penance. Particular attention will be paid to the features of public as opposed to private penance, as these are consistently reflected in the romances. The second will be an examination of the unfolding theology of sin and penance through the contributions of successive generations of Church fathers and scholars. The Contritionist school appears to have been particularly influential to the ideas of the romance-writers on the subject of penance. The third part will review the practice of penance in the later Middle Ages, in the forms in which it would have been most familiar to the authors and audience of romances, and examine some of the popular penitential manuals through which many of the contemporary views and instructions on penance were disseminated. This part will also discuss particular aspects of medieval penance, such as crusading indulgences and commutations, which are specifically reflected in the romances, and look at the relationship of these poems to other kinds of penitential literature.

## i. The Practice of Penance

### a. The Forgiveness of Sin in the Gospels and After

In the Gospels of St Matthew and St John, Our Lord explicitly gives His Apostles the commission to loose and bind, remit and retain sins.[2] On these verses was based the medieval Church's claim to play a crucial part in the salvation of every man's soul, remitting his sins on earth and in heaven. In the early days of Christianity, however, these words were not interpreted so, but were taken to mean that the opportunity for repentance and forgiveness of sins was the once-in-a-lifetime transformation undergone by the convert before the spiritual rebirth of baptism. The first Christians regarded post-baptismal sin as incompatible with Christian life, and were reluctant to admit the possibility of a second forgiveness on earth after a lapse by a Christian. In addition, it is stated in the Gospel of St Matthew that there is a sin which God Himself will not forgive.[3]

Idolatry, homicide, and fornication were the three great sins of the early Church and were regarded in the early centuries as outside the scope of earthly forgiveness.[4] However, other sins were not irremissible: St Paul, who displays a stern attitude towards the apostate in the Epistle to the Hebrews, is more lenient in the case of the incestuous Corinthian. While it is 'impossible' for the former to be forgiven, Paul advises the Corinthians to receive the latter back into the Church, forgive him, and comfort him, 'lest he be swallowed up in overmuch sorrow'.[5] The difference appears to be that the incestuous Corinthian is really repentant, while the apostate is not.

---

[2] Matt. 16: 19, 18: 18; John 20: 22, 23.  [3] Matt. 12: 31, 32.
[4] Tertullian, De pudicitia, 12, PL 2. 1002–4; Pacian, Paraenesis, 4, PL 13. 1083–4.
[5] 1 Cor. 3–5, 2 Cor. 5–11; for a discussion of the incestuous Corinthian, see O. D. Watkins, A History of Penance (London, 1920), 1. 22.

We see from these and other cases in the Gospels[6] that it was customary in the early Church for sinners detected in their sin to be expelled from the community, and that this sometimes led to repentance and readmission.

## b. The Early Church: AD 100–600

Within a 500-year period there were rapid and dramatic developments in the Church's treatment of lapsed Christians. At the opening of the period, the faithful are anxious to be received back into the Church after lapsing during the great persecutions, while at its close the Church is urging Christians to undertake penance and deploring the habit of leaving it to the last minute.

One of the earliest and most informative texts of this early period is the *Pastor* of Hermas (*c*. AD 100), written with a view to strengthening and comforting the faithful in the face of imminent persecution.[7] Hermas offers the hope of remission of sin as a special concession; it is an offer which is open only until a certain date, and it can never be repeated.[8] However, the conditions set out by Hermas were to remain fundamental to the idea of penance throughout its history. Repentance must, he says, be accompanied by suffering, or sins cannot be forgiven:

Do you think, then, that there is immediate remission from sin with repentance? Not at all. No! The one who repents must torture his soul and be thoroughly humble in all his actions and afflicted in a variety of ways.[9]

These 'ways' include losses, poverty, sickness, lack of any permanent abode, and the insults of unworthy persons.[10] Besides the patient endurance of heaven-sent tribulations and voluntary self-humiliation, the benefits of fasting are mentioned.[11] Already these features could be a blueprint for the penances undertaken by the romance heroes Guy of Warwick, Sir Gowther, Sir Ysumbras, and Roberd of Cisyle.

Hermas however never suggests that bishops or presbyters of the Church should assign penalties to repentant sinners, and it seems that by about AD 100 when the *Pastor* was written there was

---

[6] See Rev. 2: 20–3; 1 Tim. 1: 18–20; 2 Tim. 2: 19 for the casting out of sinners.

[7] Hermas, *Pastor*, Visio 2. 2, trans. Joseph M. F. Marique, *Fathers of the Church*, 1 (Washington, 1947).

[8] Hermas, *Pastor*, Mand. 4. 3.

[9] Hermas, *Pastor*, Sim. 7. 4.

[10] Hermas, *Pastor*, Sim. 6. 3. 4.

[11] Hermas, *Pastor*, Sim. 5. 3.

still no established practice. This developed apace during the second century, when penance acquired an official terminology and procedure.

There are several accounts of the harsh penances performed in Rome and elsewhere by notorious sinners.[12] Perhaps the best is Eusebius' account of Natalius' penance at Rome in about AD 200, which consisted of wearing sackcloth and ashes, prostration before the bishop, and rolling beneath the feet of the faithful with tears and entreaties.[13] According to Tertullian, it is accepted that there can only be one opportunity for repentance after baptism. He adds that contrition alone is not sufficient to win forgiveness; the sinner must expiate his sin in acts of penance:

The harder the pains of this second and only penance, therefore, the more effective it is as a demonstration; so it should not be shown in the conscience alone, but should also be directed towards some external act. This act . . . is called 'exomologesis' . . . [it] is a discipline to lay a man low and make him humble, enjoining a demeanour calculated to move mercy. And even concerning clothes and food, it commands [the penitent] to lie upon sackcloth and ashes, to cover his body in filthy rags, to cast down his spirit with sorrows, to exchange his sins for harsh treatment; to know only plain food and drink, not of course for his stomach's sake, but for his soul's: and generally to feed prayers with fasts, to groan, to weep, and to roar night and day to the Lord your God, to throw oneself at the feet of the presbyters, and kneel before those who are dear to God, enjoining all the brethren to be ambassadors for his supplications. All this exomologesis does, so that it may commend penance, that it may honour God by fear of danger; that it may by itself pronouncing against the sinner act in the stead of God's indignation, and by temporal afflictions, I will not say frustrate, but cancel out eternal punishments. Therefore, while it casts a man down, the more it raises him up; while it covers him with filth, it makes him more clean; while it accuses it excuses and while it condemns it absolves. The less you spare yourself, believe me, the more God will spare you.[14]

It is worth quoting this extraordinary passage in full, because, excluding the section from groaning, weeping, and roaring

---

[12] Irenaeus, *Contra haereses*, 13. 5 and 7, trans. Revd John Keble, *Library of the Fathers*, 40 (London, 1872), 43, 44; Epiphanius, *Adversus haereses*, 42, trans. Watkins, *History of Penance*, 1. 75.

[13] Eusebius, *Historia ecclesiastica*, 5. 28, trans. Roy J. Deferrari, *Fathers of the Church*, 19 (Washington, 1953), 344, 345.

[14] Tertullian, *De poenitentia*, 9, *PL* 1. 1243, 1244.

onwards, it describes in its major particulars the penances undertaken by the heroes of the four penitential romances.

From AD 220 onwards, when Callistus, bishop of Rome, admitted an adulterer to reconciliation for the first time, the Church became progressively more lenient towards sinners. The first of many schisms (the Montanists) resulted from the outrage this caused among rigorist factions.[15]

Origen (c. AD 185–254) distinguishes three classes of sins: those we can forgive each other (very minor), those which cannot be forgiven on earth at all (very serious), and the less serious ones which can be forgiven by a minister of God. But Origen condemns officers of the Church who presume to remit the sins of idolatry, fornication, and adultery.[16] Elsewhere he lists seven means by which sins can be remitted: by baptism, by martyrdom, by alms-giving, by forgiving sins committed against one, by converting a sinner to goodness, by fullness of love, and by penance:

In addition, there is a seventh remission of sins, though it is hard and toilsome, by means of a penance, when the sinner bathes his couch in tears, and tears are made his bread day and night, and he does not shrink from showing his sin to the priest of the Lord, and from seeking the remedy . . . if you are overwhelmed in grief and tears, and lamentations in the bitterness of your weeping; if you macerate your flesh and parch it by much abstinence and if you say 'My bones are fried as in a frying pan' . . . then . . . you are found, in accordance with the Gospel, offering the sacrifice which Israel cannot now offer in accordance with the law.[17]

From his writings it is clear that Origen held a rigorist position on the whole with regard to penance; he states that it is available only once after baptism, and that sins unto death cannot be remitted on earth, in which category he includes adultery. He claims that the commission of Our Lord to remit and retain sins can only be exercised by the bishops of the Church, and then only if they themselves are free from sin.[18]

After the Decian persecution, not only the adulterer but also the apostate was admitted for reconciliation. This move by the Church was again met with bitter opposition which led to the Novatianist

[15] Tertullian, *De pudicitia*, *PL* 2. 980–1028.

[16] Origen, *De oratione*, 28, trans. Watkins, *History of Penance*, 1. 133, 134.

[17] Origen, *Homilia in Leviticum*, 2, *PG* 12. 417, 419.

[18] Origen, *Commentaria in evangelium secundum Matthaeum*, 16. 18, trans. Revd John Patrick, *Ante-Nicene Christian Library* (Edinburgh, 1897), 25. 459.

schism. During the persecution many died, or were tortured and imprisoned, for refusing to sacrifice to the genius of the Emperor Decius, or to other more respectable pagan deities; however, in the words of St Cyprian, bishop of Carthage from AD 248:

Immediately at the first words of the threatening enemy a very large number of the brethren betrayed their faith, and were laid low not by the attack of persecution, but rather they laid themselves low by voluntary lapse.[19]

These lapsed Christians persisted in asking for reconciliation with the Church. The situation called for new measures, particularly since there was a growing abuse of the theory that martyrs could obtain reconciliation on behalf of someone else.[20] Cyprian called a Council in AD 251 and it was decided that lapsed penitents who had sacrificed could be restored at the hour of their death if they had spent their lives doing penance. If they had put off confession until they were in fear of death they could not be received back into the Church.[21]

The official Church, in opposition to the adherents of Novatian, now claimed the right to reconcile penitent adulterers and apostates. The tendency towards increasing use of the prerogative to remit sins was confirmed by council after council;[22] finally at the great Council of Nicaea in AD 325 the Church claimed her right to reconcile any sinner on earth, no matter how grave his offence, providing that he was truly penitent, appealing to 'an ancient and canonical law' as authority.[23] This decision coincided with the adoption of Christianity as the official religion of the Roman Empire, an event which changed the nature of the Church funda-

---

[19] Cyprian, *De lapsis*, 7, trans. Deferrari, *Fathers of the Church*, 36.

[20] People awaiting execution were called martyrs. Lapsed persons would visit the martyrs in prison and obtain certificates from them claiming that they were now freed from sin. A certain amount of credit was given to these *libelli* by Cyprian himself. In his *Epistola* 12, 13, 14 (*PL* 4. 265, 266, 269, 270), he states that he will not consider reconciling apostates until a council has met after the persecution and pronounced on the subject, *unless* the lapsed person is about to die, in which case if they have made exomologesis, have received the imposition of hands after penance, and possess a *libellus* from a martyr, they can be reconciled and die at peace with the Church.

[21] See Watkins, *History of Penance*, 1. 196–8.

[22] *Consilium Eliberitanum*, AD 305, canons 1–53 (Mansi, 2. 6–14); *Consilium Arelatense*, AD 314, canons 9, 13, 14, 16, 22 (Mansi, 2. 472, 473); Peter of Alexandria, *Epistola canonica*, canons 1, 2, 3, trans. Revd James B. H. Hawkins, *Ante-Nicene Christian Library*, 14. 292–6; *Consilium Ancyranum*, AD 314, canons 4–6, 16, 20–5 (Mansi, 2. 516, 519, 520–1).

[23] *Consilium Nicaea*, AD 325, canons 11, 12, 14 (Mansi, 2. 673).

mentally and forever. When membership of the Church had been entirely voluntary, the severe penalties imposed for breaches of discipline made no essential difference to members united in their devotion; but the conversion of the Empire brought a vast number of new members to the Church who joined for other reasons than religious conviction. The effect on the enforcement of penitential discipline in general was bad, but public penances of extreme severity continued to be imposed on penitent sinners in some provincial areas.[24] Not everyone was severe. St John Chrysostom was centuries ahead of his time in advocating firmly that penance should be judged not by length of time but by frame of mind, that no sin is too grave to be forgiven, and that the penitent sinner can be forgiven as often as he asks with true contrition,[25] ideas which are all reflected in the romances. This was contrary to the teaching of the Church at the time, however, and Chrysostom was reproved for it.[26]

St Jerome describes for us in detail the ceremony of reconciliation in Rome at this time:

The bishop indeed offers his oblation for the layman, imposes his hands upon the subject person, invokes the return of the Holy Spirit, and so with the pronouncement of a prayer before the people, reconciles to the altar him who had been delivered to Satan for the destruction of the flesh, that the spirit might be saved, nor does he restore one member to soundness before all the members have wept together with him.[27]

This penance is characterized by the participation of the whole congregation and probably lasts for the duration of Lent only, since penitents are customarily reconciled on the Thursday before Easter by the Bishop in Rome.[28]

To repeat penance is forbidden by Siricius at Rome, Ambrose at Milan, and Augustine in Africa.[29] There is one exception:

[24] Basil the Great, *Epistola CCXVII ad Amphilochium*, canons 56, 57, 58, 67, 73, trans. Sr. Agnes Clare Way, *Fathers of the Church*, 28 (New York, 1955), 108–13.

[25] John Chrysostom, *De incomprehensibili Dei natura*, 5. 56, trans. Paul W. Harkins, *Fathers of the Church*, 72 (Washington, 1984), 160, 161; *De beato Philogonio*, 30–3, trans. Harkins, *Fathers of the Church*, 72. 178–80; *Ad Theodorum lapsum*, trans. Watkins, *History of Penance*, 1. 331.

[26] *Synod ad Quercum habita*, AD 403 (Mansi, 3. 1146).

[27] Jerome, *Dialogus contra Luciferianos*, *PL* 23. 159.

[28] Innocent I, *Epistola XXV*, 7, *PL* 20. 559 (but on Good Friday at Milan, see Ambrose, *Epistola XX*, *PL* 16. 1002).

[29] Siricius, *Epistola I ad Himerium*, 5, *PL* 13. 1137; Ambrose, *De poenitentia*, 2. 10. 95, *PL* 16. 520; Augustine, *Epistola CLIII*, 7, *PL* 33. 655.

penitents may confess on their deathbed, in which case they receive immediate absolution without having to perform penance, and from the priest privately at home, rather than from the bishop ceremonially in front of the congregation. Many people disagreed with these late reconciliations and there was much controversy within the Church as to their value.

Eventually, partly as a result of this opportunity to leave confession until danger of death, few people would voluntarily undertake public penance. The majority of Christians were content to defer repenting of their sins until their deathbed, when the priest was forbidden to refuse them the viaticum. In such cases confession and absolution were both private and administered by the priest; the penitent need not fear either the enactment of a harsh public penance, or the severe social disabilities which were customarily imposed upon reconciled penitents after penance had been completed, and which extended to the end of their lives.[30]

Penance was by now rarely undertaken for anything other than the three capital sins.[31] At the close of the fifth century, Julianus Pomerius (c. AD 498) suggests that sinners whose sins are not public may discipline themselves as an acceptable alternative to penance imposed by the Church. Such a person must excommunicate himself; he may not receive the Eucharist until his penance is done.[32] This is a statement of great interest, since it anticipates one aspect of the penances voluntarily undertaken by the heroes of *Sir Ysumbras* and *Guy of Warwick*.

St Caesarius of Arles urges those who have committed the graver sins to undertake public penance, but says that minor sins can be atoned for by prayer and private penance,[33] or by works of charity such as visiting the sick, fasting, giving alms, forgiving enemies, and so on.[34] He puts forward the view that a life of continual voluntary penance is more likely to earn salvation than the practice of deathbed repentance. This self-inflicted discipline, interestingly, can reconcile the penitent sinner to God (in certain

---

[30] e.g. Leo I, *Epistola CLXVII ad Rusticum*, 10–13, *PL* 54. 1206–7.

[31] Leo I, *Epistola CLXVII ad Rusticum*, 19, *PL* 54. 1209; St Pacian, *Paraenesis*, 4, *PL* 13. 1083; Augustine, *Sermo CCCLII*, *PL* 39. 1558.

[32] Julianus Pomerius, *De vita contemplativa*, 2. 7. 2, *PL* 59. 451.

[33] Caesarius of Arles, *Sermo CCLXII de poenitentia*, *PL* 39. 2229.

[34] Caesarius of Arles, *Sermo CIV*, 4, *PL* 39. 1947; twelve means of remitting sins, *Homilia XIII*, *PL* 67. 1075.

cases) without confession to a priest, admission to the status of penitent, or the assignment of a specific penance.[35]

So we find that penance is increasingly associated with Lent;[36] it is still usually public; and it still consists of prostration, humiliation, the wearing of sackcloth and ashes, not washing, strict fasting, and affliction of mind.[37] But soon this will change.

## c. The Coming of Private Penance

The Celtic Church in Britain and Ireland had few links with the Roman Church on the Continent during the first centuries, and evolved an independent system of penance in isolation from Roman influence. Public penance was almost unknown in Britain and Ireland; the monastic foundations of these countries instead developed the practice of private confession to a priest, private performance of penance, and private reconciliation, also by a priest. This system enabled confession and penance to be repeated any number of times.

For the use of the priest–confessors, handbooks were compiled which prescribed the appropriate penance for every conceivable sin. The most usual penalties were fasting, vigils, prayers, tears, and almsgiving, all of which could be performed in private, though for the graver sins, especially homicide, the penalty would involve exclusion from the community—in effect, exile. It is clear that these detailed 'tariffs' for penance were the product of the idea that the priest–confessor was a spiritual physician, administering medicine to the soul weakened by sin.[38] Thus the Penitential of Finnian (c. AD 550) states that sins are to be expiated by the exercise of their contrary virtues: 'patience must arise for wrathfulness, kindliness ... for envy; for detraction, restraint of heart and

---

[35] Caesarius of Arles, *Sermo CCLVI, CCXLIX, CCLVIII*, PL 39. 2217, 2218, 2208, 2222.

[36] Eligius of Noyon, *Homilia XV*, PL 87. 647, 648; *Homilia II*, PL 87. 636; Regino of Prüm, *Disciplinis ecclesiasticis*, 1. 291, PL 132. 245, 246.

[37] Isidore of Seville, *Etymologiarum libri xx* 6. 19. 79, PL 82. 260.

[38] J. T. McNeill and H. M. Gamer, eds., *Medieval Handbooks of Penance* (New York, 1938): 'This view is developed . . . particularly in the penitentials, with special application of the medical principle advocated by the methodist school of physicians that "contraries are cured by their contraries" . . . Although most of the early Church fathers including Clement, Origen, Tertullian, and Jerome were familiar with medical thought, it was probably mainly through Cassian, a writer much used as an authority by the framers of early penitentials, that the principle of the contraries came to be integrated with the idea of penitential medicine in these documents' (p. 44).

tongue; for dejection, spiritual joy; for greed, liberality', and so on.[39] The Penitential of Cummean (c. AD 650) agrees that 'the eight principal vices contrary to human salvation shall be healed by these eight contrary remedies. For it is an old proverb: contraries shall be cured by contraries; for he who freely commits what is forbidden ought freely to restrain himself from what is otherwise permissible.'[40]

In addition the confessor was to observe carefully 'the length of time anyone remains in his faults; with what learning he is instructed; with what passion he is assailed; with what courage he stands; with what tearfulness he seems to be afflicted; and with what oppression he is driven to sin'.[41] This new attention to the circumstances attending a sinner's fault is a new feature of penitential procedure, and a significant step forward. For the first time there is an awareness that a sin can be more or less serious, depending on the manner in which it was committed. While these early penitentials do not go all the way to judging a sinner's intentions rather than his acts, it is no longer simply a question of whether a law has been transgressed or not: the process of determining what sins have been committed and what penalties incurred has become more flexible and more subtle.

MacNeill and Gamer, editors of the medieval handbooks of penance, see in this scrupulous care to let the punishment fit the crime a sound psychological basis:

There can be no doubt of the presence in them of the intention of a humane ministry. The penitentials offer to the sinner the means of rehabilitation. He is given guidance to the way of recovering harmonious relations with the Church, Society, and God. Freed in the process of penance from social censure, he recovers the lost personal values of which his offences have deprived him. He can once more function as a normal person. Beyond the theological considerations, we see in the detailed prescriptions the objective of an inward moral change, the setting up of a process of character reconstruction which involves the correction of special personal defects and the reintegration of personality.[42]

These remarks are particularly interesting and significant in view of the treatment of penance in the romances. We shall see later on

[39] McNeill and Gamer, *Handbooks*, pp. 92–3.
[40] McNeill and Gamer, *Handbooks*, pp. 100–1.
[41] From the penitential of Cummean, McNeill and Gamer, *Handbooks*, p. 116.
[42] McNeill and Gamer, *Handbooks*, p. 46.

how *Guy of Warwick*, *Sir Ysumbras*, *Sir Gowther*, and *Roberd of Cisyle* each in their own way make this idea of the therapeutic value of penance in rehabilitating the hero in society and re-integrating his sin-warped personality central to the development of the story and the moral purpose of the poem.

During the sixth and seventh centuries the Celtic type of monastic foundation spread to the Continent through the activity of Irish missionaries, of whom the most outstanding was St Columbanus. By means of these foundations the Celtic system of penance was introduced to Europe, and Columbanus himself wrote a penitential, based largely on that of Finnian. Many members of the clergy were influenced by the Irish teachers; during the seventh century these disciples in turn founded monasteries of the Celtic type, and they proliferated all over the Frankish kingdoms. Priests in these monasteries called on to administer penance would compile their own penitentials, and the numbers of these also multiplied.[43] The old public penance, with reconciliation by the bishop on the Thursday before Easter, continued to be employed side by side with the Celtic procedure.

Theodore of Tarsus, Archbishop of Canterbury from AD 668, recognized as official the private system of penance in Britain, and one of the most influential penitential handbooks ever written bore his name and contained his teachings. This was based on the same working principles as the earlier Celtic penitentials, but was fuller and more comprehensive.

The use of the private system of penance spread rapidly on the Continent during the eighth and ninth centuries. The extension of Celtic procedures which already existed, the influence of the Penitential of Theodore and the Frankish compilations based on it, the presence of English and Irish missionaries in Germanic countries, and the influence of Alcuin and his group of English scholars at the court of Charlemagne all helped to effect the transition from the cumbersome and obsolete system of public penance to one which naturally reflected the practical and emotional needs of a completely Christian society. There is evidence that from the time of Theodore onwards it became customary not only for monks and clerics, but for laymen also to repeat their penances.[44]

There was some opposition to the number of penitentials n use

---

[43] See McNeill and Gamer, *Handbooks*, chaps. 5 and 6.
[44] See Ecgbert, *Dialogus de institutione catholica*, *PL* 89. 435–42.

in the ninth century. In the Capitularies of Theodulf, the Council of Chalon in AD 813, and the Council of Tours in AD 813,[45] there is disapproval of the large numbers of penitentials now circulating, each one with different penalties for the sins, and some entirely without authority. Such penitentials, claimed the Council of Paris in AD 829, 'do not heal the wounds of sinners, but rather caress and inflame them'.[46] Attempts were made to compile a single, authoritative document which would serve everyone and end the confusion, but none was really successful.[47] Regino of Prüm wrote in about AD 906 that a visiting bishop must enquire of the parish priest 'if he have a Roman penitential, either that put forth by Theodore the bishop, or by the venerable Bede, so that in accordance with what is there written, he may either question the penitent when confessing, or impose the due measure of penance upon him when he has confessed'.[48] Regino also left a very detailed record of the standard ceremony for public penance performed during Lent, with reconciliation at the church on Holy Thursday.[49]

So at this time private and public penance were practised side by side. The priest who administered the former was expected to use an authoritative handbook at his own discretion, while the bishop who presided over the latter was performing a public ritual of a fixed and rigid nature. By about AD 950, the private system was employed exclusively in England and Ireland, and was predominant on the Continent north of the Alps, while in Lombardy and Italy the older public penance was still the normal practice. Gradually over the next 250 years public penance was almost completely superseded by private penance. It was accepted that private penance not only could, but ought to be repeated, and finally the

[45] Theodulf, *Capitularia*, 2, *PL* 105. 211; *Consilium Cabilonense*, 2, AD 813, canon 38 (Mansi, 14. 101); *Consilium Turonense*, 3, AD 813, canon 22 (Mansi, 14. 86).

[46] *Consilium Parisiensis*, AD 829, canon 32 (Mansi, 14. 559).

[47] Notably by Halitgar, bishop of Cambrai, who wrote five books based on patristic writers, and added a book known as the *Poenitentiale romanum* (*PL* 105. 693 ff.), modelled on the Penitential of Theodore (see McNeill and Gamer, *Handbooks*, p. 297); and also by Rabanus Maurus, who was invited by Otgar, archbishop of Mainz, to write a single authoritative handbook.

[48] Regino of Prüm, *Disciplinis ecclesiasticis*, 1. 95, *PL* 132. 191.

[49] Regino of Prüm, *Disciplinis ecclesiasticis*, 1. 291, *PL* 132. 245–6. That this was seen as the authoritative and standard account is shown by its being repeated in Burchard of Worms, *Decretals*, 19. 26, *PL* 140. 984, Ivo of Chartres, *Decretals*, 15. 45, *PL* 161. 867–8, and Gratian, *Decretals*, 1. 50. 64, *PL* 187. 284.

Fourth Lateran Council of AD 1215 decreed that every Christian must confess to his parish priest at least once a year.

Public penance continued to exist in a rare and specialized form. Known as 'Solemn Penance', it was imposed only for offences of a very serious nature which were notorious and scandalous. In Solemn Penance the ancient rule was maintained that it could be imposed only once.[50] Examples of these Solemn Penances abound in medieval history. The father of William the Conqueror, Duke Robert of Normandy, obtained his inheritance by poisoning his elder brother Richard, and was instructed to undertake the pilgrimage to Jerusalem barefoot.[51] Pope Alexander III sent cardinals Albert and Theodin to Avranches in 1172 to absolve Henry II of England of his responsibility for the murder of Thomas Becket. By way of restitution and penance, Henry swore never to desert Alexander or his successors so long as they acknowledged him as king, to restore certain possessions and privileges of the Church which he had withdrawn, to submit to a public flogging, and to lead a three years' crusade to the Holy Land the following year, meanwhile providing funds for 200 knights to defend Jerusalem.[52] Still more similar to a romance-penance is that imposed on Gilles, Lord of Saint-Michel in Laonnais, who had ordered the assassination of an abbé in his own cloister. Gilles had to vow to undertake a crusade against the Albigensians, and received at Rome the penance of eating only bread and water every Friday, submitting to public discipline three times a year, and endowing an abbey with a priest to pray for the soul of his victim.[53]

During this period of transition throughout the eleventh and twelfth centuries, the nature and extent of the 'Power of the Keys', the exact role of the Church's ministers in conferring pardon for sin, was the subject of keen dispute and varied speculation before the sacramental status of penance was established. Much of this theorizing will prove relevant to our discussion of penance in the romances, and it is to this that we will now turn.

[50] See Alan of Lille, *Liber poenitentialis*, PL 210. 296; Peter Lombard, *Sententiae*, 4. 14. 3, *PL* 192. 871; Thomas Aquinas, *Summa theologiae* (Rome, 1962), 3. 84. 10.

[51] He died on the way. Jean de Marmoutier, *Gesta consulum andegavorum*, ed. Louis Halphen and René Poupardin, in *Chroniques des comtes d'Anjou et des seigneurs d'Amboise* (Paris, 1913), p. 50.

[52] Ralph of Diceto, *Ymagines historiarum*, ed. W. Stubbs in *The Historical Works of Master Ralph of Diceto*, Rolls Series, 68a (1876), pp. 351–2, 383.

[53] See J. C. Payen, *Le Motif du repentir dans la littérature française médiévale* (Geneva, 1967), pp. 39–41.

## ii. The Theology of Sin and Penance

In the first centuries, before the conversion of the Empire, the Christian Church was an exclusive community whose members had redeemed themselves by their faith; in many cases by their conversion. The salvation of each member of this community was intimately connected with the fact of their belonging to it; the Church was a bastion of the true faith, a light in the great pagan darkness of the world. This community must be kept pure in order to ensure its continued redemptive efficacy. Individual members detected in sin were therefore cast out in order that they might not corrupt the whole body.

This continued to be the position of the rigorist Montanists and Novatianists, when the Church began to consider that it should readmit penitent sinners after they had performed a sufficiently exacting penance. The purpose of this penance was to take the place of the punishment incurred by sin, and also to prove the penitent's determination to mend his ways. 'Reconciliation', achieved by the imposition of hands by the bishop at the end of this penance, readmitted the sinner to the communion, but did not entail the exercise of the sacerdotal power of absolution, and the early Church never claimed that permanent exclusion from the community of the faithful absolutely prevented the sinner's repentance and penance from being acceptable to God.[54] Reconciliation concerned only the relations between the sinner and the Church; the real issue was outside the jurisdiction of any human authority, between the sinner and God.[55]

That is why we find in the early centuries that penance is not the only means of obtaining forgiveness: the patient endurance of temporal suffering,[56] the intercessory prayers of the faithful, and various acts of charity[57] were all regarded as effective means of appeasing the wrath of God, and ultimately the pardon of sin was conferred by God alone. Sin itself was a concept that was not elaborated for centuries to come. To many of the early Church Fathers, a sin was not so much that which offended God (requiring further refinement of definition), but that which transgressed the

---

[54] Augustine of Hippo, *Epistola CLIII ad Macedonio*, 7, *PL* 33. 655.
[55] See Lea, *Auricular Confession*, 1. 32.
[56] Augustine of Hippo, *Enchiridion*, 66, *PL* 33. 263.
[57] Lactantius, *Divinarum institutionum*, 6. 13, *PL* 6. 685–6.

law, that which God and His Church had forbidden. Sin was thus a state of absolute wrongness, and ignorance did not excuse the sinner from guilt.[58]

St Jerome (d. *c.* AD 420) stated positively that bishops and priests had assumed the arrogance of the Pharisees from the text of Matthew 16: 19 and 18: 18, so that they thought they could condemn the innocent and release the guilty, when really God only considers the life of the sinner and not the sentence of the priests.[59] This statement became an important source of authority for those later scholars who were reluctant to admit fully the 'Power of the Keys' and the unaided efficacy of sacramental absolution in remitting sin.

Meanwhile, reconciliation gradually began to assume the character of absolution. Influential commentators began to hold the opinion that the words of the Gospel texts meant that the power to loose and bind sins, which Christ had unquestionably committed to His Apostles, had been transmitted to their successors. Pope Celestin I (Pope AD 422–32) was horrified to hear that any bishop or priest should have refused reconciliation to the dying penitent, since this would have consigned the penitent's soul to perdition,[60] while Leo I (Pope AD 440–61) referred to reconciliation as the gate through which the sinner, having performed his penance, obtained forgiveness by the supplication of the priests.[61]

However, the opinions of the Church Fathers on this subject continued to vary almost as much as local differences in practice; much depended on the character and background of the writer, and which heresy he was attacking at the time. St Augustine himself claimed that bishops had been entrusted with the 'Power of the Keys' when arguing against the Novatianists, who denied that any man could have the power to remit sins; but when writing against the Donatists, who claimed that the priest had the power to

[58] Far from the classic theory later developed so extensively by Peter Abelard, that unless the sinner consciously and deliberately chose to commit a sin he was not culpable, Clement of Alexandria (*c.* AD 150–210), declared that to sin on purpose is as unforgivable as to lapse repeatedly after the one permissible penance, and that only the sinner who had been overborne by force or guile could hope to be forgiven. *Stromateis*, 2. 13, trans. Revd William Wilson, *Ante-Nicene Christian Library*, 12 (Edinburgh, 1869), 35–7.

[59] Jerome, *Commentarium in evangelium Matthaei*, 3. 16, *PL* 26. 118.

[60] Celestin I, *Epistola IV*, *PL* 50. 432.

[61] Leo I, *Epistola CVIII ad Theodorum*, 2, *PL* 54. 953.

forgive sins, he stated that such an opinion was heretical because Man should not presume to arrogate this power to himself.[62]

Such differences of opinion, reflecting the Church's uncertainty as to how penance actually worked, continued over the next 500 years. When public penance was so harsh and so much to be dreaded that deathbed repentance was common, the majority of theologians suggested several ways for the sinner to make his peace with God without troubling ministers of the Church, following the seven means of remission advanced by Origen.[63] This would have been quite untenable at the time when our romances were composed, yet they reflect very strongly the attitude that a man's penance is a private matter between himself and God.

Gregory the Great (Pope AD 590–604) stated that the power of the priest or bishop to absolve was only the power of manifesting what God's grace had already achieved:

We ought by our pastoral authority to absolve those of whom we know that our source of authority is making them to live by His reviving grace. And most certainly this life-giving is recognized already in the confession of the sin itself before the operation of the official sentence.[64]

Following the collapse of the Carolingian empire, there was an effort to assert and reinforce the power and authority of the Church, and forged documents began to appear, purporting to have been written by ancient authorities and claiming that the Church held the keys to the kingdom of heaven or hell.[65] In addition, the formula for the ordination of priests did not originally contain the passage in which the priest is endowed with the power to remit and retain sins on earth and in heaven, although the formula for the ordination of bishops contained a request that this power be granted. From AD 1200, however, an ordination ceremony existed which specifically granted this power to priests, and

[62] Augustine of Hippo, *In Psalmo CXVIII expositio sermo X*, 17, *PL* 15. 1336; *De poenitentia*, 1. 2, *PL* 17. 973; *Epistola LI*, 11, *PL* 33; *Epistola CLIII*, 3, *PL* 33. 655–7; *Epistola CCXXVIII*, 8, *PL* 33. 1016; *Sermo XCIX*, 8, *PL* 38. 600.

[63] Origen, *Homilia in Leviticum*, 2. 4, *PG* 12. 417 (in Latin); Eucherius, *Homilia V* and *Homilia IX*, *PL* 50. 844–7 and 854–6; Julianus Pomerius, *De vita contemplativa*, 2. 7. 2, *PL* 59. 451; Caesarius of Arles, *Sermo CIV*, *Sermo CCLVI*, *Homilia XIII*, *PL* 39. 1947, 2217, and 67. 1075; Fulgentius, *De remissione peccatorum*, 1. 6, 11, 12, 28, *PL* 65. 531–2, 535–7, 550.

[64] Gregory the Great, *Homiliarum in evangelia*, 2. 26. 5, *PL* 76. 1200.

[65] Pseudo-Clement, *Epistola I*. This was repeated by Burchard of Worms, *Decretals*, 1. 125, *PL* 140. 586 and Ivo of Chartres, *Decretals*, 5. 225, *PL* 161. 591.

this superseded the older form in which the priest could only aid the sinner by intercession.[66]

The centuries between AD 1000 and 1400 consequently inherited contradictory utterances and extremely varied practices concerning penance and the pardon of sin. Successive scholars set to work to reconcile these differences and explain according to a consistent system exactly how the practices took effect. In addition, commentators were working under the influence of those changes in the intellectual climate characterized by R. W. Southern as 'the change of emphasis from localism to universality, the emergence of systematic thought, the rise of logic . . . the emergence of the individual from his communal background'.[67] Professor Southern gives a clear account of St Anselm of Canterbury's rejection of the traditional view of the way in which Man had been redeemed by God, and of how tremendously influential it was. Anselm was concerned to establish Man's free will in choosing God and not the Devil:

But as for what we are accustomed to say—that by killing Him who was God and in whom no cause of death was to be found, the Devil justly lost the power which he had obtained over sinners; and that otherwise it would have been an unjust violence for God to make Man free, since Man had voluntarily and not through violence given himself over to the Devil—as for all this, I cannot see what force it has.[68]

Anselm replaced this notion of the rights of the Devil over mankind with that of what was due to God after the sacrifice of His Son. Christ's suffering and death must be seen, not as the final piece of strategy in the cosmic struggle between God and the Devil, but as a gift of pure love, for which God is owed love in return. This renewed emphasis on the interiority of sin was most influential; in conjunction with the adoption as standard of the Gregorian analysis of sins as proceeding from seven great vices, or infirmities, to which man's soul is liable, more attention began to be paid to the question of intention, of greater or lesser degrees of culpability for the same sinful act, depending on the sinner's state of mind at the time of its commission.

Important developments took place in the theology of penance

---

[66] See Lea, *Auricular Confession*, 1. 122–3.
[67] R. W. Southern, *The Making of the Middle Ages* (London, 1953), p. 221.
[68] Anselm of Canterbury, *Cur Deus homo*, 1. 7, ed. F. S. Schmitt (Bonn, 1929), p. 10.

in the late eleventh and twelfth centuries. It was a time of rapid growth in several crucial areas. Gratian and his followers created a systematic codification of canon law; along with this went the establishment of the seven sacraments to be administered by the Church to men, and an increasingly sophisticated theological system to support both. By the end of the twelfth century most aspects of the Church's function in standing between the sinner and God had been carefully defined and appropriate procedures instituted; the Gregorian reforms had prepared the way for asserting the necessity of the priest's role in all the sacraments. With the development of sacramental theory which followed, the Church and its ministers became essential intermediaries between the sinner and God, without whose help the sinner could not hope to be saved. However, the precise nature and effect of this role in the sacrament of penance continued to be a matter for debate.

At the opening of the twelfth century there was still a long way to go before the confident assertion was reached that sacramental absolution administered by the priest itself actually remitted sins whether the recipient was truly contrite or not, and that confession, penance, and absolution ought to be sought frequently, in order that the sinner should receive regular and effective doses of divine grace. It is worth reviewing in some detail the thoughts of the contritionist theologians who preceded this view—St Anselm, Abelard, St Bernard of Clairvaux, Peter Lombard, Hugh and Richard of Saint Victoire, Alexander of Hales—because the doctrine of penance which can be inferred from their writings is highly relevant to our romances, even though by the time the romances were composed it had been long superseded in the advancing tide of sacramentalism.

According to the theologians of contritionism, the remission of sins is achieved when the sinner consents to an infusion of divine grace, which excites in him tears of repentance. These tears are the visible sign of a divine pardon already acquired, which has loosened the bonds of eternal punishment incurred by the sin. At this point the sinner still has to pay a limited, temporal penalty for his sin, and this can only be achieved by being reconciled to the Church through penance and absolution. Thus sacramental absolution confirms a divine pardon already granted, and also fulfils a lesser role in remitting temporal punishment.

Contritionist theologians were the first to divide the functions performed by God and the priest into remission respectively of *culpa* and *poena*; God remitted the blame for the sin, which released the *debitum damnationis*, but the fault still had to be expiated in the temporal pains of Purgatory, and these were remitted by the priest pronouncing the penitent absolved, provided that he carried out his penance properly.

Those who emphasized the value of contrition in remitting sin were acting on the premiss, for which there was ample authority, that God alone actually forgives sins. Nevertheless, perfect contrition included a vow to confess; the act of confession was in itself expiatory, and the priest's function was to make manifest on earth God's pardon of the sinner, whose genuine contrition, the sign of that pardon, was marked by his sorrow at having offended God, and the tears proceeding from that sorrow.

The state of mind of the penitent was all-important; the tears were therefore essential outward signs of genuine interior grief; otherwise the Church's ministers might not be able to judge the secrets of the heart, a point noted by Yvo of Chartres (AD 1035–1115), who preceded the main school of contritionist thought. Bearing a close resemblance to the attitude of the romances, Yvo stated that repentance is the sign of divine pardon, but insisted on harsh public penance to ensure that external acts testify to the sincerity of internal repentance.[69]

The main innovation of the contritionists, spearheaded by St Bernard of Clairvaux, was the development of the concept of contrition itself—what it was, and what it meant in terms of sin and forgiveness. Contrition in the sense originally and powerfully described by St Bernard was an overpowering emotion, a detestation of sin and disgust with self which results in a changed life. It is the result of the sinner's freely chosen co-operation with an infusion of divine grace. The sinner must then act on the prompting of that grace: he must recognize his own sinfulness, his self-knowledge leading to a state of humiliation and disgust with his own weakness, accompanied by true grief at having offended God and a desire to start a new life, which amounts to a renunciation of the world and the acceptance of a life of austerity and mortification.

The necessary knowledge of one's own evil and ungrateful nature can be attained, according to both St Bernard and St

---

[69] Ivo of Chartres, *Epistola CCXXVIII, PL* 162. 232.

Anselm, by meditation upon the personal sufferings of our Saviour and reflection upon how little we have deserved them. This gave rise to a movement of devotional fervour which was to have enormous impact on all aspects of religious life.[70]

St Bernard's contemporary Peter Abelard's most influential contribution to the debate on penance was his remarks on the nature of sin itself—although these were controversial at the time. He claimed that sin consists not in the external act, for it is possible to do a wrong thing for blameless motives, but in the internal act of the will. Elaborating on St Augustine's idea that man's liability to temptation is an infirmity and only becomes a sin when it is accompanied by consent, Abelard continued to refine the degrees of culpability. Concerning the 'Power of the Keys', Abelard quoted Origen, Jerome, Augustine, and Gregory in support of the view that a bishop's decision is invalid if it is not in accordance with divine will. He even went so far as to say that if a penitent is truly contrite, his love and sorrow at having offended God are sufficient to win pardon, and so confession is not always necessary. However, the austerities of penance take the place of the pains of purgatory incurred as penalty for sin, even though God has already forgiven the sin, thus releasing the *debitum damnationis*.[71]

The definition of sin and its penalties was further developed by Hugh of Saint Victoire (d. AD 1141) in his attempt to formulate a complete theory of the sacraments. He pointed out that just as a sin is one act composed of two parts, evil intent and actual deed, so penance is of two kinds: external penance by affliction of the flesh, which remits the fact of the wrong deed, and interior penance by contrition of the heart, which remits the evil intention. Thus contrition alone is insufficient to gain pardon and the complete remission of sins. But remission, too, is of two kinds. The sinner is bound both by his sin, which has corrupted his soul, and by the penalty for his sin, the extent to which he has incurred punishment. The first of these is remitted by God when the penitent shows contrition ('first there is weeping, and then confession'), the

---

[70] Bernard of Clairvaux, *Sermo in vigilia nativitatis domini*, 3. 3, PL 183. 424; *De conversione*, 2. 5, PL 182. 836–9; *Epistola CXIII*, 4, PL 182. 258; *De gradibus humilitatis, passim*, PL 182. 941–71; *De modo bene vivendi*, 27, PL 184. 1247–54.

[71] Peter Abelard, *Ethics*, 3 and 26, PL 178. 636–47, 673–8; *Epitome theologiae christianae*, 37, PL 178. 1757–8.

second by sacramental absolution administered by the priest. Contrition may suffice to save the sinner if he has intended to confess and been unable to carry out his intention, but a sinner who has had such an opportunity and has not confessed will not be saved, because the absolution of the priest is for him the only way to efface the *debitum damnationis*.[72]

The point that sacramental absolution confirms a divine pardon which has already taken place was often illustrated with the story of the lepers whom Christ cleansed and then told to present themselves to the Levites to be declared officially clean.[73] This was picked up by Peter Lombard (*c.* AD 1100–60), who states that the prevailing attitude of his time is that the priest does not absolve, but merely makes manifest the pardon of God. He uses the story of the lepers, and of Lazarus restored from death, to extend and refine Hugh of Saint Victoire's idea that God and the Church bind and loose in different ways. God remits the *culpa* and releases the soul from the debt of eternal damnation, but although a man may be loosed in the eyes of God, he cannot be so in the eyes of the Church except by the sentence of the priest, to whom God has granted the power to remit the *poena* of purgatorial suffering.[74]

The argument was further refined and elaborated by Richard of Saint Victoire. Richard explains that penitence transforms the *debitum damnationis*, the incursion of punishment in eternity, into the *debitum expiationis*, transitory punishment in this world. The role of the priest in remitting sins is not to remove them but to mitigate their punishment; God has pardoned the sinner already, on condition that he confesses to a priest. Thus the remission of sin in all its parts is one continuous process which is not completed until the penitent has confessed, has been absolved, and has performed his penance.[75] He reiterates that the initiator of contrition is the gift of God's grace:

For there is no-one who has such a heart of stone, so hard and obstinate

---

[72] Hugh of Saint Victoire, *De sacramentis christianae fidei*, 2. 14. 1, 2, 8, *PL* 176. 554, 555, 565; *Summa sententiarum*, 6. 11, *PL* 176. 148.

[73] This is derived from the influential tract *De vera et falsa poenitentia*, 10. 25, *PL* 40. 1122; see also Alan of Lille, *Liber poenitentialis*, *PL* 210. 300, and Raymund Penafort, *Summae casibus*, 3. 34. 5 and 3. 35. 5 (Rome, 1603; republ. in facsimile, Farnborough, 1967).

[74] Peter Lombard, *Sententiae*, 4. 17. 1, *PL* 192. 880.

[75] Richard of Saint Victoire, *De potestate ligandi et solvendi*, 8, *PL* 196. 1165.

that Our Lord could not soften it into true penitence in a moment, if he wanted to.[76]

It should be noted that this moving statement could not be more forcibly illustrated than by the story of *Sir Gowther*.

Alexander of Hales (d. *c.*1245) can be seen as representing a transitional stage in the development of sacramental theory, half-way between the contritionists and their successors. On the one hand, he can properly be described as a contritionist because for him the guilt of mortal sin could not be remitted unless the penitent was truly contrite. He repeats the arguments of Richard of Saint Victoire on the role of the priest in transforming the debt of eternal punishment into a lesser bond of temporal punishment by absolution; but he also states that grace is given to the penitent on reception of the sacrament, whether he has merited it or not. Absolution is no longer simply a ratification of God's pardon, but is itself the source of sanctifying grace.[77]

The distinction between *culpa* and *poena* and the specific remissive functions of God and the priest in the performance of the sacrament, as defined by the contritionists, led to further refinements in the definition of the penitence experienced by sinners. The important development of the next generation of scholars was to distinguish between attrition and contrition. This is principally the contribution of William of Auvergne. In clarifying this point William successfully formulated the view that was to be held by the Church for centuries, that the absolution conferred in the sacrament itself remits sin.[78] The effect of this was to reduce the role of the sinner in achieving his own salvation, and increase the power of the priest. It was no longer satisfactory that the *culpa* should have been remitted by God on the penitent's experiencing contrition of heart before the priest could come to grips with the *poena*.

In effect this, too, was an adjustment of penitential doctrine which had its roots in pragmatism. The contrition advocated by

[76] Richard of Saint Victoire, *De potestate ligandi*, 7, *PL* 196. 1161.

[77] Alexander of Hales, *Glossa in quattuor libros sententiarum Petri Lombardi*, 4. 18, Bibliotheca franciscana scholastica medii aevi, 15 (Florence, 1957), 253, 322, 323, 384; see Kilian F. Lynch, 'The Doctrine of Alexander of Hales on the Nature of Sacramental Grace', *Franciscan Studies*, 19 (1959), 345–7.

[78] P. Anciaux, 'Le Sacrément de Pénitence chez Guillaume d'Auvergne', *Ephemerides theologicae lovaniensis*, 24 (1948), 107.

the contritionists, the overwhelming emotional experience signalling God's forgiveness of sin, was a phenomenon compatible only with infrequent confession:

Le contritionnisme n'implique pas seulement une pénitence larmoyante. Il correspond aussi à toute une conception de la rémission de péchés, fondée non sur la confession regulière, mais sur une conversion bouleversante qui a pour effet une expiation visible et une profonde réforme des moeurs.[79]

Once the Church had enforced frequent confession, she had to resign herself to seeing penance become a routine. It became impossible to exact in every penitent the compunction which the early contritionist writers had deemed essential for the remission of sins. 'Attrition' then made its appearance: a state of penitence inferior to true contrition, which could be made as effective as contrition for remitting sins by the divine grace accorded to the penitent through the sacrament of penance, at the bestowing of absolution. William of Auvergne distinguishes contrition, the product of sanctifying grace, which destroys sin, from attrition, the beginnings of true penitence, the product of 'prevenient grace', which starts off the process of remission that is completed by sacramental absolution:

If anyone should ask what is the difference between contrition and attrition . . . I say that attrition is to contrition as a slight wound is to a fatal one, and that prevenient, preparatory grace is to sanctifying grace as warming something up is to setting fire to it, and as illuminating something in shadow is to flooding it with light.[80]

Until William of Auvergne it was accepted that the sacrament worked in consequence of a dispensation of grace from God which had already saved the penitent. After him, it became accepted that the sacrament itself was the operative agent in remitting sin; the first movement of grace which compels the sinner to confess was no longer sufficiently powerful to save him, and only sacramental absolution by a priest could confer the grace necessary to salvation.

William notes that there are three kinds of penitent: those who resist the action of sacramental grace, preventing the sacrament from doing any good (those who confess from obligation alone or

---

[79] Payen, *Motif du repentir*, p. 73.
[80] William of Auvergne, *De sacramento poenitentiae*, 5, *Opera Omnia* (Paris, 1674; republ. in facsimile, Frankfurt, 1963), p. 445, col. 2; see also p. 464, col. 2.

habit, and are not at all sorry for their sins); those who have put themselves into a state of grace but must confess because the Church commands it, who receive an augmentation of grace; and most people, who are moved by repentance to seek remission of their sins and saving grace.[81] It is no longer necessary to be contrite, however, because if the penitence is 'insuffisant dans sa réalité psychologique, l'efficacité sacramentelle est si grande que, par la miséricorde divine, le sacrement suplée parfois aux faiblesses du pénitent'.[82]

We will complete the survey of the sacrament's theological development arbitrarily with the *Summa theologiae* of Thomas Aquinas, perhaps the apogee of that development. Aquinas states that grace is infused by repentance, and is the effect, but not the cause of it.[83] Penitence is a dispenser of grace, of which the direct source is the absolution of the priest. The sacrament is therefore essential to salvation; without it no sin can be pardoned. Aquinas agrees with William of Auvergne that although the sacrament is effective by virtue of its own action, this action is not automatically successful. The grace dispensed by absolution can only act in the soul if it finds responsive co-operation there; but it is still conferred whether it acts or not.[84] Aquinas confirms that attrition can be transformed to contrition by the operation of the sacrament. He considers contrition, which disposes the sinner to penitence, confession, and satisfaction (which achieves the work of grace), to be the matter of the sacrament, while the form of it is absolution.

Essentially the Church's position has not changed since the time of Aquinas: today it is still accepted that absolution conferred by the priest in the sacrament and performance of the penance he enjoins is the only way in which sins can be remitted on earth. Minor adjustments in theory and practice continued to be made, but reinforced the power of the sacraments and drew further away from the beliefs expressed in the romances concerning the means by which sins are forgiven.

---

[81] William of Auvergne, *De sacramento poenitentiae*, 5. 441. 1.

[82] Anciaux, 'Le Sacrément de Pénitence', p. 100.

[83] Thomas Aquinas, *Summa*, 3. 89. 1.

[84] Thomas Aquinas, *Summa*, Suppl., 18. 2, 3; 3. 62. 1, 64. 1, 84. 3, 86. 4 and 6; *Summa contra gentiles*, 4. 72.

## iii. Penance in Fourteenth-Century England

So far we have not touched upon two developments of later medieval penitential practice which are undoubtedly reflected in *Guy of Warwick*, *Sir Gowther*, and *Sir Ysumbras*: indulgences and commutations. Indulgence, in the limited and specific sense of remission of penance for warfare against enemies of the Church, can be seen in operation in all three poems. Gowther's wholesale slaughter of Saracens must be seen as an integral part of his expiation;[85] the curious fairy-tale ending of *Sir Ysumbras* shows its hero as the instrument of God chastizing the pagan hordes; and even the more thoughtful and considered *Guy of Warwick* has its hero preparing to atone for the slaughter he has done for the sake of fame with some more slaughter for the sake of God. Modern readers may find this distasteful, but there can be no doubt that it was intended to be quite acceptable to its medieval audience.

The concept of indulgence was early and unforgettably associated with the Crusades by Urban II's decree at the Council of Clermont in 1095:

Whosoever, for the sake of devotion solely, and not for the sake of renown or for the attainment of wealth, shall have furthered the deliverance of God's holy city Jerusalem, he shall have that journey set against all his penances ... moreover, whoever takes up arms against [the enemies of God] on behalf of the Christian faith, and takes on himself the burden of this travelling, we release him from all great penalties owed on account of his sins, trusting in the mercy of God and of the blessed Apostles Peter and Paul.[86]

In this early stage the Indulgence still consisted only of the remission of penance still to be performed for sins which had already been repented of, confessed, and absolved as to *culpa*. In successive calls to arms more extravagant claims were made, including remission of all penance even for those who sent substitutes on Crusade, or went at another person's expense.[87] Although officially the Church's rule was always that the indulgence remitted only the temporal penalty due after the Sacrament of Penance had absolved the guilt of sin, the common people understood somewhat more:

---

[85] See Dieter Mehl, *The Middle English Romances of the Thirteenth and Fourteenth Centuries* (London, 1968), p. 126.

[86] *Consilium Claromontis*, AD 1095, 2 (Mansi 20. 838).

[87] See Lea, *Auricular Confession*, 3. 41, 152–61, and 224–9.

... for ages there was a widespread popular belief that plenary indulgences were *a culpa et a poena*, and this belief was a considerable factor in contributing to the large revenues which the Holy See drew from their sale throughout Europe.[88]

Another kind of Indulgence, that of commuting all or part of a penance by paying money at the direction of the confessor, is referred to in *Guy of Warwick*. Felice implores Guy not to leave her, and points out that, if he must do penance, he can do it perfectly well at home by founding an abbey or church and endowing it with a monk or priest to pray for him. This practice of making gifts of money to abbeys or other religious foundations in lieu of other, more exacting forms of penance was well known and widely practised by those who could afford it from the late eighth century onwards.[89] There are even instances of clerics deliberately imposing penances which could not possibly be performed without such a commutation, as when Peter Damian gave Archbishop Guido of Milan one hundred years of penance for simony, adding the precise sum for which each year could be commuted.[90] The author of *Guy* finds this practice questionable; Guy sternly rejects it in favour of a more primitive *quid pro quo*:

> Þat ich haue wiþ mi bodi wrouȝt
> Wiþ mi bodi it schal be bouȝt
> To bote me of þat bale.[91]

Apart from these examples of specific variations of ordinary penance, the romances do not reflect exactly the kind of penitential activities we know to have been taught and practised in England in the thirteenth and fourteenth centuries. Although of course most people (and most priests) were not deeply familiar with the great complex of penitential theology, they were schooled in the basic doctrines of their religion, and particularly those concerning sin and penance. The main means of disseminating this information was through preaching, which underwent a revolution in the mid-thirteenth century after the arrival of the Franciscan friars in 1225. But increasingly there was a demand for written treatises, in

---

[88] Lea, *Auricular Confession*, 3. 60.
[89] See Lea, *Auricular Confession*, 3. 225.
[90] Peter Damian, *Opuscula V*, *PL* 145. 97–8.
[91] *Guy of Warwick*, 2. 29. 10–12.

English, both for the instruction of parish priests who knew no Latin, and of laymen who could read.

Partly as a result of the ruling of the Fourth Lateran Council in 1215 that everyone must make confession to his parish priest at least once a year, a programme of education and reform was set in motion:

Many priests, especially parish priests, were inadequately instructed in these duties, and therefore both bishops and lesser churchmen undertook to guide priests in the performance of their duties by composing manuals.[92]

The decrees of Archbishop Peckham—himself formerly a Franciscan friar—in 1281 stated that people were to be instructed four times a year in six points: the articles of faith, the ten commandments, the works of mercy, the seven deadly sins, the seven virtues, and the seven sacraments, with special emphasis on the sacrament of penance. Manuals of instruction in the vernacular began to be written, forming a tradition distinct from that of 'the more sophisticated manuals of pastoral theology [or] the increasingly complicated penitential *summas*'.[93]

It is clear that medieval people liked their moral instruction to be presented in a highly organized, systematic way, and that they were very keen on lists of things which could be numbered through like rosary beads. Although in part this way of organizing the material was derived from the original *Summas* and *Sentences* of the schoolmen with their books, parts, questions, distinctions, articles, and yet further subdivisions, the fascination of ordinary people with magical numbers is evident in the way that devotional poems on the ten commandments, the seven deadly sins, the seven sacraments, the vices and virtues, the five joys and sorrows of our Lady, the five wounds of Christ, and so on were extracted from the penitential and instructive manuals and put into medieval manuscript anthologies. In almost all the manuscript anthologies in which copies of our four romances appear there are also poems of this kind.[94]

[92] H. G. Pfander, 'Some Medieval Manuals of Religious Instruction in England and Observations on Chaucer's *Parson's Tale*', *JEGP* 35 (1936), 243–58.

[93] V. A. Gillespie, 'The Literary Form of the Middle English Pastoral Manual with Particular Reference to the *Speculum Christiani* and some Related Texts', D.Phil. thesis (Oxford, 1981), p. 2.

[94] See Appendix B, below.

A tradition of vernacular confessional manuals, intended first of all to help the priest–confessor interrogate his penitents properly, then to help the penitents prepare themselves for confession, stretched back to the seventh-century handbooks of the Celtic Church.[95] Some of these manuals were hugely popular, and survive in many more manuscripts than the most popular of romances. Most manuals are very similar in structure and subject-matter, because one book, the *Summa virtutum ac vitiorum* of Guglielmus Peraldus (written *c.*1260) provided the well-spring of this kind of literature. It was translated into the *Somme le Roi* of Frère Lorens d'Orléans in 1279, which in turn inspired other versions, translations, and adaptations, including *Handlyng Synne*, *Pricke of Conscience*, *Ayenbite of Inwyt*, *Speculum Christiani*, *Cursor Mundi*, *Jacob's Well*, the *Lay Folk's Prayer Book*, *Instructions for Parish Priests*, *Vices and Virtues*, and *The Lay Folk's Catechism* (to name but a few). They are inspired by the basic concept of an encyclopedic collection of essential doctrines for unlearned people. They usually include the following subjects, though the order varies greatly:

The Ten Commandments
The Seven Deadly Sins
The Seven Virtues
The Seven Sacraments
The Seven Gifts of the Holy Ghost
The Seven Works of Mercy
The Fourteen Articles of Faith (sometimes twelve or fifteen, however).

Some, like *Handlyng Synne* and *Cursor Mundi*, have a whole section devoted entirely to penance, which is considered in its three essential parts of contrition, confession, and satisfaction. In many the main text is supported by exempla, as in collections of medieval sermons: the authors of *Handlyng Synne* and *Jacob's Well* are particularly fond of using such stories to illustrate their moral points. *Jacob's Well* is typical in some ways, although its author chose to give it a rather quaint allegorical framework.[96] The 'well' of the title is a deep pit (man's conscience or soul) full of all kinds

---

[95] See D. W. Robertson, 'The Cultural Tradition of *Handlyng Synne*', *Speculum*, 22 (1947), 162–85.
[96] *Jacob's Well*, ed. A. Brandeis, EETS, os, 115 (London, 1900; repr. 1973).

of filth (sin) which must be removed using various tools (such as the 'skete' of contrition, the 'skauel' of confession, and the 'schouyll' of satisfaction), then reinforced with a wall of stones (good works), ready to receive the influx of clean, pure water (grace). Every detail is significant; just as the 'skete' has a handle seven spans in length, so contrition must have seven qualities: it must be meditated upon, it must be 'priue' to God alone, it must be for all your sins together, it must be in order according to the events of your life, it must be for your own sins only, not those of others, it must be the product of genuine sorrow ('contricyoun muste be bytter moornyng for þi synne, noȝt leyȝhyng ne enioying of þi synne, but in bytter heuynes'), and it must be felt inwardly, but not shown outwardly.[97]

The author is absolutely typical in insisting that contrition on its own is not sufficient for the removal of sin (unless you have intended to make confession but have been genuinely unable to do so before death), but must be followed by confession and satisfaction: 'for þi contricyoun avayleth þe noȝt but schryfte & satysfaccyoun be don, ȝif þou haue power, tyme, and space.' If you are able to make confession and for some reason you put it off, your contrition has no effect:

þou fallyst in-to a newe dedly synne, be-cause þou fulfyllest noȝt þi first purpos & þi ferst wyll to be schreuyn & to make amendys ... And ȝif þi sorwe be neuere so grete, & þou wylt noȝt be scheuyn, & do penaunce, ne make amendys, þe synne is stylle in þi soule, for þi sorwe þanne castyth it noȝt out.[98]

In support of the statement that contrition, even if accompanied by acts of penance privately undertaken, is completely ineffective in removing sin unless you go to confession, the author gives the example of a Roman lady who fell in love with her own son, bore him a child, then killed it:

... but alwey, in here herte, sche was sory & alwey preyed god of mercy, & dede scharpe dedys of penaunce, & made restitucyoun of her wrongys, saaf sche durste noȝt be schreuyn of here cursyd synne, for schame.

[This enables a fiend disguised as a clerk to accuse her before the emperor. She asks for a little time before answering the accusation, and immediately goes to a priest and confesses.]

And þanne, wyth full sorwe of herte & wepyng, sche schrof here to a

[97] *Jacob's Well*, pp. 170–1.　　[98] *Jacob's Well*, pp. 173–4.

preest. He comfortyd here, & ȝaf here in penaunce to seye a pater noster, and specyally þat sche schulde worschepyn oure lady wyth certeyn Auees.

[She completes her penance, and appears before the emperor. The fiend is unable to recognize her because she is protected by the Virgin Mary.][99]

It is clear that, for the author of *Jacob's Well* and others who emphasize the necessity of confession to a priest, self-directed penance without confession, such as that undertaken by Guy of Warwick or Sir Ysumbras, is not effective in removing sin.

In the chapter on confession itself, *Jacob's Well* again presents absolutely the standard teachings on preparing yourself for confession and what you must and must not do. Confession must be 'opynly schewyd', completely accurate in details of circumstances, performed promptly, accompanied by weeping, often repeated (in case you forget some of your sins), and undertaken freely out of love and devotion to God. The most demanding of these conditions is that the confession should be accurate in detail, and this is constantly emphasized in all confessional instruction manuals, whether designed for priest or layman. The penitent must relate all the circumstances in which his sins were committed, so that the priest can decide the degree of his culpability. The penitent must therefore ask himself, or the priest must ask him, 'Quis, quid, ubi, per quos, quociens, quomodo, quando':

> ... in þi schryfte say ryȝtly in what astat & what degre were þou, whanne þou dedyst þat synne, & in what astate or degre was þe oþer persone by whom þou synned, were þou or þe oþer persone syke or hole, chyld or of full resoun, ȝung or olde, pore or ryche or gentyl, fre or bonde, wyttyng or vnwyttyng, wyth þi wyll or aȝens þi wyll, weddyd or sengyll, of þi kyn or of straungerys, seculere or relygyous, clerk or lewyd, mayde or wydewe, of þi gostly kynrede or nay, of þin affynyte or nay, or cristen man or iewe· telle also ryȝt what synne þou hast do, & where þou dydest pat synne, in pryue place or opyn place, in holy place or oþer place, dedyst þi synne alone or wyth helpe & strengthe of oþere, or be oþeres counfort.[100]

and so on. John Myrc's *Instructions for Parish Priests* contains a similar huge passage on degrees of sinfulness, and adds that the priest must especially take note of the penitent's contrition. The power of contrition in removing sin (provided the penitent has confessed) is of great importance:

[99] *Jacob's Well*, p. 67.      [100] *Jacob's Well*, p. 184.

But fyrste take hede, by gode a-vys,
Of what contrycyone þat he ys,
ȝef he be sory for hys synne,
And fulle contryte as þou myȝt kenne;
Wepeþ faste, and ys sory,
And asketh ȝerne of mercy,
A-bregge hys penaunce þen by myche
For god hym selfe for-ȝeueth syche.[101]

Robert Mannyng points out in *Handlyng Synne* that, though contrition is not effective unless accompanied by confession and satisfaction, equally confession is not effective without contrition. He illustrates this point with the story of the devil who went to confession in the hope that he would emerge all white and spotless like the souls of human penitents he had seen. The priest spots him by the enormity of his sins, and the fact that he expresses no sorrow for them. He explains:

Þo þat þou sawe so blak wyþ ynne,
Þey are repentaunt of here synne,
And are now come to ryght gode wyl
To do penaunce & no more yl . . .
. . . But þou þat hast no repentaunce
But loue & lykyng in þy cumbraunce
To feyrhede shalt þou neuer wende,
But blak & foule wyþ outen ende.[102]

There is still considerable variation in the matter of satisfaction, of the actual penances enjoined. John Myrc says that, although of course severer penances must be given for serious sins, or for those who are uncontrite, it is better not to give penances which are so harsh that they are unlikely to be carried out at all, thus leaving the penitent's soul worse off than if he had not confessed:

Bettur hyt ys wyth penaunce lutte
In-to purgatory a mon to putte,
Þen wyþ penaunce ouer myche
Sende hym to helle putte.[103]

---

[101] John Myrc, *Instructions for Parish Priests*, ed. E. Peacock, EETS, os, 31 (London, 1868; repr. 1973), ll. 1511–18.
[102] Robert Mannyng of Brunne, *Handlyng Synne*, ed. Idelle Sullens (New York, 1983), ll. 12611–14, 12619–22.
[103] Myrc, *Instructions*, ll. 1547–50.

Myrc mentions that the penance for any mortal sin is to eat only bread and water every Friday and to go without meat every Wednesday for seven years, but 'now be fewe þat wole do so,/þer fore a ly3ter way þou moste go'.

Most penances seem to consist of prayer, fasting, and alms-giving in various combinations for various lengths of time. 'Fastyng', however, according to the author of *Jacob's Well*, is not only abstinence from food. 'In þis fastyng is vnder-stonde all manere of penaunce', including 'hardnes of clothyng on bak & in bed', 'mekenes, lownes & myldenes', and 'restitucyoun'.[104] The author of the 'Boke of Penaunce' attached in some manuscripts to the *Cursor Mundi* goes somewhat further than this, making fasting itself only a subdivision of a larger category called 'Chastiyng of flexs'. Fasting entails abstinence from food and drink, from sexual activity, and from worldly pleasures and worldly thoughts. A further subdivision of chastizing of the flesh is 'wand', and this reminds us much more vividly of the old harsh public penances:

> Þis ferth point þat i cald wand
> Es discipline at vnder-stand,
> And o þis find we four maner
> Þe first es arme o scrift to bere
> Þat es in askes and in hare,
> And weping and vneses lair;
> Þe toþer knock on brest wit hand,
> Wit knelyng and bakbetyng a-mang;
> Þe thride in pilgrimage it es;
> Þe ferth vn-hele and pin in flexs,
> In soru and site and al wa,
> Þat job him tholed, and oþer ma.[105]

But this romance-like severity of penance is rare; it is much more common to recommend less severe penances which can be performed privately and without other people noticing.

We learn from *Cursor Mundi* that while most sins can be absolved by the parish priest, there are some sins, of the more ser-ious kind such as adultery, false witness, manslaughter, witchcraft, usury, slaying your lord, harming your family, and so on, for which the penitent must go to the bishop for penance and absolu-

---

[104] *Jacob's Well*, pp. 194–5.
[105] *Cursor Mundi*, ed. R. Morris, 5, EETS, os, 68 (London, 1878; repr. 1966), ll. 29086–97.

tion.[106] In addition there are six sins which only the Pope can forgive. These are sins such as sacrilege, witchcraft, assaults against clergy, and other crimes against the Church.[107]

While God is always ready to forgive those who repent of their sins and take the proper course of confession and penance, there is no doubt about what becomes of those who die unregenerate, as illustrated by the story in *Jacob's Well* of the witch who died unshriven. She had instructed her body to be bound into its coffin with iron chains, and her children to keep watch over it with prayers. But the woman's unconfessed sins give the devils the power to enter the church, break through all the chains, and conjure the dead woman to rise from her coffin. She 'ros opynly, in sy3t of alle here wakerys, & roryng went out at þe cherche-dore, & was sett on a blak brennyng dewyl, & borne to þe pytt of helle'.[108]

The influence of the old Celtic handbooks of penance is evident not only in the attempts to define the exact nature of the sins committed, but also in the widespread reference to remedies for sin, such as the advice given in *Cursor Mundi* on combating the sin of Pride:

> Ogaines þis sin es medcyn gude
> Forto be meke and milde of mode
> And knaw oure self in alkins thing.[109]

This principle of countering tendency to sin by deliberately acting on the opposite virtue is one which informs the penances of the romance heroes. With startling relevance to *Sir Gowther* we find the following passage on the remedy for Wrath in Myrc's *Instructions for Parish Priests*:

> Agaynes wraþþe hys helpe schal be,
> 3ef he haue grace in herte to se,
> How aungelus, when he ys wroth,
> From hym faste flen and goth,
> And fendes faste to hym renneth,
> And wyþ fuyre of helle hys herte brenneth,
> And maketh hym so hote & hegh,
> Þat no mon may byde hym negh,
> And makeþ hym syche as þey arn,
> Of goddes chylde, þe deueles barn,

---

[106] *Cursor Mundi*, ll. 26204–51.   [107] *Cursor Mundi*, ll. 29241–65.
[108] *Jacob's Well*, pp. 186–7.   [109] *Cursor Mundi*, ll. 27650–2.

Wharfore he mote wyth sofferynge,
Quenche in hym syche brennynge,
A-gaynus wrathþe soferaunce
Mote be myche hys penaunce.[110]

Generally speaking, the examination which a penitent gives to himself in accordance with the instructions of these manuals is a detailed, minute, conscientious analysis of his sinful acts and the degree of intent with which they were committed. It is thoughtful, systematic, and essentially sedate. The outcome of it is a confession which will be as accurate an account as possible of the penitent's state of mind and the degree of penalty which he has incurred. Above all, the manuals are intended to train the penitent's mind, to form mental habits which will enable him to prepare for confession efficiently and thoroughly. The importance of sacramental confession is paramount; contrition is important, and highly desirable as it lessens the penalties necessary for absolution to be effective, but it is not necessary, and it is not effective without confession. It is more important to define the exact nature of the offence than to be really contrite.

It is not in the nature of the kind of romance of which our four poems are examples for the hero to indulge in minute self-examination or analysis of motive. Even at the moments when the hero is forced to come face to face with the fact of his sins and to do a certain amount of soul-searching prior to his decision to do penance, it is clear that an altogether different mental process is at work. Sir Gowther is overcome by shame and remorse and bursts into tears. Guy of Warwick, contemplating his past life by starlight, is suddenly moved by a conviction of his sinful nature. Robert of Sicily understands, after questioning himself, in a moment of revelation why he is being punished. Sir Ysumbras does not undergo any process of self-examination at all. Only Gowther actually makes confession. But all the protagonists are compelled to do penance, whether self-imposed or not, by a feeling which is forceful, spontaneous, unique. They are inspired by a deep repugnance for their former sins. There is no question of any of them returning to their old ways, or repeating their penance. These aspects bear a closer relation to the writings of St Bernard and the Contritionists than to later penitential literature.

---

[110] Myrc, *Instructions*, ll. 1567–80.

The Middle English manuals discussed above were all written more or less at the same time as three of our four romances, and in possession of the same kind of knowledge of penitential theory and practice, presumably, as that available to their authors. Yet the Anglo-Norman poem *Gui de Warewic*, source of all the Middle English versions, was probably composed between 1232 and 1242,[111] before the appearance of such manuals, and the story of the penitent sinner is already fully formed in all the aspects we have noted that are common to all four poems.

There is some evidence that the idea of a great, nobly born sinner who renounces his way of life and wanders through the world as a poor pilgrim by way of penance was deeply impressed upon the popular imagination. Some twenty years after the death of Count Baldwin IX of Flanders in 1205, a man named Bertrand of Ray was able to impersonate the dead count and raise a popular revolt against local French domination. The impostor was accepted by Flemish nobility who had known the count; a nephew of Baldwin's claimed to recognize him as his lost uncle. He was enabled to perpetrate this astonishing fraud because of a legend which had become attached to the figure of the real, dead count:

It was rumoured abroad that the count was after all not dead, but, having sinned greatly, was still discharging a penance imposed on him by the Pope. For many years he had been living in obscurity as a wandering beggar and hermit; but his expiation was now almost completed and he would very soon be returning in glory to free his land and people.[112]

This story corresponds in several significant respects with the penances described in our four poems. Firstly, it should be noted that the sin supposedly committed by the count is not really important, except as providing the occasion for his penance. In the romances, similarly, there is much greater emphasis on the penance itself, on the suffering undergone by the hero, than on defining the exact nature of the sin which occasioned it. Secondly, as in *Sir Gowther, The Romauns of Partenay*, and *Valentine and Orson*, the count's penance was imposed on him by the Pope. Thirdly, his

---

[111] See Lee C. Ramsey, *Chivalric Romances* (Bloomington, 1983), p. 48.
[112] Norman Cohn, *The Pursuit of the Millenium* (London, 1970), p. 90. The account can be found in Philippe Mouskes's *Chronique rimée*, ed. J. Reifenberg, 2 (Brussels, 1838), ll. 24463–760. Mouskes gives Nebuchadnezzar and 'duc Joisbiert' as further examples of wandering penitents later restored.

penance has compelled him to wander far from his home in a state of great poverty. Fourthly, he is expected to return in glory.

It is almost certain, therefore, that stories of this type, with fairly consistent features, existed prior to the composition of the earliest of our penitential romances, and were available for their authors to draw on. These conjectured stories may have contained a fusion of elements derived from folk-tales, from real, historical Solemn Penances, and from a consciousness of the kind of 'conversion bouleversante' described and advocated by the Contritionists. One feature of the story of the pseudo-Baldwin, however, makes it like the romances and distinguishes it from the religious ideas associated with this kind of penance; which is that the penitent, his expiation completed, returns to the world and to his former position of wealth and power (though not, of course, to his former sinful activities). It may seem an obvious remark to make, but this distinction between the ultimate goals of religious and worldly aspirations is a very important one. Susan Crane has pointed out, in her recent perceptive study of *Guy of Warwick*, that this difference, hitherto ignored by modern commentators, may be the reason behind the condemnations of these 'religious romances' along with the rest as worldly, frivolous, and vain:

> The Church's condemnation of the exemplary romances along with the rest indicates that the subordination of religious to worldly impulses in romance was evident to contemporary observers . . . [and] openly recognises that romances and religious literature are animated by different values, and ultimately endorse separate truths.[113]

The penances which the heroes of our four romances undertake, therefore, can be seen to reflect strongly the influence of religious ideas, but not to follow these ideas to their proper conclusion. The heroes feel the sentiments of self-reproach and contrition for their sins, but instead of turning from the world to God, their penances fit them for their places in the world, and it is only through the world that they reach God. The history of penance shows us that in the early Middle Ages as later, there was a distinction between the kind of penance anyone did for very minor sins and that imposed by the Church for more serious sins. Originally the former was a private matter of self-directed penitential acts such as

---

[113] Susan Crane, '*Guy of Warwick* and the Question of Exemplary Romance', *Genre*, 17 (1984), 351–74; quotation from p. 359.

alms–giving, prayer, and fasting; in the later Middle Ages this too was absorbed into the expanding control and power of the Church over people's lives, via the sacrament of penance. Meanwhile the severe public penance imposed on sinners by the early Church developed gradually into the rare Solemn Penance, imposed only for very serious offences and only once.

The romances appear to reflect a tradition developed in isolation from the more orthodox view represented in the popular devotional literature of the day, particularly penitential manuals, in the intense nature of penitence, the extreme harshness of the penalty, and the resulting reformation of character. In the following chapters we will explore how this select religious material and the literary form and techniques of romance have been successfully employed together by the authors of our four poems.

# 3

# *Guy of Warwick*

The Middle English *Guy of Warwick*, like *Sir Ysumbras*, enjoyed a position of unusual prominence in medieval popular literature and, if one may speak of such a thing, in medieval literary consciousness. Although it survives in only five manuscripts (of which two are mere fragments) and three early prints,[1] its enduring popularity[2] and its frequent mention by name in other medieval works[3] testify both to its evident fame and to the fact that, then as now, it was seen as 'the prototype of medieval romance'.[4]

As such it presents something of a problem of classification. Scholars who wish to propose a separate, hybrid genre of 'secular hagiography' for romances which are strongly religious and didactic have disagreed about the inclusion of *Guy of Warwick*; for it is too central to be divided from the main body of 'real' romances, even though its relationship with the *Life of St Alexis* has long been recognized.[5] Hanspeter Schelp, for example, includes it in his category of 'exemplary romance'; Diana T. Childress omits it from her list of 'secular hagiographies', while David N. Klausner puts it in. J. Burke Severs and Dieter Mehl place the poem in a

---

[1] Manuscripts: National Library of Scotland, Advocates 19. 2. 1 (Auchinleck MS), fos. 108a–146b, 146b–167a, 167a–175b (version in three parts) (A); Caius College, Cambridge, 107, pp. 1–271 (C); Cambridge University Library, Ff. 2. 38 (*olim* 690), fos. 161a–239a (U); BL Sloane 1044, no. 625, fo. 345a–b (fragment); BL Additional 14409 (Phillipps), fos. 74a–77b (fragment) (P). Prints: R. Pynson, London, *c.*1500; Douce fragments 20 (e. 14), W. de Worde, Westminster, 1500; W. Copland, *Book of the Most Victoryous Prince Guy*, London, *c.*1560.

[2] See R. S. Crane, 'The Vogue of *Guy of Warwick*', *PMLA* 30 (1915), 125–94.

[3] e.g. *Sir Thopas*, 2. 2; *Beues of Hamtoun*, EETS, ES, 46, p. 123; William of Nassyngton, *Speculum Vitae*, ll. 35–48; MS Harl. 7332, fo. 49.

[4] Lee C. Ramsay, *Chivalric Romances: Popular Literature in Medieval England* (Bloomington, 1983), p. 43.

[5] See Mary Dominica Legge, *Anglo-Norman Literature and its Background* (Oxford, 1963), pp. 162–71 and David N. Klausner, 'Didacticism and Drama in *Guy of Warwick*', *Medievalia et Humanistica*, NS, 6 (1975), 103–19.

group of long, episodic romances, such as *Beues of Hamtoun*, rather than with the other religious romances.[6]

In part this reflects certain obvious differences from such works as *Sir Ysumbras*, *Sir Gowther*, *Roberd of Cisyle*, *Amis and Amiloun*, or *Athelston*. In the first place, *Guy of Warwick* is a very much longer poem, and exhibits all the stylistic and structural differences which this entails, and which led Dieter Mehl very sensibly to classify romances by their length as much as by their content.[7] It may well be earlier in composition than *Sir Ysumbras* and is certainly much earlier than the other two surviving penitential romances.[8] It is based very closely on its Anglo-Norman source.[9] These are all things which must be acknowledged by anyone who wants to make of these four poems a discrete subgroup of 'romances dealing with the fortunes of regenerate sinners'.[10]

The poem's popularity has usually been accounted for by its multiplicity of adventures rather than by any literary merit; most commentators have held the view that it recommended itself to its medieval audiences as simple fare, by the entertaining nature of its episodes with their plentiful battles and dragons, offering nothing more than a thriller with a strong moral.[11] The fact that it is mentioned in *Sir Thopas* sanctioned it as a butt for ridicule, and even its champions have been compelled to admit that it contains plenty of examples of those features of Middle English romance which many since Chaucer have found absurd—crude sentiments, hackneyed clichés, tedious repetitions. More recently, however, scholars have begun to appreciate that the seemingly motiveless

[6] Hanspeter Schelp, *Exemplarische Romanzen im Mittelenglischen* (Gottingen, 1967); Diana T. Childress, 'Between Romance and Legend: "Secular Hagiography" in Middle English Literature', *Philological Quarterly*, 57 (1978), 311–22; Klausner, 'Didacticism and Drama'; Dieter Mehl, *The Middle English Romances of the Thirteenth and Fourteenth Centuries* (London, 1968); J. Burke Severs, *A Manual of Writings in Middle English, 1050–1500*, 1, *Romances* (New Haven, 1967).

[7] Mehl, *Romances*, p. 36.

[8] Severs, *Manual*, pp. 13–15, dates *Guy of Warwick* as *c*.1300, *Sir Ysumbras* as early 14th cent., *Sir Gowther* as *c*.1400, and *Roberd of Cisyle* as late 14th cent.

[9] We should be cautious about claiming this as a distinction, however; we do not have the immediate sources of *Sir Ysumbras*, *Sir Gowther*, and *Roberd of Cisyle*, but they may have been AN poems close to the surviving ME versions.

[10] Margaret Bradstock, '*Sir Gowther*: Secular Hagiography or Hagiographical Romance or Neither?' *AUMLA* 59 (1983), pp. 41 and 47.

[11] V. B. Richmond, '*Guy of Warwick*: A Medieval Thriller', *South Atlantic Quarterly*, 73 (1974), 554–63.

repetition of similar episodes is the result of a recognizable structural principle. Dieter Mehl was the first to recognize that '[Guy's] second series of adventures can be seen as a re-enactment of his former career, only in a very different spirit. The structure of the second part parallels that of the first part, but it puts a very different interpretation on Guy's exploits.'[12] A more detailed analysis is provided by Hanspeter Schelp:

Das Konstruktionsmotiv des zweiten Teil der Romanze deutet sich an: das Streben des Helden nach 'blis', das nun als die ewige Glückseligkeit zu verstehen ist. Der zweite Teil stellt äußerlich eine deutliche Parallele zum ersten dar. Die ritterlich-höfische Liebeswerbung ('þi loue') und das Lehnsverhältnis des Ritters zu seinem Herrn (wie übrigens auch zu der Dame) werden auf das Streben des Helden nach der Liebe Gottes ('his loue') und ihre Erfüllung in der ewigen Glückseligkeit und auf sein Verhältnis zu dem göttlichen Herrn sowohl begrifflich wie vorgangsmäßig übertragen.[13]

In this chapter I shall attempt to give a critical account of the poem which affords a practical demonstration of the techniques employed by its author in its construction.

Before attempting that, however, it is worth considering the poem's literary and historical context. The obvious starting-point for such a discussion is the four remarks referred to above, made about the poem in the Middle Ages. Two of these occur in romances (or at least, in fourteenth-century secular literature); and two in the context of religious writers expressing their disapproval of those very romances.

In *Sir Thopas*, *Guy of Warwick* is mentioned in a short list of 'romances of prys':

> Men speken of romances of prys
> Of Horn child and of Ypotis,
>   Of Beves and sir Gy,
>   Of sir Lybeux and Pleyndamour—
> But sir Thopas, he bereth the flour
>   Of roial chivalry![14]

---

[12] Mehl, *Romances*, p. 227.
[13] Schelp, *Exemplarische Romanzen*, p. 141.
[14] *Sir Thopas*, from *The Riverside Chaucer*, ed. L. D. Benson (Boston, 1987), p. 216 (Fragment VII, Group B2, ll. 897–902).

And in *Beues of Hamtoun* it is referred to in a similar way:

> Guy of Warwycke, I vnderstonde,
> Slewe a dragon in Northumberlonde;
> But suche a dragon was neuer sene,
> As syr Beuys slewe, I wene.[15]

The ostensible reason for mentioning *Guy of Warwick* in both these examples is to emphasize the superiority of Sir Thopas and Bevis by comparing their qualities or exploits to those of other famous heroes. This is not an unusual strategy for a romance writer to adopt; similar lists of heroes occur also in *Richard Coer de Lyon* and *Laud Troy Book*, and here, too, the names are offered as examples which are surpassed by their respective heroes. *Guy of Warwick* and *Beues of Hamtoun* appear, coupled together, in both these lists. Other lists occur in romances in which the heroes are cited as a company of exalted characters to whom the hero of the present poem is equal, but not superior.[16]

These references tell us that *Guy of Warwick* was widely known and well regarded. Guy reached the distinction, not accorded to many romance heroes, of having not only his name and his general heroic status known, but also his individual exploits. Thus the author of *Beues of Hamtoun* refers to the dragon Guy killed in Northumberland in the confident expectation that his readers, when they hear that the dragon encountered by Bevis was even more huge and horrible, will be suitably impressed. In addition, Guy's combat with the giant Colbrond became so well known as to acquire the status of historical fact.[17]

The narrator of *Sir Thopas* appears to employ the same device as the narrators of *Beues of Hamtoun*, *Richard Coer de Lyon*, and *Laud Troy Book*; but his list is not quite as straightforward as it appears. He cites three pairs of heroes. Of the first pair, Ypotis is

---

[15] *Beues of Hamtoun*, ed. E. Kölbing, EETS, ES, 46 (London, 1885), p. 123.

[16] *Guy of Warwick* is mentioned in lists of heroes in *Richard Coer de Lion*, ed. K. Brunner (Leipzig, 1913), l. 6730; *Speculum Vitae*, l. 45, see n. 23, below; *The Squyr of Lowe Degre*, ed. W. E. Mead (Boston, 1904), l. 80; and *Laud Troy Book*, ed. J. E. Wülfing, EETS, OS, 121, 122 (repr. as 1 vol., London, 1973), l. 15. Of these four only *The Squyr of Lowe Degre* does not couple Guy's name with that of Bevis of Hampton. The squire wishes he were 'so bolde in chyvalry' as Gawain or Guy, or failing that, 'so doughty of my hande/ As was the gyaunte Syr Colbrande', ll. 80–2.

[17] See R. S. Crane, 'Vogue', and Hardyng's *Chronicle*, ed. Henry Ellis (London, 1812), pp. 210–11.

the hero not of a romance but of a pious verse legend,[18] and of the third pair, 'Pleyndamour' appears to be a name which Chaucer has mischievously made up.[19] The rest are all genuine enough, and the second pair to be mentioned, Bevis and Guy, are in addition heroes of the two poems of which Chaucer made the most use in his own composition. For the audience of the *Canterbury Tales* (as opposed to the audience of *Sir Thopas*) who are able to appreciate the joke on all its levels, Chaucer points out those romances which exhibit the kind of 'drasty riming' he is parodying. Some of the choicest gems, as has been pointed out by L. H. Loomis, are lifted almost verbatim from *Guy of Warwick*.[20]

The distance in date between the two references might be seventy to a hundred years.[21] Although Chaucer shows that some readers towards the close of the fourteenth century found poems like *Guy of Warwick* unsophisticated, if not absurdly crude, they continued to be produced: *Lybeaus Desconus*, for example, was probably composed by Chaucer's contemporary Thomas of Chester, and *Guy of Warwick* itself was still being copied.[22]

The other two references are made by ecclesiastical writers speaking from the other side of the House. The first, not coincidentally, is again in a list, the list of 'gestes' given by William of Nassington at the beginning of his translation of John of Waldby's *Speculum Vitae*:

> I warne 30w ferst ate benyngnyng,
> Y wyl make 30w no veyne carpyng
> Of dethes of armes, ne of amours,
> As doth menstral and jestoures,
> That maketh carpyng in many place
> Of Octovyane and Ysambrace,
> And of other gestes,
> Namely when they cum to festes;

---

[18] *Ypotis*, ed. Carl Horstmann, *Altenglische Legenden* (Heilbronn, 1881), pp. 341–8.

[19] See note in Benson, *Riverside Chaucer*, p. 922.

[20] Laura Hibbard Loomis, 'Chaucer and the Auchinleck Manuscript: *Thopas* and *Guy of Warwick*', in *Essays and Studies in Honour of Carleton Brown* (New York, 1940), pp. 111–28 and essay in W. F. Bryan and G. Dempster, eds., *Sources and Analogues of Chaucer's Canterbury Tales* (Chicago, 1941), pp. 486–93.

[21] Severs, *Manual*, p. 13 dates *Beues of Hamtoun* at *c.*1300; Benson, *Riverside Chaucer*, p. 918 states that '*Sir Thopas* gives no clue to its date' but that it must be between 1380 and 1400.

[22] MS U is dated *c.*1450–1500 by Severs.

Ne of the lyf of Bewys of Hamptone,
That was a kny3t of gret renone,
Ne of syre Gy of Warewyke,
Alle 3yf hit my3te some men lyke.[23]

It is noticeable that, rather unexpectedly, the righteous scorn of these clerical writers falls equally upon 'religious' romances like *Guy of Warwick* and *Sir Ysumbras*, as upon 'secular' romances like *Beues of Hamtoun*, in spite of that strong tone of piety which scholars such as John Finlayson have found objectionably inconsistent with 'true romance'. It is unlikely that the writer was unaware of their edifying contents; it should be noted that three of the four romances he names are religious, and he obviously knows something about such poems and their place in popular culture.

The aptness of popular romances as a vehicle for teaching religious or moral truths in no way mitigates the writer's opposition; and it is a recognition of this aptness, the fact that a romance can penetrate the sensibilities of the common man more successfully than conventional religious literature,[24] which is the gist of our final reference to *Guy of Warwick*. In a sermon on the Gospel for Holy Week the writer uses the simile of Christ the Good Knight, donning his armour and joining battle against the Devil to free us from slavery, and reminds himself of some anecdotes to use as exempla:

And the story of the man who ... hearing the deeds of Guy of Warwick read aloud, when he came to the place where it dealt with the gratitude of the lion and how it was cut into three, wept uncontrollably. Reproving him, a brother said: O ungrateful wretch who drops so many tears for such a trifle, yet does not grieve for Christ who was condemned and put to death for your sake.[25]

[23] From MS Bodleian 48, fo. 47, quoted by J. O. Halliwell in *The Thornton Romances*, Camden Society, 30 (London, 1884), p. xx.

[24] Similar statements can be found elsewhere, e.g. from Ailred of Rievaulx, *Speculum caritatis*, 2. 17, *PL* 195. 565: 'For example, in the stories which are everywhere fabricated about the unknown Arthur, I remember myself to have been continually moved to an outburst of tears. This made me not a little ashamed of my own vanity, who if by chance those stories about Our Lord were being read aloud, or sung, or at all events told in a public sermon, would listen calmly', or Peter of Blois, *De confessione sacramentali*, *PL* 207. 1088: 'Furthermore they tell of pressures and wrongs cruelly imposed on a certain man, that is concerning Arthur and Gawain and Tristan, fabulous stories which the *histriones* repeat, on hearing of which the hearts of the listeners are convulsed by pity, and continually pricked to tears ... he who suffers with God, suffers with Arthur.'

[25] BL MS Harleian 7322, fo. 49.

One is reminded of E. Talbot Donaldson's remark that his sense of humour was 'insufficiently robust' to laugh aloud on reading *De amore* by Andreas Capellanus, as Drouart la Vache claimed to have done in the Middle Ages.[26] Perhaps, though we cannot summon up a tear for Guy's lion, we can still be moved by the delicate, understated poignancy of his deathbed reunion with Felice.

As it is, we can be left in no doubt that while contemporary ecclesiastical writers acknowledged the power of popular romances over their wayward flocks, they regretted it and opposed it. Romances of all kinds were condemned from the pulpit as 'vanite'. If 'religious' romances were seriously and orthodoxly didactic, it is difficult to imagine why they should be included—and so deliberately included—in such condemnations, along with poems relating extra-marital love affairs. If their purpose is to teach moral lessons, if they were composed by hack clerical writers aping the popular traits of romance style in order to sweeten the moral pill, then they cannot justly have been regarded as 'vayn carpyng' or 'bot fantum o þis warld'. But the fact is that they were so regarded; and this calls for a fresh examination of their religiousness. In her recent brilliant study of 'exemplary romances' Susan Crane comments:

Ecclesiastical animosity for romances is neither ironical nor strange, but rather openly recognises that romances and religious literature are animated by different values, and ultimately endorse separate truths.[27]

These observations prompt an examination of the real aims of a poem like *Guy of Warwick*. Is it really serious and didactic? Can it really have been composed by a clerical author, whose objectives and motives can be supposed to have been very different from those of most romance authors? Susan Crane observes that what she terms 'insular romances' (whether Middle English or Anglo-Norman) differ from their Continental counterparts in having absorbed religious values under pressure of competition from popular forms of religious literature, especially saints' lives, and that furthermore, these romances characteristically subvert the religious impulses they absorb to support secular values:

These pious romances do accept and incorporate Christian impulses

---

[26] E. Talbot Donaldson, 'The Myth of Courtly Love', from *Speaking of Chaucer* (London, 1977), p. 160.

[27] Susan Crane, '*Guy of Warwick* and the Question of Exemplary Romance', *Genre*, 17 (1984), 351–74; quotation from p. 354.

from hagiography, but they temper their acceptance with clearly defined resistance to those implications of religious teaching that are incompatible with pursuing earthly well-being . . . in these works, religious sensibilities sustain fundamental commitments to the importance of worldly achievement, the value of earthly life, and the centrality of the hero's power.[28]

This statement should be welcomed with relief, as it refutes some of the confusing and unhelpful arguments about how 'religious' romances supposedly differ in a fundamental generic way from 'secular' romances. A still more illuminating remark is that 'Piety enriches and broadens the importance of heroic action, but in so doing it becomes in some ways merely an attribute of secular heroism.'[29] This suggests that, instead of trying to validate a distinction between religious and non-religious romances, the proper sphere for investigation should be the extent to which the ideal discussed and exemplified in so many romances embraced piety as an essential element.

There is a strong case for arguing that most Middle English romances are, if not didactic, then certainly exemplary, and that there is no fundamental generic difference between those romances in which the hero's piety and his conscious relationship with his Maker are accepted but not explored in depth, and those in which these aspects of his heroic character are given prominence.

Susan Crane suggests that *Guy of Warwick* and the other religious romances earned their ecclesiastical opprobrium by 'substituting worldly victories for legendary transcendence'[30] and supporting such worldly values as wealth, power, and dynastic interests. The assertion made by religious romances, that virtue should be (and is in the fictional world) rewarded in this rather than the next life, and without the offices of the Church in most cases, is quite likely to have been repugnant to ecclesiastical writers, and is in direct opposition to the teachings which they themselves sanctioned and were trying to express. This has been largely overlooked. To say that the difference between a romance based on a saint's life and the saint's life on which it is based is that the saint suffers martyrdom and is rewarded in heaven, while his

---

[28] Crane, '*Guy of Warwick*', pp. 352–3, 370.
[29] Crane, '*Guy of Warwick*', p. 352.
[30] Crane, '*Guy of Warwick*', p. 368.

knightly counterpart retrieves his fortunes and enjoys the remainder of his life in comfort and security, may seem obvious and simplistic, but is actually a crucial distinction.

A comparison between *Guy of Warwick* and the *Life of St Alexis*, such as that performed most intelligently by Susan Crane shows clearly that although Guy refuses all earthly rewards and continues in penitence and (relative) poverty to the end of his days, he has not by any means abandoned worldly values in his striving for God in the way Alexis does. Not only does Guy continue to perform deeds which guarantee him an important place in the world, but he expresses his concern on several occasions that his would-be benefactors should instead of rewarding him protect and advance his son Reinbrun. Guy appears to succeed in integrating diverse interests: 'his role as a defender of secular justice, the public recognition he wins in that role, the honours offered to him, argue that spirituality is compatible with a variety of worldly interests . . . in a way that, for Alexis, is out of the question.'[31]

The chief way in which this apparent integration is achieved is through the introduction of the motif of penitence, which enables Guy to alter his way of life and behaviour in specific ways without necessitating the rejection of all the values of knighthood. Guy has been a good knight in many ways. He has sinned in his pride, his vainglory, and his neglect of God. After his penance has begun, he continues to be a good knight, but he denies himself the enjoyment of his fame. His penance leads him closer to God, and he ultimately retires from the world, but it is clear that he does not therefore reject knighthood as a way of life, since he plainly intends his son Reinbrun to be a knight.

This poem is probably the first major Middle English romance to make use of the hero's repentance and atonement in order to rework hagiographic material and themes into a romance with a fully secular frame of reference. It provides an excellent opportunity for analysis of the relation of penitence to the chivalric ideal which Guy as the hero is intended ultimately to represent.

Before we commence our detailed study of the poem, we need to look at the state of the texts. The versions in the Auchinleck MS (A) and in Caius College, Cambridge 107 (C) are generally considered to be the best, in the sense of being both the earliest and

---

[31] Crane, '*Guy of Warwick*', p. 359.

the least corrupt.[32] They are both very close translations of the Anglo-Norman poem *Gui de Warewic*, though both have important differences. The only other complete manuscript, Cambridge University Library Ff. 2. 38 (U) is a late and inferior rendering of the story which, however, retains the sequence of events and the conclusion of the AN poem, in which after Guy's death the narrative follows his son Reinbrun as he collects all the honours and rewards which Guy had refused during his life. In this version of the story it is clear that this affirmation of Guy's worldly achievements is seen as a fitting conclusion to the tale. Reinbrun is, as it were, Galahad to Guy's Lancelot; as good a knight technically, and in addition without sin. Guy himself does not, like the heroes of our other three romances, return to his former position in the world; but his son performs the same role by enjoying in proxy the rewards earned by Guy.

This version of the story bears out the opinion expressed by Susan Crane[33] that religious romances affirm worldly values such as the acquisition of wealth and the enjoyment of noble rank in a way which saints' lives do not. However, if Guy's ultimate retirement from the world of affairs is interpreted as a more saintly rejection of worldly values, then the triumphant return of his son to his abdicated glory appears to contradict the meaning of the poem. It is clear that the authors of the story told in A and C have deep reservations about the Reinbrun material. A makes the most marked and the most famous revisions to the story, by editing out the episodes concerning Reinbrun which take place before Guy's death, and uniting them with those taking place after Guy's death in a separate poem. C simply comes to a close at the deaths of Guy and Felice, leaving Reinbrun at the African king's court and Heraud in the dungeon of Amiral Persan.

There is, therefore, a case for claiming that a Middle English version of the poem exists which differs from the Anglo-Norman version in excluding the Reinbrun material. The result was a marked intensification of the pious elements of the Anglo-Norman poem, and this is reinforced by other slight alterations in tone

---

[32] A and C, edited by Julius Zupitza, *The Romance of Guy of Warwick, the First or 14th Century Version*, EETS, ES, 42, 49, 59 (London, 1883, 1887, 1891; republ. as 1 vol., 1966) are described by him in *The Romance of Guy of Warwick, the Second or 15th Century Version*, EETS, ES, 25, 26 (London, 1875, 1876), pp. v–ix.

[33] Crane, '*Guy of Warwick*', *passim*.

throughout the poem. I shall be discussing the Middle English version of A, and will quote from Zupitza's edition[34] unless lines are missing, in which case I shall quote from C. I shall discuss the first two parts of *Guy of Warwick* as they appear in A as if they were intended to be read as two halves of one whole.

## i. How the Poem Works

Considering what a long poem *Guy of Warwick* is, and how many episodes it contains, it has a clear and coherent structure. In each of the two parts there is a long introductory section followed by three main episodes or adventures. Each introductory section describes how Guy discovers his goal in life. In the first he falls in love with Felice and gradually realizes what he must do to become worthy of her. In the second he becomes aware that he has not deserved the love which God has always shown him and realizes what he must do to become worthy of it. The subsequent journeys are undertaken in pursuit of these goals.

Part 1 is longer than part 2 and appears more diffuse and less precisely structured. The introductory section contains an account of two separate journeys made by Guy on the Continent in search of fame, because it takes him some time to realize what it is that Felice expects of him, and because many of the characters who will appear later in the poem are introduced here. The first main adventure begins at about l. 1700, when Guy decides to help the besieged Duke Segyn. The second adventure concerns his relief of Emperor Ernis, under attack by Saracens; and in the third main adventure Guy helps first Tirri and then his father to regain their rights. Two extra small episodes occur at the end of part 1: that in which Guy kills the son of earl Florentine, and the famous slaying of the Northumberland dragon. Each of these is, however, equally important for completing the development of Guy's character and career before his repentance, and each is mirrored in its way in part 2 of the romance.

The introductory section of part 2 is shorter and swifter in development than that of part 1. Guy marries Felice, but leaves her

[34] *The Romance of Guy of Warwick, the First or 14th Century Version.* References to part 2 will give the stanza number as in Zupitza's edition, followed by the line number within the stanza.

almost at once to atone for his pride and neglect of God by setting off for the Holy Land as a pilgrim. In his three main adventures he helps first Earl Jonas, then Tirri again, and finally King Athelstan and his own country. He pays a brief visit, still incognito, to his own house before retiring to a hermitage, where he dies.

The three main adventures of the first part are not exactly or symmetrically reflected by the three in the second part: rather, particular scenes or situations or speeches enacted by one set of characters in one adventure will be re-enacted with a new significance by different characters later on. In this way the author creates a varied series of reverberations throughout the romance, connecting different parts of it together in order to point to unexpected similarities or to create significant contrasts. The structural pattern of the whole is determined by the two parallel and contrasting goals of Guy's life. According to Hanspeter Schelp:

Die Taten, die Guy zuvor eigenem Ruhm und eigener Ehre und mit dem Ziel, die Hand seiner Dame zu gewinnen, unternommen hatte—Taten, die er aus neuen Sicht als Ausfluß der *superbia* erachtet—stellt er nun in den Dienst des Ruhmes Gottes und seines Seelenheils. Das Werben um Gott tritt an die Stelle des Werbens um die Dame. Nunmehr wird Guy geleitet von *contritio* und Bußfertigkeit, die sich als tätige *satisfactio* äußert.[35]

When Guy repents at the opening of the second part of the poem, it is clear that he feels his past life and activities as a knight have led him into sin. Yet he has succeeded spectacularly well in what he set out to do; he is considered by everyone to be the best knight in the world. He alone finds this achievement inadequate. It is reasonable to question whether the presentation of Guy's career as a worldly knight is at all ambiguous or casts doubt on the value of his aims or activities from the outset. It would have been possible to portray Guy unambiguously as heroic. Indeed, Guy acquires a reputation for the knightly virtues of courtesy and generosity along with the more conventional qualities of personal bravery and prowess in battle. He also enjoys a fair share of divine protection,[36] which could be seen as implying divine approval. My own view, however, is that Guy's character changes and develops with each successive episode in ways which clearly show the

---

[35] Schelp, *Exemplarische Romanzen*, p. 141.
[36] See e.g. ll. 1325-6; 1501; 3993-4; 5776-7.

nature of his sin and highlight the way in which the pursuit of knightly fame has contributed to it and has in fact corrupted him.

It takes Guy some time to realize what it is Felice wants of him. Twice he mistakenly thinks he has fulfilled her requirements and tries to claim her love, only to be repulsed. Once he has begun to be the most famous knight in the world, he appears to become more interested in the winning than in the prize. His desire for personal fame and his jealous anxiety to be held in proper esteem lead him to intend abandoning the Christian Emperor Ernis to help the pagans, and then to forget Felice (albeit temporarily) and almost marry Ernis's daughter. The most secular of minstrels would have trouble presenting Guy's behaviour in this episode as perfectly heroic, since he nearly deserts the two things—his lady and his faith—which were the fundamental movers of his career, and which certainly cannot be absent from his motives if he is to become the Best Knight. There are in addition aspects of subsequent adventures, particularly the episode of Earl Florentine, which show Guy's behaviour as brutal rather than heroic, and egotistical rather than courageous.

I shall focus the discussion of the first part of *Guy of Warwick* on three topics: the development of Guy's character from ignorant puppy to man of decision and mature views; the presentation of Guy's behaviour once mature as knightly, but bad; and the use of the technique of repetition with variation throughout the poem to create significant contrasts.

The introductory section of the first part of the poem (up to l. 1709) is very long, because it describes in great detail a process of education and development in the hero. When the story opens, Guy is naïve. Though he is well loved for his courtesy and generosity, all he has to recommend him to Felice are handsome looks and fulsome ardour. He appears to have a keen sense of his own inferiority, but only on account of Rohaut's anger if he should be caught making love to Felice; he is less doubtful of his success with Felice herself (ll. 297–308). At length Guy's pangs of love overcome his caution.

The scenes in which he reveals his love to Felice repay close attention. His first protestation is remarkable for containing all kinds of hackneyed clichés uttered in a headlong rush; lack of elegance is compensated for by enthusiasm. He loves Felice more than anything or anyone else; he can't stop loving her even if it means his death; there is nothing in the world he would not do for her sake; he would die for her; she is life and death to him; he cannot be happy without her; he is dying for love of her; unless she has mercy he will kill himself; if only she knew what he suffered night and day because of his love she would have pity on him (ll. 357–76). Felice's response is somewhat crushing, and leaves us in little doubt as to the comic nature of the exchange:

> No fond I neuer man me so missede,
> No me so of loue bede,
> Noyþer kniʒt no baroun,
> Bot þou þat art a garsoun,
> & art mi man, & man schalt be.
> Yuel were mi fairhed sett on þe,
> & y such a grome toke
> & so mani grete lordinges for-soke.      (ll. 389–96)

Having poured the cold water of common sense onto the bonfire of Guy's passion, Felice warns him never to dare come into her sight again, or she will reveal his presumption to her father. Guy returns to his chamber and gives himself up to a frenzy of grief and despair. His soliloquy is similarly stereotyped and full of clichés ('"deþ," he seyd, "wher artow so long?"', l. 445; '"Acursed be þat time, seyen y may!"', l. 480; '"Y brenne so spark on glede"', l. 488, etc.); the expressions no less than the sentiments follow a conventional pattern. Guy reasons that as no one can resist the power of love, he cannot be held responsible for his actions, and he decides to risk returning to Felice against her express instructions. As he sets out, the pose of the besotted lover slips for a moment, and with it, the flowery language:

> With þis Gij arisen is,
> & to þe gate goþ y-wis.
> 'God,' quod Gij, 'y do foliliche:
> Y sle me seluen sikerliche;
> Mine owhen deþ y go secheinde.
> God,' he seyd, 'be mine helpinde!'      (ll. 551–6)

The uncharacteristic honesty of Guy's feelings at this moment are linked interestingly to his appeal to God. (I think we are to assume here that Guy is addressing God rather than casually blaspheming.) One recalls the prayers made by Sir Gowther and Sir Ysumbras at similar moments of crisis; and certainly it is at this encounter that Felice offers Guy his first hope of success. Between love and fear Guy is so overwrought that he swoons; on awakening he resolves to reveal himself to Felice once more, come what may. When he confronts Felice he is reckless and defiant. He does not care if she reports him to Rohaut and causes his death. Death will be a pleasure after the agonies he is enduring for her. Overcome by emotion, he swoons again. There follows an intriguing dialogue between Felice and one of her maidens, who points out Guy's natural aristocracy by claiming that if she were lucky enough to be loved by such a man, she would not refuse him even if she were the richest, noblest, and most beautiful princess in the world. Felice rebukes her; but it is at this moment that she begins to pity Guy, and when he awakes, she relents so far as to inform him that:

> 'No grome louen y no may
> Fort he be kniȝt forsoþ to say,
> Feir & beld to tellen by,
> Strong in armes & hardi;
> & when þou hast armes vnder-fong,
> & ichaue it vnder-stonde,
> Þan schaltow haue þe loue of me,
> ȝif þou be swiche as y telle þe.'     (ll. 667–74)

This speech is a most important indicator of Felice's character and desires, though Guy misunderstands it. The crucial line is the last: 'ȝif þow be swiche as y telle þe.' Felice, impressed at last by Guy's determination and by the recommendation of the maiden, perceives that whether he is of lowly birth or not he possesses qualities which may make him a suitable match for her. Felice is proud, beautiful, and *well educated*. She has a clear idea of what she wants, and her standards are high. She wants the Best Knight, a man whose life lived in accordance with the knightly code will turn him into a perfect embodiment of it, famed for his strength and bravery. If Guy is the man she thinks he is, he is capable of attaining that standard.

Unfortunately Guy understands her to mean that he has only to be knighted, and the improvement in rank will make him worthy of her. He recovers his health with astonishing speed and sets off to court to ask Earl Rohaut to knight him. After the ceremony, he returns to Felice and naïvely claims her love in accordance with her promise. Felice informs him that he has the name only of knight; he must now go and earn himself a reputation appropriate for that name, for 'Bot it be þurgh þi miȝt,/ Þou no miȝt chalang loue þurgh riȝt' (ll. 747–8).

Guy's first attempts to prove himself worthy of Felice's love show that his idea of knighthood is still somewhat limited. He spends the rest of the year travelling from country to country fighting in tournaments, winning 'þe priis', gaining friends and a reputation for courtesy and generosity as well as for prowess. At the end of this highly successful year Guy returns to England confident that he now has some claim on Felice's love. But once again he has underestimated Felice's exacting standard; he has not reached it even yet. Moreover, he has done just well enough to show how much better he could do if he applied himself, and Felice declares that she is unwilling to hinder him in fulfilling his great potential. Her ambition for him is greater than his for himself. He merely wants to win her love; she wants him to become peerless, the best knight in the world. Though he is 'leuest of oþer alle' to her, she will not grant him her love lest it distract him from his proper sphere of activity. In the light of future events, the speech with which Felice dispatches Guy abroad for a second time is superbly ironic. It is almost certainly an allusion to the central problem of *Erec et Énide*:

> 'No rape þe nouȝt so, sir Gij;
> ȝete nartow nouȝt y-preysed so,
> Þat me ne may finde oþer mo;
> Orped þou art and of grete miȝt,
> Gode kniȝt & ardi in fiȝt:
> & ȝif ich þe hadde mi loue y-ȝeue,
> To welden it while þat y liue,
> Sleuþe þe schuld ouercome:
> Namore wostow of armes loue,
> No comen in turnament no in fiȝt.
> So amerous þou were anon riȝt.
> Y schuld misdo, so þenkeþ me,
> & miche agilt oȝaines te,
> & ich þi manschip schuld schone,
> Wiþ me euer more to wone.'          (ll. 1132–46)

What Felice fears is what happens to Erec when he married Enide. He loves his wife so much that he spends all his time in her company, and no longer goes to tournaments. Enide is blamed for

spoiling a good knight. She reproaches herself over his sleeping
body:

> 'Lasse, fet ele, con mar fui!
> de mon païs qui ring ca querre?
> Bien me doit essorbir la terre,
> quant toz li miaudres chevaliers,
> li plus hardiz et li plus fiers,
> qui onques fust ne cuens ne rois
> li plus lëax, li plus curtois,
> a del tot an tot relanquie
> por moi la chevalerie
> Dons l'ai ge honi tot por voir;
> nel volsisse por nul avoir.'[37]

Felice's words reflect the circumstances and preoccupations of
Chrétien's characters so accurately that it is tempting to connect
Felice's much-emphasized erudition with being widely read in
romance. This would account for both her idealistic view of
knighthood and her desire to marry only the best knight in the
world, and her acute awareness of that standard paradox of courtly
romance: that the best knight, having won the fairest lady, is likely
to lose his supremacy. Uxorious bliss will destroy those very
knightly qualities which enabled him to win the lady when he was
spurred on by frustrated love.

The keen irony of Felice entertaining these scruples is that what
she fears does not in fact occur. When Guy finally marries her he
remains for only fifteen days of uxorious bliss before deserting her
to devote himself to a still higher and more demanding love.
Felice's words show the classic double meaning, of which only one
is apparent to Felice herself, but both of which are accessible to the
reader. As far as Felice is concerned, she is wilfully depriving her-
self of a husband and lover for a brief temporary period while he
perfects himself and becomes 'þe best doinde/ In armes þat ani-
man mai finde' (ll. 1157–8). In fact she is unwittingly depriving
herself of a husband and lover permanently by urging Guy to
commit the wholesale homicide for which he later repents and
leaves her for ever. In addition, her preoccupation with pre-
eminence makes him proud and influences his idea of what is due
to a knight. This is a scene which will be recalled later in the poem,

---

[37] Chrétien de Troyes, *Erec et Énide*, ed. Mario Roques (new edn. Paris, 1978),
ll. 2492–502.

when Guy tells Felice that he must leave her and she begs him to stay.

For the time being, however, Guy is unconvinced that he can ever attain the peerless eminence which Felice requires from him, and he sets off on his travels once more. The remainder of the introductory section describes the ambush prepared by Guy's enemy, the wicked Otous of Pavia, and its consequences. During the fight which follows the ambush, Guy's companions Torold and Urry are killed, and his closest friend Heraud is struck down and appears dead. Guy himself, though previously badly wounded in a tournament, kills or puts to flight all his attackers, but he is bitterly angry at the deaths of his companions. Once again we have a curious moment of candour, reminiscent of the words which preceded Guy's swoon in the garden. For in the speech with which Guy laments the untimely death of his friends, instead of blaming Otous or fate, Guy blames Felice:

> 'Allas,' quod Gii, 'felawes dere!
> So wele doand kniȝtes ȝe were.
> Al to iuel it fel to me,
> Felice, þo y was sent to serue þe;
> For þi loue, Felice, þe feir may,
> Þe flour of kniȝtes is sleyn þis day.
> Ac for þou art a wiman,
> Y no can nouȝt blame þe for þan;
> For þe last no worþ y nouȝt
> Þat wimen han to gronde y-brouȝt.
> Ac alle oþer may bi me,
> Ȝif þai wil, y-warned be.'    (ll. 1555–66)

In addition, he wishes that he had listened to his father and Earl Rohaut and stayed behind in England when they asked him to.

These sentiments are not what we should expect from a knight; he is not seeing things from a knightly point of view. His human grief for the loss of his friends overrides for the moment his determination to win Felice. He almost begins to think that the price is too high. But as yet Guy has not been initiated into the real glories of knighthood. All he has done is to travel round Europe winning tournaments; he has not yet championed the oppressed, or fought for a more weighty cause.

Guy's relationship with his older and wiser friend Heraud changes as he grows surer of himself as a knight. There are four occasions in the first part of the romance on which Heraud gives advice to his young friend. Each of these four occasions shows Guy becoming more independent of Heraud's guidance.[38] On the first occasion (ll. 1075–88), Heraud advises Guy to return to England, as they have now won 'pris' everywhere they have been and can properly introduce themselves to the king and his barons. Guy replies meekly: 'Maister, y grant wel;/ At þi wil be it eueridel.'

On the next occasion, Guy asks for Heraud's advice on whether to help the wrongly accused Duke Segyn, besieged by his angry emperor, or to return to England again, and again puts himself completely under Heraud's guidance:

> 'Þat tow redest, don y wille;
> Þi conseyl forsake y nille.'  (ll. 1899–1900)

Heraud replies:

> 'Y ȝif conseyle, & gode it is;
> Hem to help men schul spede
> Þat to help han gret nede.
> For los & priis þou miȝt þer winne,
> & manschip to þe & al þi kinne.'  (ll. 1908–12)

His 'gode conseyle' appears perhaps somewhat mercenary. Heraud is like a good actor's agent, telling him which parts will further his career, which parties to go to, and which premières to be seen at. The C manuscript emphasizes this concern for Guy's advancement, since the lines in which Heraud tells Guy that a man will prosper if he helps those who have need of help are there rendered more explicitly as:

> 'Him to helpe ye shall the better spede,
> And also therfor haue grete mede.'  (C, ll. 1909–10)

The implication is clearly that, whatever the merits of the case, it is even better for one's reputation to champion the underdog.

On the third occasion, however, Guy does not so much ask Heraud's advice as his approval: he knows what he wants to do and asks Heraud to accompany him:

> 'Heraud, mi frende, wille we gon?
> At þemperour take we leue anon.

---

[38] As was pointed out by F. X. Siciliano in his doctoral thesis, 'Narrative Technique in *Guy of Warwick*' (University of Wisconsin, 1976).

Into Costentyn-noble ichil go
To help þemperour of his wo:
Þat wiþ þe soudan biseged is he.
So siggeþ men of þat cuntre;
Þat lond destrud & men aqueld,
& cristendom þai han michel afeld.'   (ll. 2849–54)

Here Guy calls Heraud 'mi frende' instead of 'Maister', and it is
Heraud who falls in with Guy's firm plans. His reply shows once
more that he is considering the potential merits of the undertaking
only with regard to how much it will advance Guy's reputation:

Herhaud answerd, 'y graunt it be:
Miche worþschipe it worþ to þe.'   (ll. 2855–6)

These three occasions are all at turning-points in the story;
usually at the beginning of a new phase of the narrative. On the
fourth occasion Guy finds himself, in mid-adventure, in a difficult
situation, and asks Heraud's advice on how to extract himself from
it. He has been offered the hand in marriage of the Emperor
Ernis's daughter, and, having temporarily forgotten Felice, has
accepted it. In the middle of the wedding ceremony the sight of
the ring recalls Felice to his mind and he retires to his lodgings,
pleading illness. He summons Heraud and asks him what he
should do. Heraud advises him to marry the emperor's daughter,
on the grounds that he will then succeed to the empire and be the
richest and most powerful man in the world:

'More riches þe worþ bi a þousandel
Boþe of cites & of riche castel,
Forestes ful of hertes beld,
Þan þerl Rohaut haþ in weld.'       (ll. 4265–8)

Guy is angered by this counsel, which shows no understanding of
his problem, only a superficial concern for his advantage. Guy is
not interested in wealth, and explains that he would rather die than
forsake Felice. Heraud apologetically amends his advice. Of
course, if he loves Felice, 'Vn-riȝt it were & þou hir for-go'. Guy
does not ask Heraud's advice again.

At this point it is clear that Guy has matured sufficiently to
know his own mind and be independent of the guidance of Felice
and Heraud, who first set him on his way to becoming the best
knight in the world. In many ways he has become this, and most of

his adventures in this first part of the romance show Guy as truly heroic, generous, and brave. Before we proceed to examine some of the ways in which the heroic aspects of Guy's character are undermined by the presentation of less pleasing characteristics, it is worth pointing out one of the techniques by which they are established, and one in which the author of *Guy of Warwick* excels: the technique of repetition with variation. This can be repetition of a single word or phrase; Heraud's use of the words 'worþ' and 'worþschipe' in the scenes discussed above is an obvious example. Or it may be the recurrence of small motifs throughout the text; perhaps the most notable of these is the 'seen-through-a-window' motif which accompanies most of the great decisions and crises of Guy's life. At the beginning of the poem, when he is first smitten with love for Felice, and has received his first rebuff, he retires to his room to lament, and then:

> To a fenestre þan Gij is go,
> Biheld þe castel, þe tour also.   (ll. 455-6)

He then decides to return to Felice and press his suit. After the introductory section, Guy and Heraud are about to embark for England, when:

> To a windowe sir Gij is go,
> In-to þe strete he loked þo;
> A palmer he seiȝe cominge,
> Messaisliche bi þe strete walkinge.   (ll. 1801-4)

As a result of the news which the palmer gives him of the conflict between Duke Segyn and the emperor of Almayn, Guy begins his serious career of knighthood. Part of the way through the third main adventure sequence, Guy has just rescued his friend Tirri and his sweetheart Oisel and is preparing to return to England:

> It was opon a somers day,
> Gij out at a windowe lay
>
> .    .    .    .    .
>
> Wiþ þat com prikeing anon riȝt
> A kniȝt; he semed wele, apliȝt,
> Wele he semed he treuailed were.   (ll. 4939-45)

Sure enough, the knight brings news that Tirri's father Aubri has been attacked by the treacherous Duke Loyer at the instigation of the wicked Otous of Pavia, and once more Guy's plans to return home are postponed as the friends set off to the rescue again.

By now, a certain expectation has been built up in the audience, that when Guy is at leisure and looking idly out of a window, he is going to learn something which will change his plans. The next time it happens the change is the most devastating of all:

> It bi-fel opon a somers day
> Þat sir Gij at Warwike lay
>
> .　　.　　.　　.　　.　　.
>
> To a turet sir Gij is went,
> & biheld þat firmament,
> 　　þat thicke wiþ steres stode.
> On Iesu omnipotent,
> Þat alle his honour hadde him lent,
> 　　He þouȝt wiþ dreri mode;
> Hou he hadde euer ben strong werrour,
> For Iesu loue, our saueour,
> 　　Neuer no dede he gode.
> Mani man he hadde slayn wiþ wrong.
> 'Allas, allas!' it was his song:
> 　　For sorwe he ȝede ner wode.　　(20. 7, 8; 21)

And Guy is moved to undertake the penance which will change his whole life.

But perhaps the most impressive use of the technique is to transfer whole scenes from one part of the poem to another, varying minor details of character and situation in order to deepen the significance of each individual unit by placing it in counterpoint to the preceding units. The best example of this is the scene in which a party of unarmed or unprepared men are surrounded by a party of armed men. In the third adventure sequence, Heraud has been captured and imprisoned by Duke Loyer while Guy proceeds with his rescue of Tirri, Oisel, and Aubri from the wicked Otous of Pavia. Loyer is basically a good character who has been led astray temporarily by Otous; he has treated Heraud well in his captivity and Heraud undertakes to intercede with the victorious Guy for Loyer's life. He finds Guy's party unarmed and returning from a hunt. They are alarmed to find themselves approached by armed men and fear treachery:

> So mani kniȝtes þai seye coming,
> Of traisoun þai were dredeing.　　(ll. 6629–30)

This scene is the mirror-image of an earlier scene in which Guy
himself approached the emperor of Almayn to intercede for the life
of Duke Segyn. The emperor has just been hunting boar with his
nephew Tirri, when he and Tirri find themselves amid armed
men. The emperor recognizes his enemy Guy among them, and
fears the worst:

> On ich halue bisett we beþ,
> Nis her nouȝt bot þe deþ.     (ll. 2521–2)

But Guy approaches bearing an olive branch, to invite the emperor
to dine with Duke Segyn, who is willing to surrender to him. As on
the later occasion when Heraud is the messenger, Guy has only the
best of intentions, and a reconciliation is effected; but on the later
occasion it is Guy who is being persuaded to exercise mercy, in-
stead of being the one who urges it.

Both this scene and its counterpart in their turn recall a still
earlier occasion when Guy and his fellows are surrounded by
armed men whose intentions are very far from peaceful and
honourable. This is pointedly contrasted with the episode in which
Guy approaches the emperor of Almayn and Tirri on behalf of
Segyn; for Tirri beseeches the emperor, just as Heraud besought
Guy, to save himself and leave his companions to sell their lives
dearly:

> 'Sir emperour,' quod Tirri anon,
> 'For þe rode loue þat god was on don,
> Ich þe bidde, hennes go now,
> For godes loue no lenge bileue þou!
> & ichil here bileuen ay,
> & if ich Gij mete may,
> Wit meschaunce y schal him gret,
> & al his feren þat y mete.
> Ar ich be ded or nomen be
> Þou schalt passe al þis cuntre.'
> Þemperour seyd, 'for soþe, y nille:
> Here ichil wiþ ȝou duelle.'     (ll. 2527–38)

> 'Sir,' seyd Heraud þo,
> 'For godes loue hennes þou go.
> For þine loue we schul here dye,
> & defende þis pas, y seye:
> Leuer ous were her-on be ded,
> Þan þou wer ded in our ferred.'

Þan answerd Gij anon riȝt,
As gode kniȝt & ful of miȝt:
'Ȝif ȝe dye, ichil al-so;
Nil ich neuer fram ȝou go!'     (ll. 1349–58)

Here Guy is contrasted with the wicked and treacherous Otous of
Pavia. Heraud's fears for Guy were quite justified, but Tirri's for
the emperor are fortunately groundless, since this time it is not the
henchman of an envious and spiteful enemy approaching with
intent to kill, but the noble champion of an honourable and cour-
teous enemy who is anxious for reconciliation. Tirri and the
emperor are, on the other hand, likened to Guy and Heraud; their
impulses are identical—loyal, generous, noble—and this prepares
us for such future events as the successful reconciliation and
Tirri's great friendship with Guy.

The scene in which the emperor is reconciled with Duke Segyn
is masterfully handled and it shows Guy at his best. The duke,
alone, bare-headed, in his shirt, with a rope about his neck, meets
the emperor at church, and throws himself on his mercy. After his
humble plea for peace and amity, each of the emperor's captured
vassals intercedes for Segyn with their overlord. The first to speak
is the emperor's own son, Gaier, who points out that Segyn has
treated all his prisoners with great kindness and will be a valuable
ally if the emperor forgives him. In addition,

'Bot thou foryiue him thy wrath swithe,
Of me thou shalt neuere bee blithe.'     (ll. 2653–4)

Duke Reyner is the next to speak, asserting that Segyn slew the
emperor's nephew (the cause of the quarrel between them) in self-
defence, which he will prove in combat on anyone who denies it;
and he adds:

'And not if thou haue of him mercy,
Euer here-after y shalbee thyn enmy.'     (ll. 2663–4)

Gaudiner, the emperor's own constable, is even more emphatic; he
loves Segyn and is his sworn brother, and if the emperor continues
in enmity, he will personally make war on him:

'Bot thou mercy of him haue nowe,
All this y shall ayenst thy prowe.'     (ll. 2675–6)

The emperor's steward, whom Guy had captured in single combat on his first day in battle, has a similar message:

> 'Bot thou of him haue the rather mercy,
> Euere of me herafter thou shalt failly.'     (ll. 2683–4)

It is then Guy's turn to speak; but the import of his words is different:

> 'Sir, for goddis Loue y bidde the,
> Of this Duke thou haue mercy and pitee,
> And with that y shall your man become
> To serue the, Lorde, all and some.'     (ll. 2687–90)

This change from the threats of the emperor's vassals to an offer of loyal service and a reminder of divine mercy from his most feared opponent marks the turning-point of the scene. It inspires even Tirri to sue for Segyn's forgiveness, offering to make up to the emperor for the loss of his nephew by devoted service. The emperor relents, because he sees Segyn so humble and penitent, and also ' "For sir Guy, that is englissh,/ That so good knyght and curteys is" '.[39]

If this scene shows Guy behaving with great courage, courtesy, and humility, there are others in which his conduct gives the thoughtful reader cause for concern. There are disturbing signs, from the second main adventure sequence onwards, that Guy's idea of perfect knighthood has been too much influenced by Felice's and Heraud's insistence on 'los', 'priis', and 'worþ'. During this second sequence, Guy achieves what he set out to do. In the eyes of the world, he is held to be the best knight. His fame has spread everywhere; his very appearance at the scene of a conflict gives new hope to his allies and spreads dismay among his enemies. But being the best knight is not merely a question of

---

[39] This and the preceding quotations are from C, as A has had a leaf torn out at this point, losing ll. 2565–717 of Zupitza's edition. Unfortunately, where A begins again (at Otous's objections to the truce), C has lost seven lines, and goes straight from the end of the emperor's first speech to his offer of his sister in marriage to the duke. The repeated phrase 'Bot if thou haue of him mercy' and its variations, which make Guy's Christian evocation of the love of God and his generosity in offering his service such a striking contrast to the threats of the other men, is unique to this version of *Guy*. Zupitza asserts that C is substantially the same as A, but with abridgements. A tends not to differ significantly from the existing lines of C, so the repeated phrase was probably present in A. The sentiments, but not the formulaic expression, are present in the other versions of *Guy*, but only the ME versions contain Guy's appeal to the love of God.

prowess, nor is it, as Felice and Heraud seem to think, being more famous and respected than other knights.

Guy's second main adventure is a more serious affair than any he has so far undertaken. He is fighting on behalf of a Christian emperor against the enemies of his faith. Yet so little does Guy care about the real issues of the conflict that at one point he is actually prepared to offer his services to the Soudan, because the emperor's treacherous steward Morgadour has led him to believe that Ernis has turned against him. In a splendid scene of confrontation, Ernis accuses Guy of having been seduced by offers of enormous wealth from the Soudan. Guy in reply states the real reason for his desertion, which is not very much more creditable:

'Sir,' quaþ sir Gij to þemperour,
'No was ich neuer þi traitour,
And ȝif god wil, y nil nouȝt be,
Þerwhiles þe lif is in me.
Me was y-teld biforn now riȝt
Of on þat is þi priue kniȝt,
Þat þou no hadest to don wiþ mi seruise,
& þat y þe serue wiþ feyntise;
And þat ich was biwrayd to þe
(For þi nold ich no longer here be),
And þat þou wost do me to-hewe,
& mine barouns, þat ben so trewe.
For þi y þouȝt þat y go scholde
To hem þat mi seruise ȝeld me wold;
Ac for al Damas & þat cuntre
Nold ich haue holden oȝaines þe.'           (ll. 3355–70)

There is a certain dignity in the opening lines of this speech, which later breaks down into a slightly hysterical petulance. Of course Guy would never abandon the emperor for wealth or property (and indeed, it is noticeable that whenever the grateful kings he has helped offer this kind of reward he never accepts it, though he sometimes asks that his followers receive it instead[40]); but he would go because he has been told that the emperor made light of his service. Guy's pride is injured. When he is approached by the evil steward Morgadour, he realizes that someone has been telling lies to the emperor, and is furious that he believed them:

[40] See e.g. ll. 4457–66 and 7091–100.

> 'Hou schuld ich euer siker be
> Of ani bi-hest men hotes me?
> For þemperour me seyd þo,
> And treweliche me bihete þerto,
> Þat he me wold gret worþschipe,
> & now he me wil sle wiþ schenschipe
> For þe speche of a losanger,
> & of a feloun pautener.'         (ll. 3289–96)

We note at once the appearance of the word 'worþschipe'; one of
the key words of Guy's vocabulary, and one on which his image of
himself as a knight clearly depends. This speech in itself betrays
Guy's intrinsic lack of true honour; for he is doing Ernis a wrong
by believing Morgadour's tale, which the emperor refused to do
him. When Morgadour told Ernis that Guy had dishonoured his
daughter, he first of all refused to believe it, and then said that
even if it was true it was of no consequence, since she was pro-
mised to Guy in any case. Ernis makes this correct judgement
from his confidence in Guy's worth, and that natural nobility
which consists in believing other men to be as honourable as one-
self. Guy is the one who is in fact taken in by 'þe speche of a
losanger' and believes ill of the emperor when he ought to know
better. Not only that, but Guy's injured pride leads him so far
astray as to want to join forces with the Saracens, because they 'mi
seruise 3eld me wold'. As long as this criterion is met, Guy seems
not to care whom he serves.

Guy is persuaded to stay, and after performing prodigies in
battle, volunteers for the dangerous mission of bearing peace terms
to the Soudan.[41] He succeeds in ending the war by decapitating
the Soudan, and as a reward for this exploit is given the emperor's
daughter in marriage. This is the extraordinary occasion on which
Guy so far forgets the original purpose of his pursuit of glory and
personal fame that he nearly does marry the princess and accept
half the kingdom. Guy sees 'worþschipe' as an end in itself and
forgets that it was once the means to attaining Felice's love.
During the wedding ceremony, the ring presented to him by the
archbishop reminds him of Felice, and he remembers that:

> Leuer him þou3t to han hir bodi on
> Wiþ-outen siluer & gold & precious ston,

---

[41] The author derived this scene largely from the episode in the *Chanson de Roland* in
which Ganelon volunteers Roland for the rearguard.

Þan alle oþer þat were o liue
Wiþ alle þe gode men miȝt him ȝiue.    (ll. 4201–4)

and hastily withdraws from the ceremony. Guy is now faced with
the unappealing task of extracting himself from a very difficult
situation. The way in which he achieves it is far from courteous,
and not a little deceitful. He does not tell Ernis the truth—that he
has a love in England and therefore cannot marry Blancheflur. In-
stead, he adopts a tone of petulant indignation and accuses the
emperor of ingratitude because Morgadour has managed to kill his
tame lion:

'Ich haue þe serued wiþ gret honour;
Ȝolden þou hast me iuel mi while,
When þi folk þurch tresoun & gile
Haue mi lyoun to deþ y-brouȝt.
.    .    .    .    .    .    .
Seþþe þou no miȝt nouȝt waranti me,
Whar-to shuld y serui þe,
On oncouþe man in thi lond,
When þou no dost him bot schond?
Harm me is, & michel misdo;
Þer-fore ichil fram þe go,
& in oþer cuntres serue y wile,
Þer men wille ȝeld me mi while.'    (ll. 4404–22)

To say 'þou no dost him bot schond' to a man who has just offered
you his daughter's hand in marriage and half his kingdom is per-
haps unfair; and if Guy thinks that he is really at risk in Ernis's
lands when he is loved and admired by all the Greeks, he must
suffer from persecution mania. The wrongs done to him by
Morgadour have, moreover, been amply avenged, since Guy has
just cleaved him in two from head to foot. The accusation that
Ernis does not value his services highly enough is extraordinary; it
is hard to see how they could have been valued more highly, as
Ernis shows again in his pathetically anxious attempts to persuade
Guy to stay. If anyone has offended him, he may take what action
he pleases—they will all be his men one day, in any case—and
Ernis again offers Guy his daughter; he can marry her tomorrow.
Guy's response is churlish besides being untruthful: he says that
he does not want to marry Ernis's daughter, because it would make
the Greeks jealous of him and they would complain about a poor
man becoming emperor after Ernis. The emperor weeps and offers

Guy 'His grete tresour', but to no avail. Guy has succeeded in getting out of a tricky situation, not by truth and courtesy, but by lying and bluffing and behaving boorishly to a man who has always treated him with the utmost kindness.

Throughout the romance a counterpoint has been maintained between Guy's solo exploits and his reliance on his 'feren'. When he began his adventures he was one of a group of friends who did everything together, and the theme of friendship and personal loyalty is continued throughout the poem with Guy's developing relationships with Heraud and Tirri; but it is noticeable that in each successive adventure greed for fame or desire for revenge lead Guy to undertake increasingly reckless feats alone, much to the anxiety of his friends. Usually these solo heroics are spectacularly successful, as when he rides into the Soudan's tent and cuts off his head, or when he gains revenge on Otous of Pavia. However, towards the end of the first part of the romance, a strange incident occurs in which Guy once again displays the less attractive side of his character.

Guy has outstripped his friends and companions on a boar-hunt which takes him alone and unprotected into the territory of Earl Florentine. Guy kills the exceptionally large and dangerous boar and blows his horn. This alerts Florentine to the fact that someone is in his woods killing his game. In the subsequent scene Guy is concerned to protect his prerogative as a knight, and believes that to act in any other way would bring discredit to the theory and practice of knighthood. The son of Earl Florentine arrives at the scene to find Guy and the dead boar. From his point of view, Guy is a thief, and is to be treated accordingly. He attempts to take Guy into custody; Guy has killed one of his father's boars without permission and must therefore forfeit his horse. Guy replies—quite politely—that it isn't right that a knight should have to go on foot, and he may take his horn instead, if he makes the request in a respectful way. This answer enrages the young man, who seizes the reins of Guy's horse and tries to knock him out of the saddle with his staff. Guy is unable to endure the indignity of being struck:

> 'Wicke man, þou hast me smite:
> Þou schalt it abigge, god it wite!'
> Wiþ his horn he him smot,
> His breyn he schadde fot hot.

'Now, lording,' quaþ sir Gij, 'þe swin þou nim,
& alle þi wille do wiþ him.
Na more smite þou no kniȝt:
Þat þou me smot, þou dest vnriȝt.'      (ll. 6805–12)

It is just possible that if Guy had returned to his companions at
this point and we had heard no more about the incident, his con-
duct would appear, in the context of the romance, if not admirable,
then at least justifiable. But the ensuing scenes show us the con-
sequences of Guy's pride in a way which exposes that pride and its
causes and the actions resulting from it as utterly unjustifiable.

Guy in his ignorance journeys further into Florentine's terri-
tory, and asks a local man whose castle he is approaching. The man
replies:

'Y schal telle þe,
A better man no miȝt þou se:
It is þe gode erl Florentin.
Better man drank neuer win.'   (ll. 6827–30)[42]

It is clear that Florentine is no Otous. He is not treacherous or
tyrannical: he is a good man and a good ruler. He has in no way
deserved to suffer this appalling tragedy. In the light of the scenes
which follow of Florentine's grief and anger, Guy's reasons for
slaughtering his only son appear less and less substantial. Guy
enters Florentine's castle and requests a meal, which Florentine
readily and courteously grants him. While Guy sits enjoying the
old earl's hospitality, the dead body of his son is brought into
the hall and Guy is identified as the murderer. Not surprisingly
the earl and his retainers attack Guy, despite his pleas that he
killed the young man in self-defence. Guy proceeds to slaughter all
Florentine's best knights, and appeals to Florentine's sense of
honour—as a guest, Guy should be under his protection, and he is
violating the sacred laws of hospitality by attacking him. In this
grotesque and tragic situation it is scarcely heroic for Guy to
remind Florentine of his duty as a host. The earl withdraws from
the combat and utters a moving lament over the body of his son:

'Sone,' he seyd, 'what schal y do,
Whenne ich þe haue þus forgo?
Who schal now weld after me

[42] 'What praise is more valuable than the praise of an intelligent servant?', Jane Austen,
*Pride and Prejudice.*

99

Mine londes, þat brode be?
A man icham swiþe in eld:
Dye ichil, bi godes scheld.'
Opon þat bodi he fel anon:
Reuþe þai hadden þer-of ichon,
Of his gret sorwe þat he made.     (ll. 6935–42)

There is nothing left for the old earl but death, and he is deprived
of the comfort of knowing that the stability and prosperity which
he as a responsible overlord has established in his lands will be
maintained by his son. He is also deprived of the satisfaction of
punishing his son's murderer; for Guy of course escapes. The earl
allows him to mount his horse and ride off, so that he is not killed
on the premises, and catches up with him some distance from the
castle. It is an unequal fight. The earl is an old man, and has not
borne arms for fifteen years. Guy, having thrown him from his
horse, takes pity on him and, as before in tournament, returns his
horse to him. His words, however, are far from chivalrous:

'In chaumber þou schust ligge stille,
Oþer to chirche gon to bid godis wille.
Þi court ichil quite-cleym þe.
Ded ich wold raþer be,
Ar ich wold wiþ þe ete
At souper oþer at oþer mete.'     (ll. 6991–6)

This episode, brief as it is, succeeds in undermining the image
of Guy as perfectly brave and noble. It presents the unacceptable
cost of Guy's concern to maintain his status as a knight. Guy is
able to justify to himself the casual destruction of anyone who
wounds the knight's sensibilities by not according him the respect
and deference he feels is his due.

After this exploit, Guy takes leave of his friend Tirri and returns
to England, where he has his famous encounter with the dragon of
Northumberland. He presents the dragon's head to the king at
Warwick. There has been no mention of Felice since his return,
and here, in A, part 1 ends.

The break between the two parts of the romance effectively pro-
vides a space for reflection, and for the reader to collect the
impressions he has formed of Guy during the first part of his
career. Can the reader feel that Guy's progress towards knightly
perfection is entirely satisfactory? He is likely to feel strong reser-

vations on this point. It is clear that Guy has achieved his aim in some respects; he is now world-famous, is held to be peerless in battle, and he returns to a hero's welcome in Warwick. The accolade of Best Knight, however, only applies in the eyes of the world. His public virtues of courage and prowess are what the world sees. What the reader sees is that Guy lacks the more private virtues of compassion, humility, and piety. His behaviour towards Ernis, his treatment of Earl Florentine and his son, even his fight with the dragon—in which he is nearly defeated through overweening pride—together with the abrupt, unsatisfactory ending of this part of the romance point to the same conclusion. Guy's actions and attitudes, and through him, the whole concept of the knight-adventurer, are being subjected to criticism of a sensitive but uncompromising nature.

There is no direct criticism on the part of the narrator; on the contrary, it is stressed throughout that Guy is universally beloved, renowned, and praised. Of incidents such as the slaying of Florentine's son, or the abuse of Emperor Ernis, the reader can judge for himself; and sufficient sympathy is shown in the narrative for these characters to make it clear that the reader cannot always side with Guy in perfect confidence of his rectitude.

The positioning of Guy's wedding to Felice at the opening of part 2 rather than the ending of part 1 robs it of its place as the climax of Guy's worldly career, the triumphant reward for his long struggles. The wedding, rather than being the point to which everything leads, is a starting-point which leads directly to Guy's great personal crisis. It is noticeable how Guy's former impetuous wooing of Felice has become something more cold and formal. It is a measure of how far removed he has become from the passionate, naïve, hopeful young squire; and Felice is at least partly responsible for the change. When Guy is at last brought to the point of proposing to the woman he has loved for years and for whose sake he has fought over half the world, he declares his love in most unromantic terms:

> 'Ichaue,' he seyd, 'þurch godes sond
> Won þe priis in mani lond
>     Of kniȝtes strong & stiþe,
> & me is boden gret anour,
> Kinges douhter & emperour
>     To haue to mi wiue.

Ac, swete Felice,' he seyd þan,
'Y no schal neuer spouse wiman
Whiles þou art oliue.'  (5. 4–12)

He can now put a quantitative value on his love, as Felice once did when she refused him: it has been sought by many of higher rank. Felice replies in similar terms, that she has been desired '"day and niȝt/ Of erl, baroun, & mani a kniȝt"', but she loves none but Guy. After this declaration that they are willing to devote such a valuable commodity as their love to each other, they are very happy, though it still takes the interference of Earl Rohaut to get them to the altar. In Guy's reticence on the subject of marriage, is it possible to detect a slight reluctance to become a responsible husband and landowner? Now that he has won his prize, there is a suggestion that he no longer really wants it. After all, he has spent twelve years away, following Felice's instructions to become the most praised knight in the world, in order to gain her love. To this end he has poured all his energies into being the best warrior, and he has neglected other virtues, particularly those which a man needs to sustain him when a life of action is succeeded by a period of leisure and reflection. Now that Guy has achieved what he thought he wanted, and has nothing left to strive for, he discovers that there is something important missing from his life.

Once again, imagery recurs from other parts of the romance. He has been hunting, as he was after the first and third major adventures of part I—times when he became restless and felt the urge to move on. He is looking out of a window in a tower, as on numerous previous occasions. This time no human agent is the stimulus; he is looking at the stars[43] and experiences the feeling of the smallness of an individual's life and concerns in comparison with that remote and limitless splendour. The stars are a positive reminder of the greatness and glory of God, without whom, Guy now realizes, he could not have achieved any of his successes. So totally absorbed has he been in trying to become worthy of Felice that he has given no time to God. Felice's demands required him above all to increase or maintain his personal renown, and his strongest reactions—against Ernis, Otous, and Florentine's son—were to be

[43] These lines have been simplified. C adds 'And the weder that was mery and bright' (C, l. 7397) following *Gui de Warewic*, which has: 'Le pais envirun ad esgardé/ E le ciel, qui tant ert esteillé/ E le tens, qui ert serré et cler.' *Gui de Warewic*, ed. A. Ewert (Paris, 1932), ll. 7571–3.

redressed for any slight or injury which detracted from his reputation as peerless. He has in fact been proud. This is the first occasion for some time on which Guy has experienced the sensation of humility, and he fully realizes his sin.

In the subsequent monologue and scene between Felice and Guy, A is essentially the same as *Gui de Warewic*,[44] employing a somewhat Shakespearian method of adapting its source; keeping fairly closely to the meaning, but rearranging the dialogue and translating more freely than C. There is more direct speech, and Guy is more specific about the course of his future life; but in both the Anglo-Norman and Middle English poems this is a finely handled dramatic encounter.

Guy, realizing the hollowness of his victories, is struck by two things: the bloodthirstiness of his former career, in which 'mani man he hadde slayn wiþ wrong' (21. 10), and secondly the fact that 'For him þat bar þe croun of þorn/ Gode dede dede y nare' (22. 5–6); instead he was motivated throughout by his desire to win Felice's love. This thought is developed in his subsequent dialogue with Felice:

> Seþþen y þe sey3e first wiþ ayn
>
> ·   ·   ·   ·   ·   ·
>
>   Þi loue me haþ so y-bounde,
>   Þat neuer seþþen no dede y gode,
>   Bot in wer schadde mannes blode,
>     Wit mani a griseli wounde
>
> ·   ·   ·   ·   ·   ·
>
>   Ac 3if ich hadde don half þe dede
>   For him þat on þe rode gan blede
>     Wit grimly woundes sare,
>   In heuene he wald haue quit mi mede,
>   In joie to won wiþ angels wede
>     Euer-more wiþ-outen care.
>   Ac for þi loue ich haue al wrou3t:
>   For his loue dede y neuer nou3t.
>     Iesu amend mi fare!       (24. 4, 6–9; 25. 1–9)

There appears on the face of it to be some confusion in what actually constitutes Guy's sin. Either killing people is wrong, or it

---

[44] Klausner, 'Didacticism and Drama', pp. 111–12, states that there are 'important differences between the versions', with the French *Gui* repenting more of the actual homicides he has committed; but I am unable to detect them.

is only wrong if you do it for the wrong reasons. David Klausner suggests that in the Anglo-Norman poem, the hero's horror at the actual bloodshed is given more emphasis, while 'the thoughts of the English Guy in contrast are organized around the distinction between the earthly love of woman which he bears towards Felice, and which has heretofore been his primary motivation, and the love of Christ which he has neglected'.[45]

The lines in which Guy says that if he had done half what he has done for God's sake instead of Felice's he would be rewarded in heaven support the view that the motive, rather than the deed, is important.[46] They make Guy appear more consistent, since he continues to kill and wound enemies in his future life, and since he carefully instructs Felice to give his unborn son an identical up-bringing to his own, and even bequeaths him his sword. Clearly Guy is not at this point renouncing or condemning the character and activities of knighthood *per se*; it is his own personal abuse of his position which constitutes his sin. A certain amount of blood-letting is the lot of the warrior; but his own past, romping around Europe killing, wounding, and destroying for the sake of gaining fame in order to win Felice's love, he now sees, rightly, as a dis-gusting occupation, not worthy of a serious, dedicated knight. He has not been mindful of God, who lent strength to his arm; he has shed blood carelessly. The motivation lends a different moral char-acter to the act.

Felice misunderstands what Guy is telling her. This dialogue is an inverted reflection of the earlier scene in which Guy declared his love for her and she dispatched him abroad again to become worthy of her (see pp. 84–7, above). It is now Felice who begs Guy to stay with her, while he sees the necessity of becoming an outcast and exile in order to expiate his sin. The significance of this reminder is enriched by having Guy and Felice exchange positions in the argument. This time it is Guy who patiently explains to Felice the goal which he has set himself, and it is Felice who does not understand, at first objects, and finally submits to his author-ity. She is no longer spurring him on to higher achievements; to her Guy has fulfilled his potential already, and she is not aware of any goal higher than that which she set him and believes him to have attained. Felice once promised Guy that when he succeeded

---

[45] Klausner, 'Didacticism and Drama', p. 112.
[46] These lines are also present in *Gui de Warewic*.

in becoming the best knight in the world she would grant him her love. Guy now promises to share with Felice the fruits of his penance:

> 'Of alle þe deds y may do wel
> God graunt þe, lef, þat haluendel
> And Marie, his moder swete.'  (26. 10–12)

This echoes also the offers of the grateful lords whom Guy had helped—offers which Guy had consistently refused for himself throughout the romance. The major structural and thematic impulse of the poem now emerges through this network of images and associations. Unlike his hagiographical prototype Alexis, Guy is not simply rejecting his former way of life as an obstacle between himself and God. Instead, it is clear what specific aspects of his former life were sinful, and Guy in atoning for his sins applies the medical principle of things being cured by their opposites, which we have already met in the penitential handbooks of Celtic origin or influence. Guy's sin has been not homicide, but pride and neglect of God; now he returns to his former occupations, transformed by studied, thorough, deliberate humility.

Throughout the second part of the romance, details occur which recall in contrast some corresponding detail in the first part. Most obviously, Guy steadily refuses to reveal his name, something which he was only too eager to disclose in the days when he was earning himself a reputation. The idea behind this is not, as when Alexis will not reveal his name, to destroy his previous identity, but to change it. He seeks to avoid the notoriety he once courted, so he keeps his identity secret until after the performance of each of his tasks, and when he does reveal it, it is only after making the enquirer swear to keep it to himself.

Similarly, Guy now wears poor pilgrim's attire rather than 'riche array'. He is no longer concerned with maintaining his dignity as a knight. Instead of leading his band of 'feren', Guy is now alone on his travels, and even when he encounters his old friend Tirri he remains alone, for Tirri does not recognize him. Instead of the comradeship of soldiers fighting together in a common cause, Guy now engages only in single combat. Instead of telling his friends to pray for him, he now prays himself to God for help and support in his trials, an important recognition of his own weakness and dependence on God. In the first part of the romance,

Guy offered his help to strangers out of his desire to win fame; now it is those who need his help who come looking for him because of that fame.

Once again, with every successive episode Guy's attitude and feelings change and develop. During the course of this second part of the romance he is transformed by his self-imposed hardships from a robust and vigorous man in the prime of his health and strength to an aged and weary one. He undertakes his first new task for the sake of justice, his second for the sake of his friend, and his final battle in simple submission to God's will.

Numerous details link Guy's first task in part 2 with his first main adventure in part 1. The cause of the quarrel between King Triamour and the Soudan is almost exactly the same as that between Segyn and Reyner. The German emperor's nephew was named Sadok and so is the Soudan's son, and they play an identical role in causing the two quarrels—each the guilty aggressor who is killed in a fight he provoked.

It is made clear at once in his first encounter with Earl Jonas how Guy can expect to reap the rewards of his earlier fame-mongering. King Triamour, Jonas reports, has asked him if he could name anyone brave enough to undertake single combat against the formidable Amoraunt on his behalf:

> 'Ac ichim answerd þan
> In alle þis warld was þer no man
> To fiȝt wiþ þat traitour,
> Bot ȝif it Gij of Warwike were,
> Or Herhaud of Ardern, his fere:
> In warld þai bere þe flour.'     (67. 7–12)

Jonas does not recognize Guy in the garb of a poor pilgrim. Subtly an effect is created of Guy being *obliged* to undertake the combat. All sorts of pressures in addition to the single motivation of compassion for Jonas's predicament combine to make his offer of help seem to proceed not so much from inclination as from a sense of responsibility. If Jonas cannot find Guy or Heraud within the specified time, his sons will be executed. In addition, the defeat of the Soudan's champion will in a real, practical sense constitute a service to God, since if Guy wins Triamour pledges to release not only Jonas and his sons but all his Christian captives, and to permit Christians to travel freely through his lands.

Ironically, though this is the very man he seeks, Jonas is sceptical about the value of his help; for though Guy is still the best knight in the world, he no longer looks it:

> When þerl herd him speke so,
> Þat he wald batayle fong for him þo,
>     He biheld fot & heued:
> Michel he was of bodi piȝt,
> A man he semed of michel miȝt,
>     Ac pouerliche he was biweued;
> Wiþ a long berd his neb was growe
> Miche wo him þought he hadde y-drowe.
>     He wende his wit were reued.
> For he seyd he wald as ȝern
> Fiȝt wiþ þat geaunt stern
>     Bot ȝif he hadde him preued.          (75. 1–12)

The strongly moral tone of this introduces us to a topic we will find again and again in religious romances: the unlikely nature of Truth. Jonas is deceived because he puts too much faith in appearances. Though he observes that Guy is well made and strong, he doubts his ability and even his sanity, because he is poorly clad and has a long beard. King Triamour makes the same mistake. He is disappointed when Jonas appears at Alexandria with only a scruffy palmer instead—as he thinks—of the fabled warrior Guy. The exchange which follows provides a valuable insight into Guy's thoughts and feelings on the subject of his penitence. Questioning Guy, Triamour scornfully suggests that Guy's poverty reflects badly either on Guy's merit or on that of his lord:

> Þe king asked him anon riȝt,
> 'Whi artow þus iuel y-diȝt
>     And in þus pouer wede?
> A feble lord þow seruest, so þenkeþ me,
> Or oway he haþ driuen þe
>     For sum iuel dede.'          (84. 7–12)

Triamour's view is typically that of the World, and thus limited. The alternatives he mentions are reasonable enough in the context of a feudal relationship between a vassal and his lord. Either that lord is incapable of rewarding the merits of his vassals with a proportionate show of wealth, through weakness or meanness; or he has deprived his vassal of the trappings accorded a successful

knight as a punishment for 'sum iuel dede'. Guy explains that his
poverty is self-inflicted. He frames his reply in the same terms as
Triamour's question, as if he were speaking of his feudal overlord,
and that is how Triamour understands him; however, it is clear to
the audience that Guy's words hold a meaning concealed from the
king and apparent only to Guy and to us:

> 'Nay, sir, for god,' quaþ Gij,
> 'A wel gode lord ar þis serued y:
>     Wiþ him was no blame.
> Wel michel honour he me dede,
> & gret worþschipe in eueri stede,
>     & sor ich haue him grame,
> & þer-fore icham þus y-di3t,
> To cri him merci day & ni3t,
>     Til we ben frendes same.
> & mi lord & y frende be,
> Ichil wende hom to mi cuntre,
>     & liue wiþ ioie & game.'          (85. 1–12)

This important and intimate statement reveals to the reader Guy's
view of his relationship with God. This relationship is personal,
immediate, and direct. It can be related to the Contritionists'
exposition of the psychology of penitence, in that Guy is deeply
conscious of God's great goodness to him, and how little he has
deserved or appreciated it. The speech relates in stark terms Guy's
sorrow at having grieved his Lord. At the same time, though
Guy's contrition proceeds correctly enough from the conscious-
ness of his own unworthiness, he entertains few doubts of the out-
come. One day he expects to atone for his offence, and then he
foresees a future joy which will more than compensate for his
present misery.

In this and the subsequent combats, Guy is consistently asso-
ciated with God and with justice, while his opponents are equally
associated with Hell and the Devil. In addition, Guy appears to be
the underdog; Amoraunt and Colbrond are both of gigantic size
and enormously strong, while Berard, in addition to being a
doughty warrior, is protected by two suits of armour and a shield
of double thickness. Guy himself is by no means so confident of
the outcome of his battles as he used to be; and indeed, on each
occasion he is almost vanquished, and would have perished had

not God protected him. His opponents, besides being bigger or
stronger than Guy, seek to conquer him by unfair advantage.

Amoraunt, Guy's first opponent, is indeed a terrifying spec-
tacle, being four feet taller than ordinary men and so strong that
'Oȝains him tvelue men haue no miȝt,/ Ben þai neuer so strong'
(63. 2–3). His sword has been bathed in 'þe flom of helle' and no
armour can withstand it. Guy himself thinks Amoraunt is a devil
(95. 10–12), and after Amoraunt succeeds in shattering his helmet,
cutting a foot and a half off his shield, killing his horse, and knock-
ing him to the ground, Guy prays to God:

> 'Lord,' seyd Gij, 'god al-miȝt,
> Þat made þe þerkenes to þe niȝt,
>  So help me to–day.
> Scheld me fro þis geaunt strong,
> Þat y no deþ of him afong,
>  Astow art lord verray.'          (102. 4–9)

For the first time an encounter of Guy's is presented in such a
way as to make it clear that while his opponent is physically his
equal, or even his superior, he is spiritually and morally far
beneath him. Guy generously allows Amoraunt to rest and have a
drink when he is hot and weary. Amoraunt returns to the battle
completely refreshed and as strong as when he began fighting; but
when Guy in his turn asks for a rest and a drink, Amoraunt de-
clares that Guy must first surrender, despite having previously
agreed to grant Guy the same favour Guy had granted him. When
Guy appeals to the Saracen to fulfil his part of the bargain, he asks
'For godes loue now merci', and frames his request in terms of
basic fair play:

> 'Ȝeld me now þat ich dede:
> Y ȝaf þe leue to drink at nede;
>  Astow art hende & fre,
> Leue to drink þou lat me go,
> As it was couenaunt bitven ous tvo:
>  For loue y pray þe.'          (120. 7–12)

Unfortunately Amoraunt is neither 'hende' nor 'fre', and has no
love for Guy. He denies Guy permission to drink 'bi mi lord sir
Teruagaunt' (121. 2). The author thus directly associates Amor-
aunt's dishonourable behaviour with his faith, and Guy's nobility
with his Christian faith. Amoraunt gloats over Guy's weakness,

forgetting his own argument that it brings no credit to conquer an opponent weakened by heat and thirst. Guy bluntly requests him to 'do ariȝt' (121. 7) and allow him to drink so that they may see who is truly the better fighter; but this makes no impression on Amoraunt, who merely wishes to take advantage of Guy's weakness. However, he offers to allow Guy to drink if he will reveal his right name, charging him once again 'Bi þe treuþe þou owe þi lord,/ Þat þou louest so dere' (124. 2–3). But when Guy has told him, Amoraunt breaks his word again. He has already expressed a wish to meet Guy in battle, so as to pay him back for killing 40,000 Saracens at the battle of Constantinople, and for having 'destrud al our lawe' (111. 7); now he thanks Mahoun and Teruagaunt for delivering his enemy into his hands so easily. Guy in desperation rushes to the water and dives in, hotly pursued by Amoraunt, and an exciting scuffle follows. At last Guy manages to cut off Amoraunt's arms, and then his head, and the battle is over.

Guy's victory is achieved not by mere force of arms but, more than on any previous occasions, by force of justice. In addition to upholding a just quarrel, Guy represents by virtue of his nobility and generosity the right belief and the right way of life, as opposed to Amoraunt's callous and brutish paganism. The combat and its outcome are also in marked contrast to Guy's earlier victory over Otous of Pavia, the greatest traitor and felon of the first part of the romance. Guy here defeats Amoraunt in open combat, where the odds are actually against him because of Amoraunt's superior size and strength; whereas he slew Otous in an unexpected attack while he was on his way to be married, before he had a chance to draw his sword. Richly though Otous deserved his fate, it was on Guy's part not such a heroic action as his fight against Amoraunt, in which Christianity (Amoraunt addresses Guy as 'Cristen', 113. 4) comes into personal conflict with Paganism.

King Triamour is a more or less virtuous pagan, and is true to his word. He is made to illustrate the way in which Guy sets a good example by his active exemplification of Christian virtue. Triamour is so impressed that when he offers Guy a third of his kingdom to stay with him, he remarks that he will not insist on Guy forsaking his god, because 'Þou are bileueand wele afine,/ Better may no be' (136. 8–9).

Guy refuses the offer and journeys on to Jerusalem with Earl Jonas, who asks him for the love of Jesus to reveal his identity.

Guy does so, and Jonas is overcome with pity:

> 'For godes loue,' he seyd, 'merci!
> Whi artow so pouer, sir Gij,
> & art of so gret valour?'     (139. 1–3)

He offers Guy his own lands and title so that he may be restored to
what Jonas mistakenly believes is his rightful eminence and pros-
perity. Guy gently thanks him for his kindness and refuses, com-
mending him to God and explaining that 'mi way ichil ful-fille'
(140. 9). He leaves the earl weeping, and continues his journey to
Greece, to Constantinople, and finally back to Espire in Almaine,
retracing the route of his earlier adventures.

The second adventure of Guy's penance causes him to suffer
great personal anguish, and tests his resolve to abdicate from his
old life. He encounters his old friend Tirri at Espire, also impover-
ished and dressed as a pilgrim, and learns that Tirri has been
accused by Berard, the nephew of Otous of Pavia, of Otous's
murder, and unless he can find someone (Guy or Heraud) to
undertake combat for him against Berard, his life is forfeit.

Once again, a sense of obligation is created on Guy's part. Tirri
has been accused of a murder which Guy in fact committed, and
Berard is really anxious to fight Guy, not Tirri, whom he is perse-
cuting only because he knows him to be Guy's friend. Guy is
aroused to pity, grief, and anger by Tirri's plight; and these feel-
ings bring him closer to his old self than he has been since under-
taking his penitential exile. He is prevented from succumbing to
the temptations to which a full restoration of their old comrade-
ship would expose him, because he does not reveal his identity to
Tirri, and Tirri does not recognize him in his pilgrim's guise.

It is this failure of Tirri to acknowledge his old friend which is
so hurtful to Guy. That Earl Jonas should have been deceived by
Guy's appearance was not surprising; he had known of Guy only
as a great and powerful knight, and would naturally expect such a
person to wear armour and be well groomed and clad; nor would
he look beyond the visor at the man. But Tirri had been Guy's
friend and comrade, who knew him and shared danger, sorrow,
and joy with him. It is a source of bitter disappointment to Guy
that his changed exterior should blind Tirri as well, and this
enables him to leave Tirri behind him the more easily at the end of
the episode. And after all, Guy has changed inside as well as out;

he is no longer the same person Tirri knew, and the sense of this gulf between them enables Guy to continue his quest for the true friendship of God, when he sees how limited his friend's love for him is.

There is some evidence that Guy questions his motives in defending Tirri's cause. Berard, in spite of his formidable reputation (148. 2–12), shows himself to be a cowardly traitor. After the end of the first day's fight, he decides to have Guy disposed of in the night. His henchmen go to Guy's lodgings, pick up his bed, with Guy still asleep inside it, and throw it over a cliff into the sea. Some of the most beautiful lines in the poem follow when Guy awakes:

> Þe sterres on þe heuen he seiȝe,
> Þe water about him drawe.
> Þei he was ferd no wonder it nis:
> Non oþer þing he no seyȝe y-wis,
> Bot winde & wateres wawe.     (196. 8–12)

Guy assumes that he has been placed in this situation by a miracle as a divine punishment, and prays to God to save him, and explains that his motives for undertaking the combat are pure:

> 'Lord,' seyd Gij, 'God almiȝt,
> Þat winde, & water, & al þing diȝt,
>   On me haue now pite!
> Whi is me fallen þus strong cumbring?
> & y no fiȝt for to win no þing,
>   Noiþer gold no fe,
> For no cite no no castel,
> Bot for mi felawe y loued so wel,
>   Þat was of gret bounte.
> For he was sumtyim so douhti,
> & now he is so pouer a bodi,
>   Certes, it reweþ me.'     (197. 1–12)

At this point in the Anglo-Norman *Gui de Warewic* and in C, a fisherman appears on the scene, by chance.[47] In A, however, it is expressly pointed out that Jesus sent the fisherman on purpose to save Guy, in response to his prayer (198. 1–6). This prayer, which

---

[47] *Gui* has: 'Atant es vus un mariner/ Ki vint peschant par cele mer/ Le chalit vit de loiz flotant', ll. 10255–7. C has: 'Tho ther com a good fysshere/ Fyshyng be sir Gye nere./ The bed he saw far by fletand', ll. 9806–8. A (198. 1–6) departs from this.

in A does not contain the tirade against Berard which is in the other versions, recalls to the audience (and to Guy) the true action of this part of the poem: Guy's struggle, through penance, to make himself 'worþi' of God's love.

The fisherman rescues Guy, who is able to resume battle in the morning and bring it to a successful conclusion. After the battle Guy receives the emperor's pledge that the wronged Tirri will have his lands and titles restored to him, and he hastens away to bring his friend the good news, pausing only to change back into his pilgrim's clothes. Tirri is on his knees in the church praying. Guy tells him he must accompany him back to the court. Tirri immediately assumes that the pilgrim has betrayed him to the emperor, upbraids him, and wishes he had never told him his name. Guy explains that he has killed Berard and obtained the emperor's pardon for Tirri, and 'Þo was Tirri glad & bliþe' (214. 7); but for Guy to be greeted in this way at a moment when he expects joyful gratitude is a painful disappointment. Tirri uses words very similar to those Guy spoke in part 1 when he thought he had been wronged by the emperor Ernïs:

> 'To what man may men trust be,
> To chese to his make?'        (213. 2–3)

Then as now, the speaker has wronged someone whom he ought to have trusted; Guy is once again being put in the position of exchanging places with another character from a previous episode. In addition, this time, the words have another significance for Guy, which is that indeed no man is ultimately to be trusted. Who would Guy have trusted before anyone, if not Tirri, whose friendship he often mentions throughout this episode? Yet Tirri has let him down. Only God can be perfectly trusted in the last resort.

Tirri mentions several times that he believes Guy to be dead (154. 4–12, 191. 7–12, 216. 1–6), and his reason for believing this is that he can get no news of Guy anywhere. He identifies Guy so much with his fame, it is inconceivable to him that Guy can have given up his exploits as the most famous knight in the world, and fight incognito. Guy reproaches Tirri with great sorrow just before he leaves him, and voluntarily reveals his name. He recites all the things which he has done for Tirri in the past. Why does Tirri not know him (224 and 225)? Tirri reacts with grief and shame and begs to go with Guy if Guy will not stay with him. But Guy realizes that their paths must be separate; Tirri must remain in his place in the world, as the emperor's new steward, and Guy must pursue his lonely course. The parting of the friends this time is even more sorrowful than the last, for it is a final parting. They love each other, but their brotherhood is broken. Tirri has failed Guy, and the friendship becomes one more of the things binding him to this world which Guy casts off and leaves behind him in his progress towards God.

Guy returns to England, where his greatest and most famous feat of arms awaits him. When he fought Berard, the townspeople commented that Guy was no earthly man but an angel sent by God to punish the wickedness of Berard (188. 7–12). This again shows Guy as an instrument of divine justice rather than a private person. Now, on his return to England, Guy has been transformed so completely from egocentric fame-hunter to self-effacing instrument of God, that he fights the giant Colbrond entirely in compliance with God's will. His own appetite for battle has been exhausted. He does not volunteer for this task, but is pointed out by divine intervention. Though moved by England's desperate situation, Guy is doubtful of his capacity to help, and when Athelstan requests the unlikely warrior to undertake the combat, replies:

> 'Do way, leue sir,' seyd Gij,
> 'Icham an old man, a feble bodi:
>   Me strengþe is fro me fare.'   (247. 1–3)

He agrees when Athelstan and his nobles have all gone on their knees to him and begged him:

> '. . . for god in trinite,
> & forto make Inglond fre,
>   Þe batayle y nim on hond.'   (248. 4–6)

The pattern of the previous combats is repeated. Colbrond is another physically superior but spiritually base opponent; his appearance is terrifying, and Guy prays to God for help. Athelstan doubts that his divinely elected champion can succeed. The odds are against Guy, and once more his adversary seeks to win the contest by unfair means—Colbrond refuses to give him another weapon when his sword breaks. Again, the battle over, Guy resumes his pilgrim's garb and refuses rich rewards. Once more Athelstan conjures him 'for him þat made man' to reveal his name and origin. Guy does so on condition that Athelstan will tell no one else for a year. Athelstan weeps for pity to see Guy in such a wretched state, and is sorry not to have recognized him.

Guy returns to Warwick, where he receives alms from his wife Felice. Felice has undertaken to feed and clothe thirteen poor men each day for the sake of her absent lord. Now Guy himself becomes one of the thirteen. She offers to feed and clothe Guy for the rest of his life, not recognizing him and pitying his condition; but Guy declines. He seeks a more personal communion with God, in an honourable retirement. The penitential possibilities of a life of action have been exhausted. As far as the fearsome logic of 'Þat ich haue wiþ mi bodi wrouȝt,/ Wiþ mi bodi it schal be bouȝt' has been strictly followed, there are no more sins to expiate; Guy is transformed from being prosperous and proud to being wretched and humble. He is ready to retire from the world and seek solitude.

In this retirement from the world Guy of Warwick differs from the other heroes of romances of penance. Gowther, Ysumbras, and Roberd all return to their former positions in the world when their penances are complete, as changed men, and live the remainder of their lives virtuously and humbly, but in circumstances of considerable worldly prosperity. For Guy such a return is not possible, and the end of the romance resembles that of a saint's life more closely than do the endings of *Sir Gowther*, *Sir Ysumbras*, and *Roberd of Cisyle*. The visitation from the angel to warn Guy of his impending death, the miraculous tokens following his death, could be those of a saint; but the sending of the token to Felice, and the brief, touching scene at his bedside, are pure romance. These remaining details of the narrative appear as the final working-out of Guy's personal development: his education, in a sense. His initial perception of himself as sinful resulted in his rejection and denial of the worldly things he had desired. Out of his penance grew a genuine desire for higher things, a denial of self, true humility, and the love of God.

Although *Guy of Warwick* is a long and comparatively early Middle English romance, it has many features in common with the shorter *Sir Ysumbras*, *Sir Gowther*, and *Roberd of Cisyle*. These three poems, in many respects so different from *Guy*, all in their own way make use of a characteristic 'penitential pattern' which already emerges strongly in *Guy of Warwick*. The hero is in a state of sin; he is unaware of this at first, but experiences a critical revelation, usually stimulated by the influence of some external event or character. He repents and determines to atone for his sins. The penance which he undertakes is usually imposed on him by divine or earthly authority (*Guy of Warwick* differs in that Guy imposes his own form of penance and specifically rejects the more conventional recourse to the Church followed by good works and the founding of an abbey, recommended by Felice). The penance itself characteristically consists of the patient endurance of great poverty and hardship, with a long 'pilgrimage' undertaken by the penitent, followed by a period spent at court (usually his own court) incognito. The expiation accomplished, the penitent is rewarded by an assurance of salvation, and returns to his position in the world, though changed for the better. Again, *Guy of Warwick* differs from the other poems in that Guy rejects such a return, and chooses to spend the remainder of his life in retirement in a hermitage.

The sin with which Guy reproaches himself, having neglected to render God the love and worship which is His due, can be related to the forms of Pride of which Ysumbras and Roberd are guilty; and Guy's prescribed penance systematically overturns all the sources of his former pride and vainglory in just the way that Ysumbras's and Roberd's do. The course of humility undertaken by Guy, almost as a medicinal antidote to the spiritual poison of Pride, gives him an insight into the shallow and unstable nature of worldly fame and fortune. He (and the reader) gains a truer perspective on his life; he has attained through his experiences, and particularly through his sufferings, a special knowledge of himself, of his role in society, of his relationship to God.

The kind of penitence experienced by Guy is also of a kind we will find again in other romances. He realizes that he has sinned, and he responds with sorrow:

> 'Allas, allas!' it was his song:
> For sorwe he ȝede ner wode.   (21. 11–12)

but he determines at once on a course of action which will atone for his offences (22. 1–12). The consequence of his realization is logical and ineffable. He must cure a disease deeply rooted in his soul; he is very conscious of the likely result of further neglect, and of the ground he has already lost.

Guy instinctively knows what he must do. He rejects Felice's suggestion that he, like other people, could atone for his sins by more conventional and less painful means (28. 1–12, 29. 1–12). Guy's profound sense of his own sinfulness, of his own short-comings, the way in which he has failed God, and his conviction of the right thing to do to remedy this state are the significant feelings generated by the scene. These are emotions and decisions which are fundamental in human experience; they recur in other romances; and they correspond exactly with the psychological stages of penitence described by the contritionist theologians. Here as we have seen the sorrow felt by the penitent sinner and the strength of his determination to atone for his sins and to alter his future conduct are seen as the really potent factors in the operation of the sacrament of penance, the actual forgiveness of sin (rather than, as later, the form of the sacrament and the role of the priest).

Guy's refusal to accommodate his own conviction to what is done by the world in general is an explicit statement of an impor-tant element of romance. In this partially ideal world, where there are no compromises and no half-heartedness, it is not acceptable to buy your way out of the consequences of your sins, even if every-one else thinks it is. Of course, the founding of abbeys is a good thing in itself, and indeed, at the end of the poem, the faithful Tirri does found an abbey in Lorraine, where he inters the bodies of Guy and Felice, and endows priests to 'sing for hem to/ Euermore til domesday' (298. 11–12). Sir Gowther also founds an abbey on the completion of his penance. But while this may be a virtuous deed when performed in addition to a romance penance, it will not do instead of one. The implication of Guy's decision is that the inspiration which guides him has far more force than the conventional forms of penitence proposed by Felice, although he does not make this explicit in his reply to her (29. 1–3). It is not necessary to do so, because the reader who has been following Guy's thoughts and feelings will recognize that for Guy to acquiesce in Felice's perfectly proper suggestion that he go to con-fession and commute his penance by founding churches and abbeys would be a gross violation of the truth which Guy (and the reader) has just perceived.

*Guy* is a long, discursive poem, and not all of its lengthy epi-sodes are consistently treated in accordance with the didactic aim of the poem. It contains more scenes of dialogue and description, treated in a more realistic manner, than short romances, which are inherently more concise and symbolic in mode. In terms of style and narrative technique, *Guy* has little in common with these shorter works, being like a gigantic landscape painting filled with different scenes, while they resemble a fine miniature of a knight, in which every detail, from the crest of his helmet down to the herb under his foot, is a clue to a deeper symbolic significance. Yet the major elements that appear in Guy's penitence and atonement are taken up in these poems and reworked in the manner appropriate to them. It is to these poems that we now turn.

# 4

## Sir Ysumbras

*Sir Ysumbras*,[1] like *Guy of Warwick*, was widely read and popular.
Its fame is attested by the large number of surviving manuscripts
and prints[2] and by its twice being mentioned by name in other
medieval writings. In addition to appearing in the short list already
quoted[3] from the *Speculum Vitae*, *Sir Ysumbras* is also mentioned
in a longer list of 'iestis' given at the opening of *Cursor Mundi* as
examples of the kind of tales which foolish men want to hear:

> Man yhernes rimes for to here,
> And romans red on maneres sere,
> (Of Alexander, Caesar, Greece, Troy, Brut, Arthur,
> Gawain, Kay, King Charlemagne, Tristram)
> O Ioneck and of ysambrase,[4]
> Of ydoine and of amadase
> Stories als o ferekin thinges
> O princes, prelates and o kynges

. . . . . . . .

[1] *Sir Ysumbras*, ed. G. Schleich and J. Zupitza, *Palaestra*, 15 (1901). All quotations will
be from this edition, which is based on MS C (see n. 2, below), with variant readings from
other manuscripts.

[2] *Sir Ysumbras* was probably composed in the early 14th cent. near the northern border
of the East Midlands. There are eight early manuscripts: Caius College, Cambridge 175,
fos. 98b–107b, *c*.1425–50, 780 lines with lacunae (C); Thornton MS, Lincoln Cathedral A.
5. 2, fos. 109–14, *c*.1440, 794 lines (T); BL Cotton Caligula A. 2, fos. 103a–134b, *c*.1450–
1500, 794 lines (L); Bodleian Library, Ashmole 61, fos. 9a–16b, *c*.1475–1500, 822 lines (A);
National Library of Scotland, Advocates 19. 3. 1, fos. 48b–56a, *c*.1475–1500, 837 lines (E);
Royal Library of Naples (now Biblioteca Nazionale) XIII. B. 29, fos. 114–18, MS dated
1457, fragment, 122 lines (N); London, Gray's Inn 20, *c*.1350, fragment, 104 lines (G);
University College, Oxford 142, *c*.1450–1500, 1 leaf, opening 15 lines (U). Two manu-
scripts exist which are transcriptions of printed versions of the poem: MS Douce 261, fos.
1a–7b, dated 1564, 372 lines (D); and Harvard University, Percy Folio MS Eng. 748, vol. 3,
*c*.1767. There are also three early prints: Copland's, BL C. 21. c. (61), *c*.1550 (c); a leaf in an
old print in Douce's fragments 78, Bodleian Library, *c*.1550 (d); Malone 941, Bodleian
Library, fo. 9, fragment of an old print, stanzas 37. 11–41. 10. D, c, and d share some dis-
tinctive readings and will be referred to as a group, cDd.

[3] See above, pp. 74–5.

[4] A variant reading in some manuscripts gives 'King John' instead of 'Ioneck'.

Þe wisman wil o wisdom here,
Þe foul hym draghus to foly nere.[5]

Again we must draw the conclusion that the pious and edifying nature of the poem, assuming that the authors of *Speculum Vitae* and *Cursor Mundi* were aware of it, and its close relation to the Legend of St Eustace did not sufficiently distinguish *Sir Ysumbras* from other romances for ecclesiastical commentators to exclude it from their condemnations of foolish 'rimes'. Nor is this surprising, in view of the thorough 'secularization' of the structure and motifs of the story which *Sir Ysumbras* has undergone.

*Sir Ysumbras* belongs to two distinct and clearly defined groups. The first group is that of versions of the Legend of St Eustace; the second is a group of romances known as the 'Eustace–Constance–Florence–Griselda' legends, in which the main story motif is that of 'The Man Tried by Fate'.[6] In addition, it has been connected with a group of romances, said to be the product of a Midlands 'school', many of which fall within the 'Eustace–Constance–Florence–Griselda' group, and all of which share such features as the tail-rhyme stanza, vocabulary, formulae, and dialect.[7] Critics have been divided as to whether *Sir Ysumbras* should be considered primarily as a member of the first or the second group.

G. H. Gerould gives summaries of all the analogues, both Western and Eastern, of St Eustace's life, concluding that its origins were in the East. Of *Sir Ysumbras* he says that it is 'more closely related to the other romance versions' than to the legend itself.[8] A. H. Krappe concluded that the Western analogues (*Guillaume d'Angleterre*, *Die gute Frau*, *Wilhelm von Wenden*, *El Caballero Cifar*, *Boeve de Hamstone*, *Sir Ysumbras*, and *Der Graf von Savoien*) are derived from a Balkan version of the story of Near-Eastern, and ultimately Indian, provenance, although the saint's legend was certainly instrumental in the final shape they have assumed.[9] Laurel Braswell argues persuasively that *Sir Ysumbras*

---

[5] *Cursor Mundi*, ed. R. Morris, EETS, os, 57 (London, 1874), p. 9, ll. 1, 2, 19–22, 28, 29.

[6] Or its female counterpart, 'The Calumniated Wife'. See J. Burke Severs, *A Manual of Writings in Middle English, 1050–1500* 1, *Romances* (New Haven, 1967), pp. 120–32.

[7] Laurel Braswell, '*Sir Isumbras* and the Legend of Saint Eustace', *Medieval Studies*, 27 (1965), 132–3.

[8] Gordon Hall Gerould, 'Forerunners, Congeners and Derivatives of the Eustace Legend', *PMLA* 19 (1904), 335–448.

[9] A. H. Krappe, 'La leggenda di S. Eustachio', *Nuovi studi medievali*, 3 (1928), 223–58.

is more closely related to the legend of St Eustace than are the other romances which resemble it (the 'Eustace–Constance–Florence–Griselda' group: *Sir Triamour, Octovian, Eglamour of Artois, Sir Torrent of Portyngale, Emare, The King of Tars,* and *Le Bone Florence of Rome*) or the related works extant in other vernaculars (*Guillaume d'Angleterre,* etc.).[10]

*Sir Ysumbras* is, however, unique among both groups in adapting the story of St Eustace or 'The Man Tried by Fate' to accommodate the theme of the penitent sinner, originally foreign to it,[11] something which has been overlooked by many commentators. In the process, it comes to resemble *Sir Gowther* and *Roberd of Cisyle* in several respects.

Laurel Braswell gives 'Isumbras' trial for reasons of penance' as an example of the poem's 'especially important links' with the legend, but this is not the case. The misfortunes inflicted on Eustace and Ysumbras must be either a trial or a penance, but cannot be both. St Eustace's misfortunes are specifically stated to be a trial of his faith after the manner of Job.[12] Similarly the protagonists of the 'Eustace–Constance–Florence–Griselda' poems are all virtuous men and women, whose patience, fortitude, and faith are tested and rewarded. The saint-like passivity which such a story necessarily imposes on its hero or heroine has excited comment.[13] *Sir Ysumbras,* however, is different. Ysumbras is specifically said to be sinful (ll. 31–6); he says that his misfortunes are a direct consequence of that sin (ll. 112–14); and the actions he performs during his wanderings are stated to be a penance for his former deeds (ll. 526–8).

---

[10] Braswell, '*Sir Isumbras*', pp. 128–51.

[11] The empress in *Octovian* (ed. Frances McSparran, EETS, os, 289 (London, 1986), when falsely accused by her mother-in-law and cast into exile with her children, responds:

> 'Lorde, the sorowe that y am ynne,
> Well y wot hyt ys for my synne:
> Welcome be thy sonde.' (ll. 397–9)

a speech almost identical to (and surely influenced by) Ysumbras's words at ll. 112–14. In *Guillaume d'Angleterre* (ed. Maurice Wilmotte (Paris, 1927)), Guillaume is advised by his chaplain after hearing the heavenly voice to give away all his goods in reparation for wrongs he has done (ll. 92–105). The empress and Guillaume, however, are not sinners, but innocent and virtuous.

[12] See e.g. *St Eustace,* ed. Carl Horstmann, *Altenglische Legenden* (Heilbronn, 1881), pp. 211–19, l. 187.

[13] See Diana T. Childress, 'Between Romance and Legend: "Secular Hagiography" in Middle English Literature', *Philological Quarterly,* 57 (1978), 317–18.

In a romance as short as *Sir Ysumbras* we should not expect to find the detailed discussions and psychological developments so realistically created in *Guy of Warwick*. There is no room for explanations or descriptions of mental states in a poem which is a mere 800 or so lines long and covers fifteen years of action. The absence of a more fully realized scene of penitential revelation has perhaps deceived some critics into discounting the theme of penance in the poem. Gerould misses it altogether in his account,[14] while Dieter Mehl describes the action of the plot as 'the trial and salvation of the hero by suffering' and feels that, while the poem represents a 'very successful attempt' to combine 'the punishment and purification of a sinner and the prolonged demonstration of patience and constance in adversity' in terms of structure and plot, it is much less successful in terms of character development, because Ysumbras does not appear to undergo the change of character seen so clearly in *Roberd of Cisyle*.[15]

Laurel Braswell, misunderstanding the difference between Eustace's trial of faith and Ysumbras's penance for his sins, accounts for the introduction of penance to the story as a device of the plot to cover the fact that Ysumbras, being Christian already, cannot undergo the conversion with which the story of Eustace begins:

> Essential differences between the Life of St Eustace and the romance are determined by the fact that Isumbras is depicted as already Christian. He therefore suffers because of his sins, not because he may thereby acquire martyrdom.[16]

This is of course not necessarily so. There is no reason why Ysumbras should not simply be informed that God is going to make trial of his virtues, just as He did of Eustace. Octavian, Eglamour, Guillaume d'Angleterre are all Christians at the openings of their stories, as are the heroes and heroines of the other Middle English romances related to this group, who are simply made to suffer many hardships and are subsequently rewarded for their exemplary patience. In *Sir Ysumbras*, then, the fact that the hero suffers in penance for his sins is not the inevitable consequence of

[14] Gerould, 'Forerunners of the Eustace Legend', p. 365.
[15] Dieter Mehl, *The Middle English Romances of the Thirteenth and Fourteenth Centuries* (London, 1968), p. 133.
[16] Braswell, '*Sir Isumbras*', p. 132.

his having been born a Christian. The theme of penance is not introduced at random, but is consistently worked out through the action of the poem, and creates a moral impetus which is radically different from that of its analogues.

Dieter Mehl's reservations about the success of Ysumbras's characterization perhaps reflect the difficulty with which we, conditioned by the literary conventions of our age, can assimilate a fictional world in which realistic details are to varying degrees combined with an impressive symbolic power. In *Roberd of Cisyle*, to which Mehl compares *Sir Ysumbras* in the realization of the penitent's change of heart, the external, symbolic means of expressing the essential action of the poem is hardly employed at all; in *Sir Ysumbras* it is unusually strong. Here the transformation which Ysumbras undergoes is expressed not so much by what he says or by an account of how he feels, as by the things which happen to him and the things he does. This is a phenomenon observed much more readily in short romances, particularly where, as in *Sir Ysumbras*, a fairly long and complex story is compressed down to a few hundred lines. W. R. J. Barron comments:

The need to express fundamental human concerns in the heightened terms of idealism leads the authors of romance to exploit a technique of superlatives: extraordinary, even supernatural, incidents, exotic settings, fabulous trappings, and properties which function as images as much as objects ... In the medieval romance, these expressive conventions ... draw much of their evocative power from their continuous corporate use. Their dual nature, mimetic and symbolic, puzzling to modern readers, presented fewer problems to an age accustomed to see all physical, mental, and spiritual phenomena as inter-related expressions of the divine will and to read all narratives at more than one level of meaning.[17]

It is worth noting at this point a version of the Eustace legend which appears in the *Gesta Romanorum*, where an explicit moralization is added to the end of the story. A knight, on his way to a great tournament held by the Emperor Averyos, hears a nightingale singing sweetly and wonders what the song means. An old gentleman approaches and tells him that before he arrives at the emperor's feast he will 'suffre gret persecucion'. The knight sets forth with his wife and two sons; after they have crossed the sea in a ship, his wife is kept by the shipmaster in lieu of payment. Soon afterwards, at a river crossing, the knight loses his two sons, one to

[17] W. R. J. Barron, *English Medieval Romance* (London, 1987), p. 5.

a lion and one to a bear. He proceeds in great sorrow to the tourna-
ment, which he wins. Soon he must raise an army for the emperor,
and the wife and sons are reunited with him exactly as in the
legend of St Eustace, though they do not suffer martyrdom after-
wards. The *moralite* reads:

Dere frendis, this Emperoure is oure lord Ihesu Crist, the which callith
us to the turnement of penaunce, wherthurugh we mow come to euerlas-
tyng ioy . . . the two childryn bethe reson and wille . . . they mow sekirly
come to the tournement of penaunce . . . the Ship in which vs owe to
entre is penaunce . . . [etc.][18]

A romance rarely veers so close to allegory, but the unexpressed
meaning of images and events is there to be explored by the reader.
This has not been fully realized until recently, with the result that
some assessments of *Sir Ysumbras* have been undisguisedly con-
temptuous[19] and have typically viewed the theme of penance as a
transparent device which enables the author to get on with the real
business of the romance, that is, the wanderings, the fabulous
beasts, miracles, and marvellous reunion. Thus Laurel Braswell:

The general tone of the work is naturally that of a romance. It is filled
with wondrous elements and mythical beasts, and the author indulges in
the usual topoi of such romances, e.g. praise of minstrelsy, emphasis
upon physical prowess, and descriptions of armour or battles.[20]

It is not difficult to interpret the events of *Sir Ysumbras* in this
way: nowhere is the motif of penance articulated with any force;
nowhere does Ysumbras express remorse or sorrow for the sins he
is supposed to have committed. He does weep, on seeing the
'gamen and glee' at his wife's castle, but this is interpreted as
Ysumbras feeling sorry for himself and comparing his former life
of luxury unfavourably with his present wretched state.[21] The
moral point of the didactic story is simply, as in other 'Eustace–
Constance–Florence–Griselda' stories, the exemplary patience
and fortitude, the resignation to the will of God, displayed by the
hero throughout his long trials. The word 'penance' is only men-

[18] *Gesta Romanorum*, ed. S. J. H. Herrtage, EETS, ES, 33 (London, 1897), p. 91.
[19] See e.g. George Kane's account of the poem in *Middle English Literature* (London, 1951), p. 13.
[20] Braswell, '*Sir Isumbras*', p. 135.
[21] Thus Laurel Braswell, who cites these lines as evidence of the author's 'praise of min-strelsy', '*Sir Isumbras*', p. 135.

tioned once (at l. 527), and the nearest Ysumbras himself comes to uttering the standard formula of repentance is to inform his bewildered family:

> For alle þe bale, þat we aryn in,
> It es for oure wyked syn;
> We are worthi wele mare!     (ll. 112–14)

Here is no sense of the sinfulness of the heart. Thus it is felt that the identity of the penitent sinner does not fit well with the character and circumstances of Sir Ysumbras; throughout the romance he behaves in an exemplary manner: 'The carefully graded sequence of his trials does not correspond to a significant development in him and he remains rather static in his perfect submission.'[22] Ysumbras does not take the initiative and go searching for absolution, as does Sir Gowther. On the other hand, the tribulations inflicted on him do not appear to make him conscious of, and sorry for, his sin, as in *Roberd of Cisyle*. Ysumbras accepts from the first that he has sinned, and is then plunged into deeper and deeper sufferings, from which he may be spectacularly restored at the end of the poem.

However, another interpretation of the poem is possible, in which a strong symbolic coherence can be seen in the treatment of Ysumbras's penance throughout the poem. This is achieved chiefly by rigorously controlled structural patterns and the repetition and manipulation of symbolic motifs. Through these a convincing portrayal of Ysumbras's penitential re-education and spiritual rebirth are created.

A comparison between the Legend of St Eustace and *Sir Ysumbras* is instructive in highlighting the small but important changes to the plot made by the latter (or its lost source):

| ST EUSTACE | SIR YSUMBRAS |
|---|---|
| 1. Opening Circumstances ||
| Placidas is a Roman general in the army of the Emperor Trajan. He has a wife and two sons and, though not a Christian, is a virtuous man. | Sir Ysumbras is a good knight, handsome, wealthy, courteous, and generous, especially to gleemen. He has a wife and three sons. He becomes proud and forgets God. |

---

[22] Mehl, *Romances*, p. 134.

## 2. Message from God

While hunting Placidas chases a fine stag, becoming separated from his companions. When the stag turns at bay he sees a vision of Christ crucified between its horns and is converted to Christianity. He is baptised, along with his family, and takes the name Eustace.

Ysumbras is riding through his forest 'him to pleye' when he hears a bird singing in a tree (an angel in the sky in cDd). It tells him that he has lapsed from his former virtue 'for pride of gold and fee'.

## 3. The Choice

In a second vision Eustace is told that he must be tried like Job and suffer extreme deprivation in order to be rendered worthy of the kingdom of Heaven; he may choose whether to suffer now or later in life. He chooses to suffer now.

Either in his youth or in old age Ysumbras must suffer in penance for his sins; he may choose which it shall be. Ysumbras, considering that he will be more capable of enduring hardship while he is young and strong, chooses to take the penance now.

## 4. Loss of Goods

A series of disasters overwhelms him: he finds on his return home that all his servants and livestock have died of pestilence. After moving away, robbers steal all his goods. For shame of poverty, Eustace and his family flee, intending to travel to Egypt.

Ysumbras's horse drops dead under him, his hounds go mad and run off. Walking home, he is met by a small boy who tells him that his property is all burned down and his cattle are slain. He meets his herdsmen, who lament his losses, and his wife and sons, fleeing naked from the fire. He shares his clothes with them, and decides to go to the Holy Land. With a knife he cuts a cross in his shoulder.

## 5. Separation of the Family

After two days they come to the sea and embark on a ship. As Eustace has no money to pay for their passage, the captain decides to keep his wife Theospita instead. When Eustace objects he is thrown into the sea. Soon after he comes to a river; having carried one of his sons across he is returning for the other when a lion comes and carries away the first, and a wolf the second.

At a river crossing, Ysumbras loses his two elder sons, one to a lion, one to a leopard. Coming to the shore the remainder of the family see a ship and approach it to beg for food; but it contains a heathen king who is attracted to Ysumbras's wife. On his refusal to sell her and become the Sultan's vassal, Ysumbras is beaten and made to accept a mantle full of gold. In a last interview Ysumbras and his wife exchange rings and vow to slay the Sultan. Ysumbras goes on his way; an eagle steals his gold, and while he gives chase a unicorn abducts his youngest son.

## 6. Period of Suffering

In despair Eustace likens himself to Job. He arrives at Badyssus and there remains for fifteen years as a poor labourer. Meanwhile his sons are rescued from the lion and the wolf by shepherds and ploughmen and are brought up unknown to each other in the same village. Theospita escapes from the sea captain and lives as a seamstress in the country to which she had been taken.

In despair Ysumbras prays to God to guide him to 'some towne'. God guides him to a smithy, where he works as a smith for seven years. Having forged his own armour, he goes to help a Christian king who is fighting the Sultan. He slays the Sultan but is himself badly wounded. After recovering at a nunnery he spends a further seven years of agonizing hardship as a pilgrim, at the end of which an angel appears and tells him his sins have been forgiven.

## 7. Reunion and Restoration

Trajan sends in search of Eustace to lead his army. He is recognized by a scar on his forehead, returns to the emperor's service and raises an army. Two of his new recruits are his sons. During the campaign the army is encamped in the town where Theospita now lives. The two sons tell each other their life stories and realize that they are brothers; Theospita overhears them and recognizes them as her sons. She comes to Eustace and requests to return to Rome; she then recognizes him, they are all reunited, and after the defeat of the enemy return to Rome.

Ysumbras arrives at the castle in which his wife now lives as queen. He is taken in and receives alms. After living there for some time unrecognized he recovers the mantle of gold and hides it in his room. Suspicious knights raid his room while he is out and show the gold to the queen, who recognizes it as that given to her husband in payment for her. A reconciliation with Ysumbras follows and he is made king. The neighbouring kingdoms attack him as a Christian; his pagan retainers desert, leaving Ysumbras and his wife to face battle against 30,000 Saracens. The three sons appear, riding the lion, leopard, and unicorn, and together they conquer the pagans.

## 8. Conclusion

Unfortunately Trajan has been succeeded by Hadrian who, on their refusing to sacrifice to Apollo, has the family roasted in a brazen bull.

Ysumbras and his family conquer and convert the neighbouring kingdoms. They live in great virtue, wealth, and happiness, and go to heaven when they die.

This comparison demonstrates that the romance follows the story of St Eustace in its basic outline, but differs in small but important details. Laurel Braswell emphasizes the point by comparing the plot of *Sir Ysumbras* with those of *Sir Triamour, Octavian, Sir Eglamour of Artois, Sir Torrent of Portyngale, Emare, The King of Tars, Le Bone Florence of Rome,* and *The Erl of Toulous.* It clearly owes more to the story of Eustace. But somewhere in the evolution of the poem *Sir Ysumbras* as we now have it, a process of

drastic compression and skilful reorganization of the plot material
has taken place.

*Sir Ysumbras* has a narrative structure of almost symmetrical
precision. Exactly half-way through the poem Ysumbras plumbs
the depths of misfortune. He has lost his wife and three children;
he is battered, starving, and penniless. In stanza 33 he is about to
make his complaint to God:

> Ofte he was in wele and woo,
> Bot neuer half, as he was thoo:
> He sett hym on a stone.     (ll. 385–7)

Towards the close of the story, Ysumbras has recovered his for-
tunes, his wife, his sons, and has just won a great battle against
overwhelming odds. At the opening of stanza 65 he is about to ren-
der thanks to God:

> Ofte was he in wele and woo,
> But neuer so wele, als he was tho:
> One knees he hym sett.     (ll. 769–71)

These two stanzas relate respectively the moments of deepest
sorrow and greatest joy experienced by the hero in the poem. His
response to each is a heartfelt prayer to God. The correspondence
of the formulaic lines is unlikely to be fortuitous.

Similarly the appearance of the two heavenly messengers is sig-
nificant in terms of the narrative structure. At the beginning of the
poem God sends Ysumbras a 'steuen' via a bird:[23]

> He herde a fowle synge hym by
>     Hy vpone a tree,
> And said: 'Welcome, sir Ysumbras!
> Þou hafes forgetyn whate þou was,
>     For pride of golde and fee.
> The kyng of heuen gretis the soo:
> In ȝouthe or elde þou sall dry woo;
>     Chese, whethir es leuer to thee!'     (ll. 41–8)

At stanza 45, God sends an angel to Ysumbras at midnight where
he sits beside a stream, weeping with exhaustion and hunger:

---

[23] The group cDd however reads:

> He sawe an aungell in the skye
> Which toward hym dyd flye     (ll. 40–1)

> And, als he sett, abowte mydnyghte
> Þare come an angelle faire and bryghte
>   And broghte hym brede and wyne.
> 'Palmere', he saide, 'welcome þou bee!
> The kynge of heuen wele gretis the:
>   Forgyffen erre synnes thyn.
>
> Rest þe wele, sir Ysumbras:
> Forgeffen es alle thi tryspasse,
>   For sothe, withowttyn layne.
> Wele the gretis heuen kynge
> And gyffes the his blyssynge
>   And byddes the torne agayne.'          (ll. 535–46)

After the first message Ysumbras loses first his possessions and then his family, one by one; after the second, he gradually regains all he had lost. The poem settles itself into regular sections about these crucial points:

Opening (st. 1)
Prosperity/pride (sts. 2–3)
First message (st. 4, response 5)
Loss of everything (sts. 6–32)
Nadir—complaint (st. 33)
God directs to expiatory actions (sts. 34–41)
Second message—forgiveness (sts. 45, 46)
Regains everything (sts. 47–64)
Zenith—thanks (st. 65)
Conclusion (sts. 66, 67)

One development consequent on the introduction of the hero's penance as the dominant motive force in the plot is that the action of the poem, unified and simplified, focuses much more on Ysumbras himself. Dieter Mehl comments:

... the whole tale centres round the hero and every episode throws some light on his career. For this reason, the fate of Ysumbras' wife and children is practically passed over; they vanish completely from the scene and suddenly make their appearance again when the time of the hero's trials is over ...[24]

The disappearance of Ysumbras's wife and children will be seen to have its place in the penitential scheme of the poem. Other changes, such as the number of children and beasts, the Sultan and

[24] Mehl, *Romances*, pp. 131, 132.

his gold, Ysumbras's labour as a smith, his slaying of the Sultan, his reconciliation with God and reunion with his family, the rewards of his labours, have all been created in a singularly purposeful and consistent manner. A straightforward account of the poem will demonstrate this best.

At the opening of the poem there is a fairly conventional description of the hero in terms familiar to romance readers as those of approval. We are told that he is a knight (l. 7), brave (l. 8), incomparable (ll. 11, 12), physically powerful (ll. 13, 14), handsome (l. 15), tall (l. 16), universally beloved (l. 17) because he is 'so hende' (l. 18). Three lines characterizing Ysumbras's activities follow:

> Glewmen he luffede wele in haulle
> And gafe þam riche robis of palle,
> Bothe golde and also fee.       (ll. 19–21)

The author goes on to inform us that Ysumbras was courteous (l. 22), not niggardly (l. 23), was in fact the most generous man in the world (l. 24); that his wife was very beautiful (ll. 25–7) and his three children also as fair as could be (ll. 28–30). These could be taken as instances of what a good man Ysumbras was before he was corrupted by the sin of pride, providing a contrast with the lines that follow describing Ysumbras's sin; before and after. Dieter Mehl perceptively remarks:

All these perfections of body and mind, which add up to a conventional portrait of an ideal knight, are, however, deceptive, because they have made him proud and forgetful of God's grace ... the poet consciously stressed this contrast in order to interest his audience in the hero and at the same time to criticize traditional ideals of knighthood.[25]

However, the lines can also be seen to show why Ysumbras was proud, and what form his pride took. The author has adopted exactly the same strategy for pointing this out as we have already seen in *Guy of Warwick*: that is, to subvert or undermine what appears at first sight to be a character portrayed in an approving style. Both Guy and Ysumbras are presented initially as if they were ideal figures—though each has flaws which cause uneasiness to the careful reader—but their status is then dramatically undercut by a sudden revelation of their sinfulness.

[25] Mehl, *Romances*, p. 133.

Ysumbras's flaws are perhaps less obvious at first glance than Guy's; but nevertheless, they are there. Of particular interest are the lines about minstrels, which have been cited as examples of 'praise of minstrelsy' as a common feature of romances. Recent commentators have been less happy with the assumption of L. A. Hibbard that *Sir Ysumbras* was composed by a 'humble minstrel author',[26] and have suggested more clerical origins for that elusive figure.[27] It is certainly worth noting that giving money to minstrels was not an activity smiled upon by churchmen. Particularly apposite here are the words of John Bromyard describing how:

*Histriones* perform before the mighty who, like lapdogs and prostitutes, get rich food and presents when they ask for them, while the poor go empty away. At the tables of kings and other great lords, he tells elsewhere how those guests who seek their favour bestow upon their minstrels (*menestralius*) gifts of robes in their honour. 'For largess! For largess!' is the insatiable cry of the *histrio*. Assuredly, to give to such persons, adds the preacher, 'is not largess, but vice'.[28]

This is almost certainly the implication of Ysumbras's gifts of clothes and money to 'Glewmen'; for only a few lines later the bird describes his sin as 'pride of golde and fee' (l. 45).

The penance which befalls Ysumbras subsequently 'trifft Isumbras in der Eigenschaft, durch die er gesündigt hat'.[29] Details of the sufferings he undergoes consistently recur as deprivations of clothes, food, and money. One of the first pointedly significant things to happen is that Ysumbras's wife and children flee *naked* from the fire. He then shares his own clothes with them. (This detail is unique to *Sir Ysumbras*.) A further reference to the fact that Ysumbras ought to have been giving alms to the poor instead of robes to minstrels may be found later in the poem, when he himself is able to benefit from his wife's alms-giving—the proper application of wealth. When he is invited by the queen to talk with her, what he says is described as 'his laye' (l. 600). He tells it 'so nobilly' (l. 601) that she rewards him with clothes and food and accommodation for life (ll. 604–9). We cannot help comparing

---

[26] Laura A. Hibbard, *Medieval Romance in England* (New York, 1960), p. 4.

[27] Mehl, *Romances*, pp. 134, 135.

[28] G. R. Owst, *Literature and Pulpit in Medieval England* (Oxford, 1961), pp. 10, 11. See John Bromyard, *Summa praedicantium* (Venice, 1586), Eleemosyna, iii. 7 (p. 229).

[29] Günther Blaicher, 'Zur Interpretation der Mittelenglischen Romanze *Sir Ysumbras*', *Germanische Romanische Monatschrift*, NS, 21 (1971), 136.

Ysumbras's treatment at his wife's hands with his own treatment of the minstrels on whom he formerly wasted his revenue.

The squandering of his money on minstrels is, however, only a part of that 'pride of golde and fee' of which the bird speaks. It stems from the same foolish belief in his self-sufficiency which leads Roberd of Cisyle to claim that no god is more powerful than he; and the terms in which this is expressed in the poem are reminiscent of the reproaches uttered by Guy of Warwick against himself for neglecting God:

> In his hert a pride was broghte:
> Of goddis werkes gafe he righte noghte
> His mercy for to neuen.  (ll. 31–3)

Sir Ysumbras is so engrossed in the good life, spending freely and being generous and well loved, that he forgets to praise God. There is a hint that Ysumbras's open-handedness is the cause of his great popularity; at any rate, when his wealth has vanished he shows a remarkable lack of faith in his friends:

> Owre frendis of vs will son be irke  (l. 166)

These same friends weep copiously at parting with Ysumbras, but here the MS variations make the reading somewhat ambiguous.[30]

Ysumbras himself is aware of what his sin has been. His immediate response to the message of the bird is to promise ' "Werldes welthe I will forsake/ To goddes mercy I will me take" ' (ll. 52–3). The subsequent events reflect a penance tailor-made for the sin. After the loss of his worldly wealth and the division of his clothes between his family, Ysumbras determines to lead them ' "þare god was qwike and dede" ', because ' "Who so hym sekes with herte fre,/ He sendis þam lyues fode" ' (ll. 128, 131–2). Much is made of the fact that they must beg for their food:

> With þam þay bare full littill gude
> To helpe þam to þaire lyues fode,

[30] In Schleich's edition the lines read:

> Alle þay, þat his frendis ware,
> They wepid faste and syghede sare:
> Payre sange was 'waylawaye'.  (ll. 136–8)

Most manuscripts agree in substance with this; L however offers a reading which suggests that 'ware' means 'used to be' rather than 'still were':

> They þat wer here frendes byfore
> They wepte . . .

> Nowþer golde ne fee,
> Bot in þe lande to begge þaire mete,
> Were þat þay myghte any gete
> For saynte Charite.
>
> . . . . . .
>
> Þay, þat was wonte to wele and wyn,
> The pouerte, þat þay were in,
> Grete dole it was to see.　　　　(ll. 145–50, 154–6)

From this and the preceding speech of Ysumbras's it is clear that 'lyues fode' does not simply mean meat and bread, just as the journey is more than just getting from A to B. Günther Blaicher's illuminating article points this out:

In diesen Versen [Ysumbras's words to his family] wird gleichsam das Programm der Romanze gegeben: die Gottsuche. Dies bedeutet im Wortsinn die Pilgerschaft zum irdischen, im allegorischen Sinn die Wanderung der menschlichen Seele zum himmlischen Jerusalem . . . Die allegorische Bedeutung von 'lyues fode' kann nicht übersehen werden.[31]

Ysumbras loses his two eldest sons crossing a river (we will come back to the separation of the family later) and proceeds to the 'greckes see' with his wife and youngest child. Another slight but significant change in detail from the Eustace legend is that Ysumbras does not approach the ships he sees in order to travel to the Holy Land, but in order to beg for food. Ysumbras, whose money spent freely bought friendship, is offered gold in payment for his wife by the Sultan:

> He saide: 'Wil þou thi wyffe selle me,
> I will gyff the golde and fee
> More þan þou kane neuen.
> I will þe gyffe ane hundrethe pownde
> Of florence, þat bene rede and rownde,
> And riche robes seuen.'　　　　(ll. 280–5)

Note that Ysumbras is offered 'riche robes' as well as 'golde and fee'—the exact words used of his gifts to minstrels and of his pride. Ysumbras has already refused payment for service as a warrior in the Sultan's army, on the grounds that he is a pagan; he now refuses to 'selle awaye' his wife, but he is forced to accept the gold. He is helpless and his will counts for nothing. In sight of his wife and youngest child he is savagely beaten and cast ashore with

---

[31] Blaicher, 'Interpretation', p. 138.

the gold wrapped up in a red cloak. After the final interview with his wife, at which she gives him enough food to keep him and their little son alive for a week (ll. 349–51), he sits down to eat with his son, and then 'in his mantill of skarlet rede/ Ymange his golde he did his brede' (ll. 370–1). It is perhaps for this reason that he pursues the eagle which steals the cloak, and thus loses his last remaining son to a unicorn. Neither the gold nor the red cloak appear in the legend of St Eustace, in which the ship's captain keeps Theospita in lieu of the fare which Eustace cannot pay.

Günther Blaicher, arguing that the poem should be read as an allegory, suggests that the Sultan's offer of gold in exchange for his wife is a temptation which Ysumbras successfully resists, but that when he chases the eagle which has taken his mantle and gold, 'Sein Verhalten zeigt, daß er sich noch nicht ganz von seiner Liebe zu irdischen Gütern befreit hat'.[32] There can be no doubt that the spiritual overtones of the 'lyues fode' would have been clear to medieval readers of the poem, but it is perhaps demanding too much to suppose that the whole poem can be interpreted in an entirely consistent allegorical manner, and certainly wrong to suppose that its medieval readers would have sought out these other levels of meaning at the expense of the literal level of the story. The spiritual significance of all the motifs which are repeated throughout *Sir Ysumbras* lend depth and meaning to the literal story, but do not at any point supersede it, unless perhaps at the finale, where the mere account of events and the meanings apparent behind those events transcend either story-telling or allegorical interpretation because of their climactic emotional power.

Having lost his youngest son, Ysumbras is utterly broken in body and spirit. His prayer to God is a confession of his own helplessness, and places him entirely in God's mercy. Just after this Ysumbras comes across a smithy and begins seven years of labour as a smith. This detail is again unique to *Sir Ysumbras*: Eustace spends the fifteen years of his separation from his family working as a peasant in the fields; Guillaume d'Angleterre becomes a merchant, Wilhelm von Wenden a pilgrim, Cifar a hermit. The idea of making the hero work for his living is not new, but his becoming a smith gives it a certain force. Ysumbras forges for himself a suit of armour. He does this in order to be able to obey his wife's parting injunction to kill the Sultan, becoming by the work of his own

<hr>

[32] Blaicher, 'Interpretation', p. 136.

hands the Christian warrior. Meanwhile the Sultan has been lay-
ing waste to Christendom (ll. 421–3), and at length a great battle is
fixed between 'þe crystyn and þe haythen' to which Ysumbras
rides in his home-made armour, on the horse 'þat coles broghte'.
Before joining the battle, he prays to Jesus for victory, ' "Þe
heythen kyng þat I myght ȝelde/ The woo he hase me wroghte" '.
Ysumbras turns the tide of battle (like Guy of Warwick and Sir
Gowther) almost single-handed. The version in L comments:

> Hit was seene ther his stede yode;
> The knyghte slewe all that byfor hym stode,
> Bothe lesse and more.                    (ll. 448–50)

C however makes of these lines a miracle in Ysumbras's honour:

> The beryns he hitt appon the hode,
> And ȝitt es sene, whare his horse ȝode,
> And sall be euer mare.                    (ll. 460–2)[33]

Ysumbras succeeds in killing the Sultan, and is praised by the
Christian king, who offers to reward him with knighthood (l. 489).
But Ysumbras, like Guy of Warwick, conceals his identity, telling
the king that he is only 'a smethyman' and retiring to a nunnery
until his terrible wounds (ll. 477, 491) are healed. He then puts on
the garb of a poor palmer (ll. 505–6), like Guy of Warwick, and
sets off for the Holy Land:

> When þay were in Acris lenede,
> With wery bones vp he wenede
>   In to þat haythen stede.
> Seuen ȝere was he palmere þore
> With hungre, thriste and bones sore.   (ll. 517–21)

As elsewhere in the poem, great emphasis is placed on Ysumbras's
physical sufferings. During this time, however, the resignation
which Ysumbras has always shown (ll. 191–2, stanza 16b, etc.)
grows into the true penitent's active co-operation in humility with
the will of God:

> Goddes werkes for to wyrke

---

[33] It is interesting to note that in MS E, the account of Ysumbras's prowess in battle has
been expanded. He is not wounded until the end of the battle, nor is his horse killed as it is
in other MSS; the final battle against the Saracens too is expanded. This MS also contains
the longer version of *Sir Gowther*, in which the battle scenes have been given a similar
heroic amplification.

Of penaunce was he neuer irke
For his are-mysdede.            (ll. 526–8)[34]

At the end of seven years, he finally arrives at Jerusalem; weary,
poorly clad, hungry, and thirsty. The following stanza, relating
one of the great moments of crisis in the poem, is worth quoting in
full for the austere beauty, typical of the best style of short
romances, with which it relates Ysumbras's symbolic absolution:

> All þe cete he hase thurgh gone,
> Mete ne drynke ne gat he none
> Ne house to herbere in.
>
> Besyde þe burghe of Jerusalem
> He sett hym by a welle streme
> Sore wepande for pyne.
>
> And, als he satt, abowte mydnyghte
> Þare come an angelle faire and bryghte
> And broghte hym brede and wyne.
>
> 'Palmere', he saide, 'welcome þou bee!
> The kynge of heuen wele gretis the:
> Forgyffen erre synnes thyn.'            (ll. 529–40)

The significance of this moving scene has often been overlooked,
but Günther Blaicher is almost certainly correct in connecting the
angel's gift of bread and wine, and his message of forgiveness to
Ysumbras, with formal reconciliation after penance:

> könnten wir von einer Exkommunikationsstruktur sprechen. Es geht also
> in dieser Romanze nicht nur um den allmählichen Entzug weltlicher
> Güter und ihre anschließende Rückgewinnung, sondern auf der Ebene
> das allegorischen Sinnes um den Ausschluß Isumbras' aus der Gemein-
> schaft, sein Weg in die Anonymität des Büßerlebens und, nach erfolgter
> *reconciliatio* durch die Überreichung von Brot und Wein, den Symbolen
> der Kommunion, durch den Engel, die Wiederaufnahme in die
> Gemeinschaft der Christen.[35]

Public penance, it will be recalled, involved exclusion from the
community—spiritual if not actual exile—fasting, the wearing of

---

[34] MS L reads:

> Of that penaunce wolde he not yrke
> Forto fulfylle Goddes werke
> And lette all his evell dedes.

[35] Blaicher, 'Interpretation', p. 138.

137

rags, public humiliation, and so on. At the ceremony of reconcilia-
tion the penitent was permitted to partake of the Communion
bread and wine and this was the sign of his readmission into the
Christian community. The practice of excluding persons not in a
state of grace from the Sacrament is still followed.

However, Ysumbras's reintegration into the Christian com-
munity, like his exclusion from it, is gradual and delicately drawn.
The absolution conferred by the angel does not make any imme-
diate difference to the hard life Ysumbras is enduring:

> Bot wyste he neuer, whedir to gone:
> For he had no beter wone,
>    Bot aye to walke in payne.          (ll. 550–2)

However, from this point on, Ysumbras gradually regains his lost
family and fortunes; though it is by no means the end of suffering
for him. Having arrived at the castle where his wife is now living as
queen, Ysumbras queues up with the other poor folk in the hope of
receiving alms (again like Guy of Warwick). He is taken into her
household, where he lives for some time unrecognized. On first
entering the hall, Ysumbras is seated in a high place at the table:

> Mete and drynke was forthe broghte:
> Þe palmere satt and ete righte noghte,
>    Bot luked abowte the haulle,
> So mekill he sawe of gamen and glee
> And thoghte, what he was wonnt to be;
>    Terys he lete downe falle.          (ll. 583–8)

These lines are usually understood to mean that Ysumbras is wish-
ing for the old days, nostalgically recalling when he indulged in
'gamen and glee' himself. His tears in this case would be tears of
self-pity, brought on by the pathetic contrast between his former
wealth and ease and his present indigence. Another interpretation,
and one more consistent with the didactic aims of the poem, is that
he recalls his former life with regret because it led to the loss of
those he loved and all his sorrow. When at the end of the poem
Ysumbras's worldly fortunes have been retrieved he does not
return to his old ways of 'gamen and glee' but sets about establish-
ing Christianity in the neighbouring kingdoms.

During Ysumbras's sojourn at the court, he is mocked by the
pagan knights. They respect and admire his strength (ll. 616–18),
but make him take part in a tournament riding on 'a crokede

stede', after which he performs great feats of arms. This episode bears some resemblance to the stories of *Sir Gowther*, *Robert the Devil*, and *Roberd of Cisyle*, when those heroes are treated as fools at court. The queen laughs to see her best knights unhorsed by the poor palmer, and comments that he is 'worthi to fede!' (l. 636).

Ysumbras next recovers his lost gold. The lines describing the scene (ll. 637–42) are similar to those in which the bird first gave him God's message at the beginning of the poem. It is noticeable that it is just as he begins to 'playe' again 'Als it was are his kynde' (ll. 638–9) that Ysumbras recovers the mantle full of gold, which causes him to remember his lost wife and children, and 'To pyne torned his playe' (l. 654). Günther Blaicher, intent on a consistent allegorical interpretation of the poem, sees in these lines evidence of Ysumbras sliding into sinful ways again, for which his subsequent grief is a punishment. But Ysumbras's grief has a more important narrative than symbolic function; it arouses the suspicions of the knights and leads to the discovery of Ysumbras's identity by his wife.[36] The gold becomes the means of their reunion, and provides a symbolic link throughout the poem of the sin, the punishment, and the reward of Ysumbras. Although the stages of Ysumbras's reward are not yet complete, he takes a large step towards happiness here. Having abandoned the identity of 'sir Ysumbras' for that of 'þe poure palmere' after the battle against the Sultan, he now changes back to his true, knightly self, with the improvement also of being crowned king (ll. 706–8).

Now wealthier than ever, Ysumbras proclaims Christianity throughout his new kingdom, which causes the neighbouring pagan kingdoms to attack him, and his own retainers, also pagans, to desert him. Ysumbras must face battle alone; but in a touching scene his wife asks to be armed and to fight beside him, ' "ʒif god wolde vs grace sende,/ Þat we myghte togeder ende,/ I kepe þo lyffe no mare" ' (ll. 742–4). The scene is set for a glorious demise; readers familiar with the story of Eustace might well expect that Ysumbras and his wife will suffer glorious martyrdom fighting for the Christian faith, as 'Agayne thrytty thowsandez and maa/ Come þere nane, bot tay twaa' (ll. 748–9), but at the very last possible minute, 'Righte als þay solde hafe taken bee', the three lost sons appear, miraculously riding upon the beasts which stole them and

---

[36] In L, the rings which were exchanged at their final interview before separation serve as tokens of recognition for Ysumbras and his wife. No other MS contains this motif.

looking like angels. The miraculous aspects of this scene are enhanced in C and T by having an angel lead them to battle. Together they rout the pagans. This astonishing denouement is the more effective in *Sir Ysumbras* because nothing has been mentioned about the three children since they were abducted, while in most analogues the children are rescued by herdsmen, etc., and brought up apart.

After a prayer of thanks and scenes of joyful reunion the victorious warriors repair to a nearby castle for a miraculous victory feast. They go on to conquer all the neighbouring kingdoms for the three sons to rule over, live virtuous lives, and go to heaven when they die.

There are some episodes in the poem which remain puzzling and which have resisted attempts to fit them into an allegorical interpretation. Günther Blaicher observes that it is only in *Sir Ysumbras* that three beasts steal three children, riding on which the children reappear at the end of the story to the aid of their parents. He makes the fruitful suggestion that this 'sinnvolles Abweichen von dem in der Tradition Bereitgestellen' is an attempt on the part of the author to bring a precise allegorical significance to these episodes.[37] He tries hard to prove that the three beasts which abduct the three sons represent three cardinal sins, and that when the sons reappear riding on the beasts at the finale, this symbolizes the conquest of those sins by Ysumbras, or rather, by his reason, will, and body. This will not quite stand up in the final analysis, because although Blaicher is easily able to identify the Lion as Pride, and rather less easily the Unicorn as Wrath, he is compelled to admit that 'Der Leopard steht in der mittelenglischen Devotionsliteratur nicht für eine bestimmte Sünde', and has to make do with the unsatisfactory 'Instrument und Inkarnation des Bösen' for the leopard.[38]

There is therefore as yet no hard evidence that three children and three beasts are more suitable for sustaining the allegory than two, as in all other versions of the story (including, as we have seen, the version in the *Gesta Romanorum*, in which the *moralite* is supported perfectly well by two children). Blaicher supposes medieval people to have been very familiar with, and sensitive to, this kind of animal symbolism; and this is not unlikely, but in a romance like *Sir Ysumbras* the meaning of individual animals

---

[37] Blaicher, 'Interpretation', p. 140.     [38] Blaicher, 'Interpretation', p. 143.

probably operated in a much less specific way. The return of the
sons as conquering heroes, riding on the beasts which formerly
stole them away, is enriched by an association with the idea of the
sons as human faculties and the beasts as sins, which have been
tamed and controlled in the psyche of the reformed sinner, but it is
more importantly a reflection in a more general way of Ysumbras's
spiritual well-being. This point is enhanced in some manuscripts
by the appearance of the sons, who 'In angells wede were . . .
clede'.[39]

One episode which is difficult to assimilate into Blaicher's
allegory is the 'time-out' which Ysumbras takes from his penance
to kill the heathen king who abducted his wife. One of the chief
differences between *Sir Ysumbras* and the legend of St Eustace is
the replacement of the ship's captain by the pagan Sultan, and the
consequent opposition of Christians and Saracens throughout the
poem. The Sultan is the enemy of Christendom, as is made clear
by ll. 421–6. His having made Ysumbras's wife his queen is the
cause both of Ysumbras killing him in the earlier battle, and of the
later confrontation when Ysumbras and his wife must defend
themselves against 30,000 pagans. Initially Ysumbras pursues the
Sultan for reasons which have not much to do with expiating the
sin of pride. In the first place, Ysumbras's wife, Lady Macbeth-
like, instructs Ysumbras to follow her to the country of the Sultan:

> 'The haythen kyng sall we slaa.
> Þan sall ȝe be kyng of þat lande
> (And alle men bowe vnto ȝoure hande)
> And couer all ȝoure waa.'     (ll. 345–8)

This puts the killing of the Sultan in the context purely of ambi-
tion and worldly aspirations. Ysumbras obediently apprentices
himself as a smith, forges his own armour, and rides to battle
against the Sultan. Before joining the fray, he prays to Jesus:

> To sende hym grace in þat felde,
> 'Þe heythen kyng þat I myght ȝelde
> The woo, he hase me wroghte.'     (ll. 442–4)

which prayer is equally clearly motivated by a desire for revenge.
It is only after accomplishing this deed that Ysumbras puts on his

---

[39] l. 757; however this appears only in T, E, and A; in Schleich's edition the lines are
supplied from T.

'poure palmeres wede', travels to the Holy Land in fulfilment of his original intention, and begins to undergo the sufferings which we recognize as truly penitential. The seven years of hard labour which culminate in his slaying of the Sultan do not appear to constitute part of his penance, except insofar as they are seven years of grinding poverty, but are rather part of the rise and fall of Ysumbras's fortunes which accompany the penance.

Günther Blaicher has not much to say about the presence of the Saracens, and passes over the slaying of the Sultan without comment. However, in the light of comparison with other penitential romances we may be able to shed light on this morally dubious area. Firstly, we have already seen how in *Guy of Warwick*, more Christian versus Saracen incidents occur in the second, penitential part of the romance than in the first, and how Guy himself, quite apart from his personal penitential sufferings, is gradually subsumed by the role of instrument of divine justice in combating anti-Christian forces. The same will be observed in *Sir Gowther*, where the hero, whose penance consists of not speaking, eating only what he can snatch from dogs, and the attendant discomforts, is enabled by direct divine intervention to fight against the Saracen hordes which threaten to overwhelm the Christian army of his host, the emperor of Germany.

It is not inconceivable that in this use made of the hero to combat heathens there is a hint of the idea (mistakenly inferred from crusading indulgences) that defending Christianity against heathens atones for or cancels out sins. What is more certain is a general identification of the Saracens with the forces of evil. Emphasis is placed in all three poems on the fact that the Saracens threaten, or harm, or destroy, or despise Christianity. Their inspiration in doing so is, of course, the Devil himself, whom they worship in the form of their gods. The Devil's aim, through his servants the Saracens, is to destroy Holy Church, and the frustration of this aim, whether or not it is accompanied by personal ambition or the desire for revenge, is a good and laudable thing. It may also be implied that the sufferings incurred in the course of such conflicts, such as Ysumbras's serious head-wounds and Gowther's bruises, are in themselves expiatory. It is moreover possible to see in the prolonged combats which take place in all three poems a symbolic dimension, that of the forces of good struggling against the forces of evil in the penitent's soul. This is more likely in the case of *Sir Ysumbras* and *Sir Gowther*, where the narrative mode is predominantly non-literal. Looked at in this way, the combat with the Saracens and the slaughter of the Sultan in *Sir Ysumbras* take their place beside more conventional manifestations of penance, in constituting service to God and the fulfilment of His designs.

Although the scenes of Saracen slaughter can be fitted into the symbolic infrastructure of the poem, we must make the reservation that Ysumbras's unsaintly motives remain unpalatable to modern tastes and unreconciled with conventional moral theory. Susan Crane comments:

> Isumbras strives to rewin his wealth and family by supplementing a humble acceptance of God's punishment with plucky social initiative ... [His] dramatic ascent through the ranks of society to a final royal reward substantiates Isumbras' belief that Christian faith can support personal initiative and commitment to earthly goals. Like Guy of Warwick, Isumbras incorporates his faith successfully in a secular structure of values.[40]

Because of the theme of penitence and the consequent changes of emphasis in the action of the poem, *Sir Ysumbras* now has several details in common with *Sir Gowther* which related romances do not. Both heroes are informed from outside that they are in a state of sin of which they were previously unaware. Both the informers (the bird in *Sir Ysumbras*, the faithful old earl in *Sir Gowther*) act by the grace of God, who actively intervenes to save the sinner. Both heroes *choose* to do penance immediately, and what form the penance takes is imposed on them, Ysumbras's by God, Gowther's by the Pope. Both are conscious of doing penance and strive to act in accordance with God's will. Both fight battles for Christianity against pagans, in which both play a crucial role in the final victory and both receive injuries. When the commander of the Christian forces asks after each of the heroes, wishing to praise and reward them, both conceal their identities. Both suffer hunger, and both refuse food. Both spend time at a court incognito. Both heroes are told by miraculous means that they are forgiven; both are fed by miraculous means when in extremity. We shall now turn to *Sir Gowther* and see how that poem in its turn exploits the theme of the penitent sinner.

[40] Susan Crane, '*Guy of Warwick* and the Question of Exemplary Romance', *Genre*, 17 (1984), 364.

# 5

## *Sir Gowther*

*Sir Gowther* differs from *Guy of Warwick*, *Sir Ysumbras*, and *Roberd of Cisyle* in being relatively obscure. It survives in only two manuscripts; it does not appear in contemporary lists of romances and is not mentioned by name in other medieval literature. Yet the romance, though late, is a highly developed version of the story of the penitent sinner, and it shares many features with the other poems.

The poem is generally reckoned to have been composed towards the end of the fourteenth century in the North Midlands.[1] The two surviving manuscripts[2] date from the second half of the fifteenth century. The poem has been edited four times;[3] the two manuscripts exhibit numerous differences, but are of such equal merit that the editors have been exactly divided in preferring one or the other. Those who favour MS B do so on the grounds that it is 'courtlier' and more 'refined' than A,[4] while those who prefer A argue that it is less corrupt than B, and that its omissions are due to damage to the manuscript rather than to a process of deliberate editing which seems to have taken place somewhere along the line of B's transmission.

I agree with E. M. Bradstock that the structural pattern of the poem is crucial to an understanding of the author's methods of

[1] J. Burke Severs, *A Manual of Writing in Middle English, 1050–1500* (New Haven, 1967), I, *Romances*, 14, 141.

[2] National Library of Scotland, Advocates 19. 3. 1 (A); BL Royal 17. B. 43 (B). Breul is of the opinion that B is later than A, see his edition (details in n. 3, below), p. 1.

[3] E. V. Utterson, *Select Pieces of Early English Popular Poetry* (London, 1817) I. 157 (B with omissions uncorrected). Karl Breul, *Sir Gowther: Eine englische Romanze aus dem XV Jahrhundert* (Oppeln, 1886) (A corrected with B)—all quotations given will be from this edition. Thomas C. Rumble, *The Breton Lays in Middle English* (Detroit, 1965) (B, with omissions supplied from A). Maldwyn Mills, *Six Middle English Romances* (London, 1973) (A supplied with the opening fourteen lines of B).

[4] See Shirley L. Marchalonis, '*Sir Gowther*: The Process of a Romance', *Chaucer Review*, 6 (1971/2), 24, 27.

accomplishing his didactic aims, and that 'the various discrepancies between the A and B manuscripts indicate that it is in A that this pattern emerges more distinctly'.[5] Since this point is of some importance to my interpretation of the poem, further consideration is given to the two manuscripts and their respective merits in Appendix C.[6]

I shall begin the discussion of the poem's treatment of the theme of penitence in the traditional manner by comparing the poem with its main sources, in order to determine the nature and extent of the poet's originality in reshaping his material. I shall argue that the structural and thematic changes made to the story of *Sir Gowther* are radical, purposeful, and skilful, and that they serve the poet's didactic aims in an artistically successful way. The author's strategy in presenting his material is quite clear. It is not simply that the author 'has made prominent, and structurally important, those features of the legend which reinforce his homiletic message';[7] he adopts a quite different artistic procedure from that of his main source, the Old French poem *Robert le Diable*. This poem is presented very much from the hero's point of view, at least from the moment of his repentance; it is dramatic in mode and attempts a certain degree of psychological realism in its depiction of a repentant sinner. *Sir Gowther*, on the other hand, having drastically simplified the narrative, becomes spare, lean, cryptic, allusive, almost ballad-like in places. Given to making statements rather than descriptions, its events and characters symbolize rather than enact the moral truths it wishes to teach.

In her seminal article on *Sir Gowther*, E. M. Bradstock suggests that the poem operates on more than one level and should not be read in a simple, literal manner. She argues that 'the subject-matter, apprehended at a symbolic level, ceases to be improbable and effectively exemplifies the theme . . . the knightly exploits . . . give visual expression to the process of regeneration . . . the rise in

---

[5] Margaret Bradstock, 'The Penitential Pattern in *Sir Gowther*', in *Parergon*, 20 (1974), 3. However, in Ms Bradstock's subsequent article, '*Sir Gowther*: Secular Hagiography or Hagiographical Romance or Neither?', *AUMLA* 59 (1983), 26–47, she remarks that 'B is reputedly the superior text' (p. 33).

[6] In the ensuing discussions, where my interpretation rests on A's readings only, B's variations will be given in the footnotes. I hope it will appear that B's grasp of the major thematic concerns of the poem is weaker and more confused than A's.

[7] Bradstock, 'The Penitential Pattern in *Sir Gowther*', p. 3.

[Gowther's] heroic status is dependent upon the improved state of his soul and is thus a symbolic statement of it.'[8] The kind of reading proposed by this article is essential for a proper understanding of the poem and the richness and subtlety of the author's narrative techniques.

Stories exemplifying the moral that God's grace is sufficient to forgive even the gravest sins are abundant, particularly in the forms of sermon exempla and miracles of the Virgin and saints.[9] The variation of this popular theme which is found in *Sir Gowther* and its main source, *Robert le Diable*, has some interesting affinities with the presentation of the theme in *Gregorius*.[10] Gregorius, like Robert and Gowther, is a knight. Like them, he commits a sin for which he cannot really be held responsible; like theirs, his sin is a particularly serious one; and, like them, he is forgiven after a long and arduous penance, and rewarded with great happiness and worldly success.

The message—that even the most grievous sinner can be saved, provided that he is truly repentant—is perhaps even more explicit in *Robert le Diable*, where the Pope himself, and even the Pope's own confessor, dare not attempt to impose a penance on such a heinous sinner as Robert, and it has to be done finally by direct divine intervention. In the idea that the hero was not responsible for his sins, however, *Sir Gowther* is closer to *Gregorius* than to *Robert le Diable*. Gregorius marries his own mother while unaware of her identity and her relationship to himself. There is nothing intrinsically sinful about marrying a lady; Gregorius's intentions are innocent. It is his misfortune to commit incest unintentionally; but it is suggested to a certain extent that he is fated to do so, because he is the offspring of an incestuous union between brother and sister. While there is something intrinsically sinful about the murder, arson, rape, and so forth committed by Gowther and Robert in their unrepentant states, it is suggested that both heroes are compelled to do these things.

Robert is not quite in the same position as Gowther. The Devil has power over him and directs him to do evil, because his mother gave him, body and soul, to the Devil at his conception. In the

---

[8] Bradstock, 'The Penitential Pattern in *Sir Gowther*', p. 9.

[9] See e.g. J. C. Payen, *Le Motif du repentir dans la littérature française médiévale* (Geneva, 1967), pt. 4, chaps. 1 and 2.

[10] Hartmann von Aue, *Gregorius*, ed. and trans. S. Z. Buehne (New York, 1966).

earlier couplet version of the poem[11] it is stressed that because of this Robert is not really responsible for his actions; he observes that every time he wishes to do good, another thought assails him and compels him to do evil. *Sir Gowther*, on the other hand, is unique among versions of Robert the Devil stories in that he is actually the son of the Devil rather than owed to him as a debt. This puts Gowther in a position more similar to that of Gregorius, because the poet encourages the reader to consider Gowther's behaviour as 'working his father's will'; and obedience to one's father is not in itself a sin.

The fact that Gowther is the son of a devil introduces new aspects of the problem of sin and atonement to *Sir Gowther* and gives the poem a different moral direction and emphasis from those of its source. Robert is an ordinary human being who has been forced away from his natural moral condition by the consequences of his mother's rash vow. When he repents he returns to his true human nature, which was always inherent in him, but overwhelmed by the power of the Devil. Gowther on the other hand is presented as having inherited from his father a really evil nature, from which he must struggle to escape. When Gowther repents, he throws off a state of sin which is natural to him, and struggles to become a new man, which is clearly an altogether different portrayal of the idea of a sinful man.

*Sir Gowther*, *Robert le Diable*, and *Gregorius* have important themes in common, and each relates a special story sequence of a sinner's repentance and penance, which was very familiar to medieval readers in its various forms. Each of them however has its own ideas about the problem of atonement for grave sin and the role of God's grace in initiating repentance and forgiving sin. The attitudes discernible in *Sir Gowther* and the techniques by means of which its author presented his point of view in his story form the substance of the following discussion.

A considerable number of the existing studies of *Sir Gowther* concern themselves with the question of sources and analogues. In his

---

[11] *Robert le Diable*, ed. E. Loseth, *SATF* (Paris, 1903), ll. 373–8. This motif is lost in later versions of the poem, where the attention given to Robert's unruly childhood and to the notion that he cannot be taught shifts the moral focus from the case of the unintentional sinner to the hardened, habitual sinner.

edition of the poem Karl Breul devotes almost all of the long intro-
duction to an exhaustive survey of the various versions, the devel-
opment, and the geographical spread of the story of Robert the
Devil (a study which has proved invaluable to later scholars).
Breul states that the 'lai of Breyten' (l. 28) from which the author
of *Sir Gowther* claims to have drawn his story is unknown to us;
but it is clear that *Sir Gowther* is based on something similar to a
very early version of *Robert le Diable*: that is, not the stanzaic *Dit
de Robert le Diable*,[12] but the much longer *Robert le Diable* in
couplets, which its editor describes as a *roman*.[13] The *Dit* differs
from the *roman* in several important details, and it is clear that the
story offered in *Sir Gowther* corresponds more closely to the
latter.[14]

Florence Leftwich Ravenel and M. B. Ogle identify as *Tydorel*
the Breton lai referred to in lines 28 and 753 of *Sir Gowther* as its
source.[15] Miss Ravenel claims that 'the points of contact between
*Tydorel* and *Sir Gowther* are too numerous to be the result of
chance.'[16] In fact the only element which *Sir Gowther* shares with
*Tydorel* which is not in any other known version of *Robert le Diable*
is the episode in which the Devil seduces Gowther's mother,
begets Gowther, and foretells the nature of the unborn child.
Tydorel's father similarly seduces his mother (though not in dis-
guise) and makes a prophecy concerning Tydorel's future and
characteristics. In the context of the folk-tales from which both
*Tydorel* and *Robert le Diable* are derived, it is certainly significant
that the hero should actually be the son of the supernatural being,
instead of the supernatural being intervening in the lives of the
hero's parents to bring about his conception. However, this feature
is not unique to *Tydorel*, and in addition important dissimilarities
between the seduction scenes of the two poems lessen the likeli-
hood of *Tydorel* having served as a model.

[12] *Le Dit de Robert le Diable*, ed. Karl Breul in *Abhandlungen Herrn Professor Dr Adolf
Tobler* (Halle, 1895), pp. 464–509.

[13] Breul, *Sir Gowther*, Introduction, pp. 45–132.

[14] The *Dit* was the more popular form of the story and was translated into English at the
end of the 15th cent. and printed by Wynkyn de Worde. Thus when Shirley Marchalonis
compares the plot of *Gowther* to that of the English version of *Robert* her conclusions are not
accurate.

[15] Florence Leftwich Ravenel, '*Tydorel* and *Sir Gowther*', *PMLA* 20 (1905), 152–77;
M. B. Ogle, 'The Orchard Scene in *Tydorel* and *Sir Gowther*', *Romanic Review*, 13 (1922),
37–43.

[16] Ravenel, '*Tydorel* and *Sir Gowther*', p. 153.

Miss Ravenel calls attention to the fact that the heroes of both poems are made aware of their supernatural origins by a pointed remark made to them by an outsider. The young goldsmith in *Tydorel* observes that the man who does not sleep is not of mortal birth; the faithful old earl in *Sir Gowther* also notes the legacy of Gowther's father—his wickedness—and comments more directly that Gowther cannot have been sired by a Christian and must be kin to the Devil. Nothing like this survives in any extant version of *Robert le Diable*, but the Latin version of Étienne de Bourbon does contain a similar remark made by the hero's mother, which precipitates his violent reaction:

One day, when angered by him and moved to bitter complaint, his mother had told him that she would trouble herself no more about him, because he was the sort of person who did nothing except evil, he attacked her with drawn sword, saying that either he would kill her, or she would tell him why she had said that to him, and why he was so evil.[17]

Such a remark could easily have been a feature of the version, now lost to us, which was used as a source by the author of *Sir Gowther*, since it is associated with the legend of Robert the Devil at this early stage.

Other features mentioned by Miss Ravenel as points of contact between *Tydorel* and *Sir Gowther*—the long and childless marriage of the mortal parents, the 'marked characteristic' which distinguishes the hero from other children, his extraordinary strength, vigour, and beauty, the way in which he forces the truth from his mother with drawn sword—are all features of *Robert le Diable* as well, and therefore cannot be considered as conclusive evidence that *Sir Gowther* was derived from *Tydorel*. This duplication of features is not surprising since, as Miss Ravenel herself remarks, both *Tydorel* and *Robert le Diable* are derived ultimately from the '*Kinder-Wunsch*' motif of folklore.[18]

Breul's suggestion that the poet simply found his material in a real 'lai of Breyten' which is now lost cannot of course be dismissed; but if this was the case, then the grafting of the orchard seduction scene and its consequences onto *Robert le Diable* was still done by someone, even if not by the author of *Sir Gowther*, since

---

[17] Breul gives the whole text on p. 208 of his edition.
[18] Ravenel, '*Tydorel* and *Sir Gowther*', p. 155 and *passim*.

*Sir Gowther* is unquestionably based on *Robert le Diable*, and the orchard seduction scene unquestionably does not belong to that poem. I regard Breul's suggestion as unlikely, however. The poet refers to a Breton lai because he wants his audience to think his poem is one, and he has gone to some lengths to provide it with features characteristic of Breton lais; but really it is a very clever forgery.

Apart from the events concerning Gowther's conception, the main plot of *Sir Gowther* follows that of *Robert le Diable* quite closely, particularly if the author was using a version of the latter in which the hero does marry the princess in the end.[19] There are some striking correspondences of detail between the two poems. The most extensive alterations made by the author of *Sir Gowther* are omissions of various characters and events in order to simplify the narrative; thus the hermit to whom the Pope sends the penitent Robert, and who reappears at the climax of the story to tell him that his penance is ended, the angel who brings and removes Robert's white armour, the knights who wound Robert, and the wicked seneschal who pretends to have been the mysterious champion and tries to marry the princess do not appear in *Sir Gowther*. The effect of this trimming away of minor characters and episodes is to focus the story more clearly on the hero's predicament. The story of Robert is sprawling and circumstantial—an accumulation of small episodes, in keeping with its pretension to be the history of a real person. The exclusion of these distracting elements from *Sir Gowther* results in the plot becoming stark and monumental, with two great movements of sin and atonement at its core.

Besides this tendency to concentrate on the central issues of the tale, other small but significant changes have been made to the story. Both the duchesses, for example, must produce heirs for their husbands in order to save their marriages; but the Duchess of Normandy knowingly invokes the Devil when she has become impatient of God's help, and deliberately dedicates her child to him if he will enable her to conceive. The Duchess of Estryke, on the other hand, conforming less closely to the folk-tale underlying the story, prays to the Virgin for a child. Her prayer is desperate and

---

[19] In the *Dit*, Robert refuses the hand of the Emperor's daughter and departs to live with the hermit in the forest, where he remains until his death, serving God. His death is marked by miracles and he is held to be a saint. In later versions, however, Robert does marry the princess and inherits her father's kingdom, as in *Sir Gowther*.

reckless, however; instead of the proper humility of the supplicant who says, 'Not my will, but Thy will be done,' she begs for a child, 'on what maner scho no roȝth' (l. 66). The consequences of the two acts differ as well. The Duchess of Normandy has committed a deliberate sin, for which she later pays dearly. The seduction of the Duchess of Estryke is the result, it is hinted, of her carelessly worded prayer; this, and the fact that the Devil takes the form of her husband, greatly lessens her guilt and her responsibility for her son's nature. She does tell her husband a shocking lie about being visited by an angel, but nevertheless, the guilt of the mother, which is a strong element of *Robert le Diable*, is made less in *Sir Gowther*.

Gowther forges himself a sword at the age of 15, which becomes throughout the poem an important motif. There is nothing to correspond with this in *Robert le Diable*. When he decides to set off for Rome to seek penance and absolution from the Pope, Robert 'S'espee si rue mout loing' (l. 466). By contrast, the fact that Gowther takes his sword with him to Rome and wherever he goes is strongly emphasized.

Robert is seen to progress in his crimes from the childish breaking of stained-glass windows and putting ash in the mouths of yawning knights, to the more serious crimes of his maturity. With his band of outlaws he ravages the countryside, torturing pilgrims and merchants and raping women. Gowther's crimes are more selectively perpetrated, almost exclusively against the clergy. He 'men of holy kyrke dynggus down,/ Wher he myȝt hom mete' (ll. 170–1). He makes friars leap from cliff-tops, hangs parsons on hooks, slays priests, burns hermits, and so on. His antipathy towards the Church is marked:

> Masse ne matens wold he non here
> Nor no prechyng of no frere,
>   Þat dar I heyly hette;
> Erly and late, lowde and styll
> He wold wyrke is fadur wyll,
>   Wher he stod or sete.        (ll. 172–7)[20]

[20] In B, ll. 175–7 read:

> And tho that wold not werk his will
> Erly and late, lowde and still,
>   Ful sore he wold hem bete.

Gowther is performing a specific task at the orders of his father, the Devil; he injures the Church and the institution of marriage by his deeds. Robert's wickedness, on the other hand, finds expression in a more random way. Robert also tries to amend his behaviour, but fails to do so.[21]

When Robert receives an invitation to be knighted from his father he is overjoyed; he disbands his gang of robbers and promises to mend his ways. He seems to be sincere in his desire to be good, but is unable to carry it into practice. This failed attempt at reform has been omitted from *Sir Gowther*, and all that remains of the episode is the cryptic remark that the Duke of Estryke 'made hym knyȝt þat tyde' (l. 150). In later versions of *Robert le Diable* Robert is knighted, goes berserk at the tournament held in his honour, and then leaves for the forest and forms his outlaw gang, making this episode part of a sequence of Robert's increasing wickedness, and missing the point of it in this version: that Robert's attempt to reform his conduct and be good without repenting of or atoning for his past sin is bound to fail.

The scenes in which the heroes repent of their sins exhibit some differences, but the basic sequence is the same. Robert is on his way back to the Chateau d'Arques, where his parents live. He has just slaughtered a whole convent full of nuns and is covered in their blood. His appearance is so horrible that even the grooms won't take his horse. It is this which stimulates Robert to reflect that he has never been able to do any good, and he decides to elicit the truth about himself from his mother, whom he suspects of hiding something from him:

Pense que cele mesestanche
Li soit venue de naissanche,
E que coupes i ait sa mere,
Qui onques ne fu vers lui clere.   (ll. 383–6)

At first he is angry and violent; then, after he hears the truth from his mother, he is overcome with horror and shame and breaks down. He and his mother weep together, and then he decides to renounce the Devil and all his works:

'Diables en moi plus n'avra;
Ja tant pener ne s'en savra,

---

[21] *Robert le Diable*, ll. 253–64.

> Que il or mes en nule guisse
> Ne puist avoir en son servisse:
> D'un des siens li dessaisirai.'    (ll. 455–9)

Essentially this sequence is repeated in *Sir Gowther*; Gowther's repentance differs from Robert's in only two respects. Firstly, he is told of his diabolical origins by someone else, rather than realizing it from his own feelings and observations; and secondly, while Robert sees the Devil as a feudal overlord in whose service he has been and from whom he must now 'dessaisirer', Gowther's relationship with the Devil is necessarily more personal:

> To save hym fro is fadur þo fynde
> He preyd to god and Mare hynde
> Þat most is of poste.    (ll. 241–3)[22]

He will go to Rome to 'lerne anodur lare' (l. 237). More emphasis is placed on Gowther's turning to God; in *Robert le Diable*, on Robert's turning away from the Devil. Gowther's paternity is not an element introduced at random; it is thoroughly worked out and enriches the theme of repentance as the tale unfolds. Gowther often refers to the Devil as 'my father' during the course of the poem.[23]

The faithful earl is also more than a narrative device for enlightening Gowther. Leaving aside the possibility that he might be derived from the young goldsmith in *Tydorel*, it is not so great a step from the reactions of the people to the blood-drenched Robert to the action of the earl in *Sir Gowther*. The response of the former communicates the same message to Robert as the earl gives more explicitly to Gowther: that he is inhuman and horrible. The courageous earl does not then disappear from the story. Gowther pauses before leaving for Rome to commit the country to his care, and when he returns after his penance is accomplished, he rewards the earl by marrying him to his mother and making him Duke of Estryke in his stead.

Once in Rome, the penances given to the two heroes differ slightly. Gowther, who is directed by the Pope himself, is told to be silent and to eat only what he can snatch from dogs, but he is

---

[22] These and the following three lines, i.e. the first half of stanza 21, are missing from B.

[23] After the scene of Gowther's conception, the Devil is referred to as his father in ll. 97–9, 176, 209, 212, 231, 241, 274–6, and 748. Of these lines, 176, 241, 276, and 748 are different in B.

not, like Robert, told to feign idiocy, provoke the populace, or obey any order he is given by someone who knows about his penance.[24]

A curious episode present in *Sir Gowther* but missing from *Robert le Diable* is Gowther's three-day sojourn in the wilderness when he is miraculously fed by a greyhound. Robert only has to return to Rome, while Gowther travels from Rome to Germany, and thus Robert's story has no place for such an episode. It does not appear to serve much purpose in terms of the plot, unless it is to mark the passage of time between Gowther's leaving Rome and finding his way to the emperor's castle; but it has thematic resonances which should not be overlooked. It shows that God is looking after Gowther; it recalls Elijah in the wilderness fed by ravens with bread and flesh;[25] it anticipates the way in which the princess later rewards Gowther by sending him bread and meat via two greyhounds. It is surely a sign of that reintegration of Gowther's personality which we expect to be a result of his repentance. On the fourth day, Gowther arises from the hillside where he has been lying, 'And lovyd god in his þoʒt' (l. 318).[26] It is impossible not to be reminded by this of that moment in *The Ancient Mariner* when the mariner 'beholdeth God's creatures of the great calm' and spontaneously blesses them from his heart. From that moment he is able to pray, and the burden of the dead albatross falls from his neck into the sea.

Gowther's greyhound also recalls the episode in *Sir Ysumbras* when, after seven years of wandering as a palmer in the Holy Land, Ysumbras is visited by an angel who gives him bread and wine and tells him that his sins have been forgiven. This sacramental meal marks the end of Ysumbras's penance proper, while the 'meyt' and 'whyte lofe' which Gowther receives come at the beginning of his penance. Yet there are clear parallels. Ysumbras, like Gowther, is in extremity. He has been wandering through the city of Jerusalem all day without finding food or drink. He sits down by a well, 'sore wepande for pyne'. After the appearance of the angel, Ysumbras kneels and gives thanks to God. In addition, though Ysumbras has received God's forgiveness this does not mark the end of his sufferings, and the next thing that happens to

---

[24] *Robert le Diable*, ll. 894–906. This makes a considerable difference to the way in which the hero's part in the war against the infidel relates to the expiation of his sins.

[25] I Kgs. 17: 6.  [26] B: 'And thankid god in thoght'.

him is that he finds his way to his wife's castle, where he is received as a beggar, given alms and food, and where his wife's retainers make fun of him.

It is not impossible that the author of *Sir Gowther* knew the romance of *Sir Ysumbras*, which was very famous and which probably originated, like *Sir Gowther*, in the Midlands.

To return to *Robert le Diable*; when the emperor is attacked by heathens, both Gowther and Robert pray to God. The import and results of these prayers are similar, but their positions in the moral context of the story are distinct. Robert prays to God to help the emperor and destroy the Turks (ll. 1725–44); he wants to go and fight, but he stays behind because of his penance. Subsequently an angel appears with a white horse and armour and *commands* Robert to fight for God's sake, giving proof that he is to be obeyed by relating the details of Robert's penance. Robert obeys the order gleefully. Gowther's desires are identical; he wants to be on the field of battle slicing into Saracens with his 'fauchon'. But his prayer is more specific:

> Syr Gwother went to a chambur smart
> And preyd to god in his hart,
>  On rode þat boȝtt hym dere,
> Schuld sende hym armur, schyld and speyr,
> And hors to helpe is lord in weyr,
>  Þat wyll susstand hym þere.        (ll. 403–8)

Horse and armour appear at once 'at his chambur dor', but unaccompanied. Gowther does not mention, as Robert does, the arrogance and pride of the enemy; he wants to fight 'to helpe is lord', out of gratitude for his kindness, not because he hates Turks. He receives the armour because he has prayed for it, and thus is able to fight; Robert fights because he has been ordered to, in a manner which indicates that the whole thing has been pre-ordained by God. Gowther is permitted to fight in order to expiate his sins; Robert is allowed to fight partly as a reward for the ten years of hard penance he has already done, and partly as an instrument of divine justice. Robert's armour is always white; Gowther's is black in the first battle, red in the second, and white in the third,[27]

---

[27] The battles in *Sir Gowther* take place on three successive days, so that his different coloured armour recalls the traditional three-day tournament at which the hero appears in disguises and wins, as in *Ipomedon* or *Richard Coer de Lion*. A good account of the colour symbolism can be found in Marchalonis, '*Sir Gowther*', pp. 20–3.

expressing symbolically that Gowther is being cleansed of his sins as the battles progress.

The relationship between the hero and the emperor's daughter is subtly different in *Sir Gowther*. The princess is carefully brought into the narrative; her growing love for Gowther is a quiet, private business, conducted away from the noise and bustle of the court. The emperor in *Robert le Diable* notes perceptively, when his daughter has tried to identify Robert as the knight who saved him in battle:

> Saves por coi boin ceur li porte
> Al fol? Por che que ne parolle,
> L'a ename ma fille fole,
> Car ele est ensement muele.
> Li vilain dist en sa quarele
> D'un proverbe qu'il nous retrait:
> Li samblant a son sanblant trait.    (ll. 2386–92)

The same is clearly true in *Sir Gowther*, but it is never stated. The relationship between Gowther and the princess is separate from the court, a private bond of sympathy brought about by their shared affliction and the princess's secret knowledge. In *Sir Gowther* she does not feel compelled to share this knowledge until the end of the poem, where it has the authority of a divine revelation. Her father never knows of her kindness to the fool, and is not put in the position, like his counterpart in *Robert le Diable*, of abusing his daughter for telling him the truth.

Robert is often an object of attention at court (see e.g. ll. 2785–92) because of his position as Fool; he escapes from this to his little garden, where he can be alone. No one seems to take much notice of Gowther after the novelty of his eating habits has worn off, except the princess, and their growing sympathy is delicately evoked. After the third battle, when the princess is unconscious after her fall, and Gowther is battle-sore and weary, the narrator states with characteristic understatement, 'Þen myssyd he þat meydon schene' (l. 648).

It is, however, the end of *Sir Gowther* which shows the most radical alterations to the story of *Robert le Diable*. The dénouement of the latter is rather like the final scene of *Cymbeline*: what with the princess and the false seneschal and the spearhead and the hermit and the Pope, it is all rather confused. In *Sir Gowther* matters are much simplified by making the miraculous cure of the princess the sign which announces Gowther's forgiveness. Instead of the exposure of the false seneschal and the substitution of Robert as the princess's bridegroom at the eleventh hour—though this undoubtedly generates more suspense—in *Sir Gowther* we have a metamorphosis of funeral to wedding. This is concerned as much with the theme of transformation as with completing the plot; again, the ending of *Sir Ysumbras* is analogous. It is comic in the sense of that cathartic obliteration of all troubling and unhappy elements in the work by a blatantly artificial Happy Ending. The shadows of death and misery are lifted from the characters, and each is rewarded according to his deserts. This is something characteristic of romance, essentially a comic form; it is this sense of transformation and emergence which we find in Shakespeare's comedies and romance plays, achieved in a directly similar way.

However, like the best romances and like Shakespeare's comic plays, *Sir Gowther* shows a keen awareness that the period of heightened happiness and the sense of goals achieved is not permanent. Life goes on, and while it has increased in blessings, it is also tinged with more sombre perceptions. Gowther, on his return to Estryke, is stricken with remorse when he recalls the crimes of his past:

> All yf þo pope had hym schryvyn
> And god is synnus clene forgyvon,
>   Yett was his hart full sare,
> Þat ever he schuld so yll wyrke,
> To bren þo nunnus in hor kyrke
>   And made hor plasse so bare.    (ll. 697–702)

Gowther attempts to compensate for this by founding an abbey and endowing it with priests and monks to pray for the souls of his victims. Later versions of *Robert le Diable* have an ending which is more similar to that of *Sir Gowther*, and it is likely that the version used by the latter's author ended with the hero marrying the princess and returning briefly to Normandy before becoming emperor, rather than retiring to the forest as a hermit. *Sir Gowther* seems to reconcile the Robert who returns to the world and whose sinful past is forgotten with the Robert who continues to repent and pray; perhaps the author knew both versions.

Thus a review of the differences between *Robert le Diable* and

*Sir Gowther* shows that a number of systematic and purposeful alterations have been made by the latter. The beginning and ending have been changed, two important motifs added, and all characters and incidents not relevant to the central concern of the hero's penitence have been removed from the story. The tale becomes less anecdotal, less novelistic in terms of relating the characters' reactions to particular pre-ordained or random events, and instead becomes the illustration of a theme—becomes, in fact, a highly stylized exemplum. The alterations to the beginning and end emphasize the hero's relationship with the Devil, his escape from it, and his new relationship with God. Gowther's being a knight is extended from being a mere circumstance of the story, to becoming a metaphor for the condition of his soul and his progress towards salvation. His sword is in its turn a symbol of Gowther's potential to do good or evil, the emblem of that prowess which is the medium both of Gowther's sin and of his salvation.

Yet *Sir Gowther* is more than an exemplum; it is also a highly crafted romance. As we have seen, the narrator says that he got the story from a 'lai of Breyten' (ll. 28, 753);[28] and it is noticeable that many features of its style and of its altered plot make it more like a Breton lai. It is of course not certain that the audience of late Middle English romances were aware of the kind of generic distinction which is now meant by the term 'Breton lai'. Certainly not all the poems which claim to be Breton lais bear any resemblance to the group of French poems we know by that name. But it is at least possible that the features which seem to us to be characteristic of this kind of poem were also so regarded in the thirteenth and fourteenth centuries, and that the presence of some of these features in *Sir Gowther* would have made a medieval reader believe the narrator when he claimed a Breton lai as his source. Such a medieval reader might well have been familiar with the fairy seduction beneath the tree as a feature of several lais; if he was, he might also have agreed that *Sir Gowther* was similar to most lais in being short, tightly structured, and in containing a love story; he might well have recognized in Gowther's sword a symbolic object to compare with Orfeo's harp or Le Freine's mantle.

These features are only superficial likenesses, for the core of the poem is much more religious and didactic than any Breton lai. Yet

---

[28] But note that 'Lai' is Breul's amendment. A reads 'law' in both these lines; B has 'Yn the bayes of Bretyn' in l. 28, and 'laye' in l. 753.

the sword as a symbolic object unites the structural and stylistic features with the deeper meaning of the poem, for Gowther is a knight, and the medium of his sin and his salvation is knighthood.

Gowther's sword epitomizes his potential to do good or evil. When he is wicked in his youth it is with this sword that he murders men of God; when he repents he takes it with him into exile, but does not use it (just as Orfeo takes his harp, but at first does not play it). When he is called to fight the Saracens, he wins back his salvation wielding it. The sword is mentioned ten times altogether in the poem. Gowther's father prophesies his son's formidable nature at the time of his conception—he will be 'full wylde' and will 'weppon wyȝtly weld' (ll. 76, 78).[29] Gowther accordingly forges himself a sword when he is 15 years old, which no one else can wield. It is 'A fachon boþe of styll and yron' (l. 142),[30] and with it Gowther terrorizes the country. By the time he has been knighted he has become invincible in arms; there was 'no knyȝt in all þat londe/ Þat dynt of hym durst byde' (ll. 152–3). Gowther slays his mother's soldiers 'with his fachon' (l. 166), and when he forces his mother to reveal the truth about his birth, 'He sette his fachon to hur hart' (l. 223).[31] When Gowther sets off on his quest for forgiveness it is stated that he leaves everything behind *except* the sword (unlike Robert the Devil, who throws his sword far away):

> His fauchon con he with hym take,
> He laft hit not for weyle ne wrake,
>    Hyt hong ei be his syde.        (ll. 259–61)

He shows the same insistence on keeping the sword even when the Pope himself has asked him to lay it down, a refusal which is all the more striking since he has just sworn 'At þi byddyng beyn to be' (l. 286):[32]

> 'Lye down þi fachon þen þe fro;
> Þou schallt be screvon or y goo,
>    And asoylyd or y blyn.'
> 'Nay, holy fadur,' seyd Gwother,

---

[29] Breul's version. A reads 'weppons', B 'weppen'.

[30] ll. 139–44 are missing from B. B tends to weaken the sword motif, as if unaware of its significance.

[31] B: 'He sette the poynt to her brest'.

[32] B: 'That what penaunce ye me yeve/ I shall do that if y may leve'.

'Þis bous me nedus with mee beyr;
My frendys ar full thyn.'          (ll. 289–94)[33]

Whether the Pope is amused by the grim humour or not, he proceeds to give Gowther's penance without commenting on the penitent's surprising lack of obedience.

The last three references to the sword occur during the battles, when Gowther is fighting the Saracens with it. Although he prays to God for 'armor schyld and speyr/ And hors to helpe is lord in weyr' (ll. 406–7),[34] he is usually described as fighting with a sword, for example, at line 475, 'He hewde insondur helme and schelde', or at line 430, where he 'mony a heyþon hed of smott'.[35] On the second day of battle, the emperor remarks 'His fochon is full styffe of stele:/ Loke, he warus his dyntus full wele/ And wastus of hom never won' (ll. 493–5). Gowther continues to devastate the besieging army with the sword:

All þat he with his fawchon hytte,
Þei fell to þo ground and rosse not yytte     (ll. 604–5)

With his fachon large and long
Syche dyntus on þem he dong
Hor lyfus my3tte þem lothe.          (ll. 619–21)[36]

In almost all these references the weapon is named as a 'fachon' or 'fauchon', denoting a particular kind of sword with a curved blade, commonly regarded as being of pagan origin.[37]

The accounts of the three battles are detailed, with more attention devoted to each successive encounter (even without A's extra stanzas). Their position in the story is important, the way in which they are described climactic; not only are the battles themselves an integral part of Gowther's atonement and spiritual regeneration, but they lead directly on to the resolution of the plot through the princess's fall from the tower. Again, *Sir Orfeo* suggests itself as analogous; Orfeo's successive encounters with the fairy hunt lead up in the same way to that sudden meeting with Heurodis which precipitates his decision to win her back, the real crisis of the story.

[33] At l. 293, B reads: 'This fauchon most y with me ber'.
[34] Breul has amended A's 'armus' to 'armur'.
[35] On the other hand, B's 'Many helmys there he hitt/ Upright myght thei not sitt' clearly describes combat with a spear or lance.
[36] These lines are from one of A's 'extra' stanzas, no. 52 in Breul's edition.
[37] *MED* fauchoun (OF): a large, broad sword with a curved blade.

The most important element of the Breton lai to be found in *Sir Gowther* is the account of his conception. Here all the circumstances—the lady in her orchard encounters a man 'Þat hur of luffe beso3th' (l. 69), who makes love to her 'Undurneyth a cheston tre' (l. 233)—recall those lais in which ladies are approached by fairy men who either win their love, seduce, rape, or abduct them. The association of such an event with the lady's sitting down under a tree, particularly an 'ympe-tre',[38] a grafted tree in an orchard, is particularly striking. *Sir Gowther* here imitates a Breton lai and departs from *Robert le Diable*; Gowther is the son of his mother's seducer, as Tydorel and Yonec are the sons of fairies. But Gowther's father is not a fairy; he is a devil. Nor is his behaviour similar to that of his fairy counterparts. He assumes the identity of the lady's husband in order to seduce her; something which we are told in the opening stanzas that the Devil often does in order to harm and mislead women, and something the fairy seducers never do.

In *Tydorel*, which as we have seen, resembles *Sir Gowther* so closely as to have been considered one of its sources, the hero's father approaches his mother in his own person in order to win her love. Far from disguising his fairy nature, he is at pains to point it out, entering his fairy kingdom under the lake to prove it. In such a liaison there would be no point in the fairy obtaining the lady's love by trickery; on the other hand, the Devil in *Sir Gowther* is unlikely to be successful by any other means. But why does the devil assume the likeness of the lady's husband, rather than that of a handsome stranger? Had he adopted the latter course, we might well agree with G. V. Smithers when he remarks that 'the peculiar point of this story would be that it was a salutary warning against the dangers of entering into such liaisons, or at any rate, of attending to stories about them'.[39] As it is, this does not really apply to *Sir Gowther*; the Duchess thinks she is with her husband, and therefore commits no (intentional) sin, while Gowther himself comes at last to a good end, as the whole story is designed to show.

Smithers also points out that in Breton lais, 'when a son is introduced into the story, his experience is normally treated as pendant

[38] *Sir Orfeo*, ed. A. J. Bliss (2nd edn., Oxford, 1966), Auchinleck MS, l. 70, 'Vnder a faire ympe-tre'.

[39] G. V. Smithers, 'Story Patterns in Some Breton Lays', *Medium Ævum*, 22 (1953), 77, 78.

to the main interest, which is the relationship between the parents and its vicissitudes.' This is the case with *Tydorel* and numerous other lais, but in *Sir Gowther* the son is the protagonist and the circumstances of his birth are important only in relation to him, and not in their own right. In spite of the comment in stanza 9:

> Þei servyd never of odyr þyng,
> But for to tempe wemen yyng;
> To deyle with hom was wothe.    (ll. 100–2)

it is clear that the point of the Devil's dealings with the Duchess of Estryke is the begetting of Gowther; the interest of the incident is in no way dependent on the relationship between the two of them, or even on the temptation of the duchess to be unfaithful.

The narrator is at pains to point out that the father of Sir Gowther is not a fairy, but a fiend, and a particular type of fiend. He is in fact an incubus, a fiend which specializes in seducing mortal women. Incubi, present at the very inception of Judaeo-Christian demonology, bear a resemblance which is not the result of either imitation or coincidence to the fairy lovers of Celtic myth, in that they do the same things, though not for the same reasons. The author of *Sir Gowther* was not the first to perceive this resemblance: the father of Yonec had to take the Host in order to prove to his lady that he was not a demon, while Desiré's fairy mistress reproved him for fearing that she had cast a spell over him, and for confessing their liaison to a priest as if it were a sin.

There is a peculiar point in *Sir Gowther* in placing an incubus, a demon which seduces women, in a literary context in which a fairy commonly does the same thing. This point depends to some extent on reversing the expected consequences of such a beginning. As G. V. Smithers points out, 'Tydorel does not go through the ecclesiastically conceived adventures of Gowther; he is in orthodox style reunited with his father (while for Gowther a reunion with his father was, to say the least of it, not desirable).'[40] If it was 'orthodox', as Smithers suggests, for the offspring of such a liaison to seek out or join the lost fairy partner, then making the Devil into Gowther's father gives added emphasis to the evasion of his fate achieved by the folk-tale hero whose parents have made a pact with the Devil, or with some supernatural being, in order to conceive a child.

[40] Smithers, 'Story Patterns', p. 78.

Breul traces the legend of Robert the Devil back to its foundation, and finds it to be a clerical redaction of two ancient folk-tale motifs, the *Kinder-Wunsch*, or wish-child, and the *Grindkopf*, or male Cinderella.[41] The essence of the first tale type is that a couple who have long been childless are desperate for an heir; the conception of the child is granted as a wish by some supernatural character, on condition that the child is to be handed over to him or her by a certain date. The rest of the tale is then concerned with the efforts of the child to escape its fate. The Devil is eminently suited to the role of supernatural wish-granter; he does not need to claim his part of the bargain in person, he simply waits for the child to die, and receives its soul, predestined to damnation.

In another form of this tale, the *Enfant voué au diable*, the child is promised to the Devil because it is unwanted, and is destined for hell because of this in spite of living an exemplary life. In *La vie du saint Sauveur l'ermite*,[42] the hero is saved by the intervention of the Virgin after undertaking a penance sufficiently arduous to compensate for his mother's rash vow. Many tales of this type were made into legends of the miracles of the Virgin, most notably that of Theophilus. Elements from all these versions can be found in the legend of Robert.

*Sir Gowther*, in addition to the folk-tale heritage of its main source, in which the hero is expected to try to escape his parent's inhuman creditor, bears the opposite expectation, from its analogy to Breton lais, that the hero, who by some marked characteristic shows his supernatural parentage, will at the end of the story be willingly united with the absent parent. Gowther does not fulfil this expectation; he recoils from his father when he has learned his identity, and sets out to earn the right to call himself the son of God.

The author of *Sir Gowther* has quite a lot to say about incubi and clearly means his readers to attend to it. The first thirty lines of the poem repay close attention:

> God, that art of myghtis most,
> Fader and sone and holy gost,
>    That bought man on rode so dere,
> Shilde us from the fowle fende,

---

[41] *Sir Gowther*, Introduction, pp. 115–17.
[42] P. Meyer, '*L'Enfant voué au diable*', *Romania*, 33 (1904), 163–78.

That is about mannys sowle to shende
   All tymes of the yere!
Sum tyme the fende hadde postee
For to dele with ladies free
   In liknesse of here fere,
So that he bigat Merlyng and mo
And wrought ladies so mikil wo,
   That ferly it is to here.

A selcowgh thyng that is to here,
Þat fendus niȝyt wemen nere
   And makyd hom with chyld,
Þo kynde of men wher þei hit tane,
For of hom selfe had þei nan,
   Be meydon Mare mylde.
Þerof seyus clerkus, y wotte how,
Þat schall not be rehersyd now,
   As Cryst fro schame me schyld:
Bot y schall tell yow of a warlocke greytt,
What sorow at his modur hart he seyt
   With his warcus wylde.

Iesu Cryst, þat barne blyþe,
Gyff hom ioy, þat lovus to lyþe,
   Of ferlys þat befell.
A lai of Breyten long y soȝght
And owt þerof a tale have broȝht,
   Þat lufly is to tell.      (ll. 1–30)

In the dedication of such a short poem no words are to be wasted; yet it is not until some thirty lines into the poem that the narrator gives the appetite-whetting 'I'm going to tell you a Breton lai full of marvels.' The opening, in which the poet invokes the protection of God against the power and cunning of the Devil (ll. 1–6) is conventional enough, but it is interesting that the first note is one of anxiety, and that what follows is set against a background of the great cosmic struggle between God and the Devil for the possession of men's souls.

In the following lines the poet draws our attention to one especially dangerous trap laid by devils for unwary souls: the seduction of women by demons in the shape of men. He makes four distinct observations on incubi: (1) the devil can assume the likeness of a lady's 'fere' in order to seduce her, and (2) in this way he begot Merlin; (3) incubi have to steal 'þo kynde of men',[43] because they are themselves incapable of generation; and (4) the writer knows, but will not repeat (because it is improper) what scholars have to say on the subject of incubi.

The lore of demons and angels had been steadily developing in complexity since before the birth of Christ, springing largely from the much-discussed verse of Genesis:[44]

and there were giants on the earth in those days and after that the sons of God came in unto the daughters of men and these bore their children, and these same children became mighty men which were of old, men of renown.

The Book of Enoch also tells of angels who disobeyed God, took mortal wives, and begot giants, letting loose evil on mankind.[45] In romances this early connection between giants and incubi is preserved; for example, the Roman Emperor in *Morte Arthure* has in his army 'Sexty geauntes . . . engenderide with fendes',[46] and in *Torrent of Portyngale* we find:

> There ys a gyant of gret Renowne,
> He dystrowythe bothe sete and towyn
> And all that euyr he may;
> And as the boke of Rome dothe tell,
> He was get of the dewell of hell,
> As his moder on slepe lay.[47]

Philo of Alexandria established the nature of 'angels' as spiritual, and their dwelling-place as the air between the moon and the earth.[48] Justin Martyr identified wicked demons with false pagan gods, and accused them of defiling women and begetting children called demons.[49] Isidore of Seville associated these incubi with Roman fauns and Gallic dusii,[50] while St Jerome made a substantial contribution to the standard concept of a devil as being half-goat, hairy, and horned, in his account of St Anthony's desert

---

[43] *OED* Kind (noun) 6. c. 'The semen' (Obs. rare).      [44] Gen. 6: 4.

[45] *The Apocrypha and Pseudepigrapha of the Old Testament*, ed. R. H. Charles (2 vols.; Oxford, 1913), 2. 191 ff., Book of Enoch, 6: 1, 2 ff.

[46] *Morte Arthure*, ed. V. Krishna (New York, 1976).

[47] *Torrent of Portyngale*, ed. E. Adam, EETS, ES, 51 (London, 1887; repr. 1973), ll. 921–6.

[48] Philo of Alexandria, *On Giants*, 2, 3, 13 in *Works*, trans. C. D. Yonge (London, 1854), 1. 331–2, 340–1; and *Questions and Answers on Genesis*, 1. 92 (4. 334).

[49] Justin Martyr, *Apology*, 1. 5, 2. 5, *The Ante-Nicene Fathers*, trans. A. Roberts and J. Donaldson (New York, 1980), 1. 164, 190.

[50] Isidore of Seville, *Etymologiarum libri XX*, 8. 11. 103, 104, *PL* 82. 73.

encounters in *The Life of Saint Paul the First Hermit*.[51] St Augustine accepted the existence of incubi, albeit reluctantly:

And since it is so very frequently reported, and many confirm both from their own experience and that of others, who cannot be doubted, to have heard that Silvans and Fauns, which are commonly called incubi, have often appeared to women, and the shameless things have tried to lie with them, and have accomplished it; and that certain demons, whom the Gauls name the Dusii, continually both attempt and carry out this filthy deed, is so earnestly declared by such people, that it would seem impudent to deny it.[52]

St Thomas Aquinas put the finishing touches to the theory of incubi, and expressed what was probably the most widely accepted view. He affirms that the demons took no pleasure in their carnal activities, but were motivated entirely by envy. While they were spirits and composed of air, they could assume living bodies, and do what living bodies could do:

Certainly it is seen that these [demons] are capable of generation, not through semen from the assumed body of a dead man, nor by virtue of their own natures, but through the semen of a man made use of for generation, in that one and the same demon acts as a succubus to a man, and transfers the semen received from him to a woman to whom it acts as an incubus ... Whence a man begotten in this way is not the son of the demon, but of the man whose semen it was.[53]

Aquinas goes on to state that, since demons are capable of observing an auspicious astrological season, and choosing just the right circumstances and temperaments of both parents, the offspring of such a conception would necessarily be greater and more illustrious than ordinary mortals. This belief is repeated in Ranulf Higden's *Polychronicon*:

*Genesis* Godes sones took men douȝteres, and gete geantis.

*Petrus 29* And hit myȝhte be þat Incubus, such feendes as lieþ by wommen in liknesse of men, made geantes be i-gete, in the which geantes gretnesse of herte answereþ and acordeþ to þe hugenesse of body.[54]

---

[51] Jerome, *Vita S. Pauli primi eremitae*, PL 23. 23, 24.

[52] Augustine of Hippo, *De civitate Dei*, 15. 23, PL 41. 468.

[53] Thomas Aquinas, *Quaestiones de potentia Dei*, 6, 'De miraculis', 8, *Opera omnia* (Antwerp, 1612), 8. 132. He repeats this in *Summa theologiae*, 1. 51. 3. 6 (Rome, 1962), p. 254, citing Augustine as his authority.

[54] Ranulph Higden, *Polychronicon*, trans. John of Trevisa, ed. Churchill Babington (2 vols.; London, 1865), 2. 230 ff.

It is significant that, of all the things he might have chosen to say about incubi, the author of *Sir Gowther* mentions that they have no 'kynde' of their own and must steal it from men. If, as St Thomas Aquinas affirmed, the offspring resulting from the seduction of women by incubi were human, then they were capable of being saved; indeed, they were even capable of great good, since the chief result of the Devil's sinister experiments in breeding a master-race is that such men must be outstanding in some respect. The essential humanity of Gowther is important when it comes to his chances of salvation and his potential to do great harm or great good.

There are other examples of demon offspring in romances who come to good ends; the hero of *Richard Coer de Lion* has a female demon for a mother, and while he is extraordinarily savage, his ferocity is directed against the enemies of God. Merlin is also the son of an incubus, and is clearly intended to be compared with Gowther. The author takes the trouble not only to mention that Merlin was begotten in the same way as his own hero, but also to point out that

> Þis chylde within hur was no nodur,
> Bot eyvon Marlyon halfe brodur,
> For won fynd gatte hom bothe.     (ll. 97–9)

This unusually specific reference to another poem has not so far been explored. It is likely that the poet is referring to the story of Merlin as it appears in *Arthour and Merlin* and as told by Robert de Boron.[55] The Devil in the former is made to state his intentions and give his reasons for them. Robert de Boron's *Merlin* and the English translations of this actually open with an account of the devils holding council in Hell. They want to create an Antichrist; one who will do as much harm to mankind as Christ did good:

> Ac þe develen of whom y said
> Seiȝe hou Ihesu of a maide
> Þurth his milce was ybore
> And bouȝt al þat was forlore,
> Þerto þai hadden gret ond

---

[55] *Arthour and Merlin*, ed. O. D. Macrae-Gibson, EETS, os, 268 (text) and 279 (introduction, notes, glossary) (London, 1973, 1979). Only the opening (*c*.500 lines) of Robert of Boron's poem remains, edited by W. A. Nitze in *Le Roman de l'Estoire dou Graal* (Paris, 1927), Appendix, pp. 126–30.

And sayd þat þai wolden fond
To ligge bi a maidenkin
And biȝeten a child her in
Swiche schuld acomber also fele
So þat oþer had brouȝt to wele.[56]

The Devil in *Arthour and Merlin* sets about this task by destroying the family of a young girl, so that she is defenceless. Her confessor, the hermit Blaise, aware of her danger, tells her to perform certain charms every night before she goes to sleep which effectively keep the Devil out of her room. One night she forgets to do this, and the Devil gets in and lies with her. When her child is born he is 'black' and 'rouȝh as a swyn'—so ugly that the midwife is appalled. Luckily Blaise arrives and, taking stock of the situation, baptises the baby at once. The Devil's power over it is by this means destroyed, and instead of becoming the dangerous and evil magician Antichrist, Merlin grows up to become good and helpful. He inherits his extraordinary powers from his father, but God turns him to good.

This story bears a relationship to *Sir Gowther*. It is clear from the Devil's prophecy at Gowther's conception that he expects him to be spectacularly harmful to mankind—as indeed he is, until he repents. When the narrator of the poem tells us that the devil who begot Gowther is the same one who begot Merlin, he may well mean us to understand that the Devil is making another attempt to create Antichrist—this time a little more successfully. Antichrist must act in opposition to the true Christ; he must destroy instead of establish those institutions which help men to order their lives so that they come closer to God—the Church and marriage—and he must bring souls to damnation instead of salvation. Gowther, as we have noted, has a particular antipathy to churchmen and women, and delights in spoiling marriages (ll. 196–8). When Gowther kneels before the Pope and reveals his name, the Pope replies that he was just about to come and make war upon Gowther, 'For þou hast holy Kyrke dystroyed' (l. 283). At the close of the poem, when Gowther is stricken with remorse for his former wickedness, he is anxious to have masses said for the souls of those whom he sent to their deaths unshriven (ll. 703–7).

In the story of Merlin which we have been discussing, the basis

[56] *Arthour and Merlin*, Auchinleck MS, ll. 665–74.

of the devils' plot is to create a sort of monstrous parody of the conception and birth of Christ; each element is to be mimicked and perverted in order to achieve a perfect polarity in design and intention. The classic concept of Antichrist[57] cannot take place in *Sir Gowther* because Gowther's mother is not a virgin, but the element of perversion and parody is undoubtedly represented by the shocking lie which the duchess tells her husband about her supernatural visitation:

> 'To ny3t we mon geyt a chyld,
> Þat schall owre londus weld.
>
> A nangell com fro hevon bryght,
> And told me so þis same nyght,
> Y hope was godus sond.'        (ll. 83–7)

This is the opposite of the truth, and as such comes very close to sounding like the Annunciation.[58] However understandable the duchess's motives may be, desperate as she is to save her marriage and terrified of the consequences if the truth gets out, this statement (especially to a reasonably devout audience) carries a double shock: it is not only a barefaced lie, but a blasphemous lie. Blasphemy and the opposite of the truth—not merely the truth in the sense of an accurate and honest representation of the facts, but also the Truth that is God—are the essential ingredients in the idea of Antichrist.

If it is the case that the author has deliberately modified his material in this way to introduce this idea of the Devil's motive in begetting Gowther, then he has introduced an idea which leads away from the human predicament of Gowther struggling to win redemption, and places the action of the poem in the context of the unending battle between Heaven and Hell. The reader's attention is focused on Gowther himself for most of the poem; yet, in addition to the presentation of his story in a way which demands the sympathetic imaginative involvement of the reader, one is also aware of this added dimension. Gowther, more so than Robert, is not just a particular individual, but a great Type, acting out a familiar and timeless role.

[57] See e.g. *The Homilies of Wulfstan*, ed. Dorothy Bethurum (Oxford, 1957), p. 288. The Pseudo-Wulfstan, *De temporibus antichristo*, says that as Christ is true God and true man, so antichrist must be true devil and true man.

[58] See Ogle, 'The Orchard Scene', for an interesting interpretation of the seduction scene and its association with biblical and apocryphal accounts of the Annunciation.

He begins, when 'Erly and late, lowde and styll/ He wold wyrke is fadur wyll' (ll. 175–6), to be a splendid destroyer of Holy Church, a possible Antichrist, the worst sinner in the world. He is then transformed, not into the perfect ascetic, like the desert saints who repented of their early misdeeds and like the original Robert the Devil, nor into the Good Sage, magician, and prophet, like Merlin, but into the type of the Good Knight. At the end of the tale, when Gowther has succeeded his father-in-law as Emperor of Almeyn, we find that he has become 'Of all cryston kny3ttus þo flowre' (l. 713), the dread of the Saracens, that whatever a man bids him do for God's love he is 'ey redy bown þer too', that he protects poor folk, maintains the rights of rich folk, and helps Holy Church with all his might (ll. 714–20). The coincidence of these last good deeds with the traditional vows of knighthood[59] is not by chance.

It is in this delicate balance between our interest in Gowther's personal predicament and our awareness of his symbolic status that the author's strategy in presenting his moral lesson is most successful. The Gowther we see to be the son of a devil and the most sinful man imaginable—perhaps even the Antichrist—is moved to escape the burden of his inherited sinful nature and attain grace; but he is also Everyman, who has inherited Original Sin, and seeks to escape from the burden of his naturally sinful flesh. In this respect the poet differs in his tactics from *Guy of Warwick* and *Sir Ysumbras*; one must be fairly scrupulous to detect the sins of which these two have been guilty, but Gowther's sins are as bad and as obvious as they can be. Gowther exemplifies all the more effectively the moral that even the most sinful can be saved, by God's grace and a full repentance.

It is possible to discern from the presentation in the poem of Gowther's sin, repentance, penitential exile, and rehabilitation into society, that the poet's views on the subject of penance are essentially humane, and his message one of hope. To begin with, the poet in the opening stanza of the poem invokes God's protection against the wiles of the Devil, who is 'about mannys sowle to shende/ All tymes of the yere' (ll. 5–6). Such a view is in accordance with the tradition of penitential literature represented by the *Vie du Pape Gregoire*, the *Vie des Pères*, and the story of Theophi-

---

[59] See e.g. John of Salisbury, *Policraticus, PL* 212. 743–4 and *The Vision of Piers Plowman*, B text, ed. A. V. C. Schmidt (London, 1978), 6. 11. 24–36.

lus the clerk. The Devil entraps human beings into sin; he is irresistibly cunning and strong, and is prepared to go to endless trouble to deceive and ensnare his victims. Fallen man is almost incapable of avoiding sin, because he is so far removed from the natural state of grace in which his perfect virtue endowed him with the clear understanding necessary to perceive the true Good, and the uncorrupted will to desire it above all else. Fallen man's perceptions are clouded and impaired; he may be repentant, he may earnestly desire to please God, but he will be unable to achieve this unaided against the great power of the Devil and the weakness of his own flesh. God, or the Virgin, or a saint, must actively intervene to rescue him.

On the other hand, God is infinitely careful of His creatures and by His grace even the most heinous sins can be wiped clean, provided that proper repentance is shown.[60] Thus the vigilance and cunning of the Devil and the incapacity of man to attain virtue without the aid of God's grace must necessarily be compensated for by an enormous Divine generosity. The opening of the poem illustrates the first two facts. The Devil, hoping to entrap unwary souls, may go to the trouble of becoming an incubus, stealing 'þo kynde of men', and seducing a woman. The weakness of mankind in the face of such diabolical machinations is amply demonstrated by what happens to the duchess.

The part played by God in Gowther's repentance is not directly stated in the poem. While Gowther is sinning, and during his repentance, the Devil is frequently mentioned in connection with him. For the first time at his repentance, and more often during his penance, God is introduced into the narrative in a way which shows that He is taking over the role of the Devil in guiding Gowther's actions and manipulating events. This is done very subtly. It is obviously God who sends the greyhound with bread and meat to feed Gowther on his long journey from Rome, and who sends horse and arms before the first battle with the Saracens in answer to his prayers; but this is not stated. These things simply happen:

> A greyhownde broʒt hym meyt untyll
> Or evon yche a dey.          (ll. 311–12)

---

[60] See Payen, *Le Motif du repentir*, pt. 4, p. 519: 'toute cette littérature tend a démontrer qu'il n'est pas défaute si grave qu'elle ne puisse être pardonée.'

> He had ne ner is preyr made,
> Bot hors and armur boþe he hade,
> Stode at his chambur dor.          (ll. 409–11)

The following day, however, 'God sende Syr Gwoþer þro is my3th/ A reyd hors and armur bry3th' (ll. 466–7). Gowther thinks on God, and on his penance, while the lords and ladies of the court are celebrating victory that evening (ll. 538–40). He 'lovvyd god in hart ful feyn' after rescuing the emperor and killing the sultan during the third battle. More explicitly than ever before, as the princess lies, seemingly dead,

> Syche grace god hur sentt,
> Þat scho raxeld hur and rase
> And spake wordus þat wyse was,
> To syr Gwother, varement.
>
> Ho seyd: 'my lord of heyvon gretys þe well
> And forgyffeus þe þi syn yche a dell.'          (ll. 657–62)

The Pope gives thanks to God and tells Gowther:

> ... 'now art þou goddus chyld:
> Þe þar not dowt þo warlocke wyld,
> Þer waryd mot he bee.'          (ll. 673–5)

The conclusion of the poem makes all plain. Gowther will do anything he is asked to for God's sake (ll. 715–16); after he has died he becomes a saint and God performs miracles for his sake (ll. 729–30). God has promised that 'Who so sechys hym with hart fre/ Of hor bale bote mey bee' (ll. 733–4). No one prays to Gowther in vain, 'For he is inspyryd with þo holy gost/ Þat was þo cursod kny3t' (ll. 737–8). Gowther makes the blind see, the dumb speak, the crooked straight, the mad sane, 'And mony odur meracullus yytte/ Þoro þo grace of god allmy3t' (ll. 743–4). Finally, 'Grace he had to make þat eynd/ Þat god was of hym feyn' (ll. 749–50).

Correspondingly, while God is absent from the text during the early part of his life, Gowther manifests nothing of what could be called 'character'. We are informed of his deeds, which are indeed too wicked for their perpetrator to be imaginatively realized as a flesh-and-blood fellow being. Unlike Robert the Devil, Gowther performs his horrible sins methodically and in silence. It is this sense of Gowther's alien-ness which leads the earl to the conclusion that he 'come never of cryston stryn' (l. 208). This is the first time we get a glimpse of Gowther responding to the world around him personally, rather than Gowther the agent of the Devil working his father's will. He is stung into anger; he threatens the earl, and he threatens his mother; he shows anxiety to learn the truth about himself. The scene in which his mother's confession brings about Gowther's conversion is masterfully handled. Gowther demands to know who his father was; he places his sword at his mother's heart:

> Ho onswarde hym þat tyde:
> 'My lord', scho seyd, 'þat dyed last'.
> 'Y hope', he seyd, 'þou lyus full fast'.
> Þo teyrus he lett don glyde.          (ll. 225–8)[61]

These tears come as a shock, placed where they are. They are the first sign of Gowther's humanity, the first sign of a softening of his heart. With acute psychological insight, they follow an outburst of violent anger. A's reading, in which Gowther's mother reveals the truth to him after seeing his tears, rather than as a consequence of his threats, seems to me to be superior to that of B; and indeed the whole scene is more delicate and moving in A. In stanza 20, Gowther's mother tells him the true story of his conception—the first time she has spoken of it since it happened, perhaps twenty years before. At this point A has 'Þen weppyd þei boþe full sare', while B has the more non-committal 'Tho sythed Sir Gowghter full sare'. So different is B's account that Gowther does not shed a tear throughout the whole experience. In addition, B lacks the first half of stanza 21; Gowther begs mercy of Jesus and sets off at once to see the earl. In A his prayer is extended:

> To save hym fro is fadur þo fynde
> He preyd to god, and Mare hynde,
>     Þat most is of poste,
> To bryng is sowle to þo blys
> Þat he boght to all his
>     Apon þo rodetre.          (ll. 241–6)

A's treatment of the scene shows far more vividly that Gowther's crisis of conscience is an emotional crisis, which deeply affects his feelings; it is overwhelming. It is reminiscent of the penitence

[61] B reads: She said: 'Sone, the duke that dyed last/ That is owt of this world past;/ He weddid me with pride.' This is immediately followed by her admission of the truth in stanza 20; Gowther does not accuse her of lying.

described by the contritionist theologians of the twelfth and thirteenth centuries, for whom repentance was not valid unless accompanied by bitter tears.

This introduction of Gowther's personal life—his thoughts, feelings, fears—into the poem coincides with the first sign that God has entered Gowther's life. In place of the cold brutality which characterized him while he was inspired by 'is fadur þo fynde', Gowther now displays passionate sorrow and fear. Throughout the rest of the poem, we see a great deal more of the inner Gowther—necessarily, since he cannot speak, but in any case his thoughts and motives are revealed to us as they have not been before. Gowther becomes more human as his penance progresses; he grows a soul. The reader is made aware through this way of presenting the story that the mortal sinner is a fractured, tortured creature who cannot function as a normal person, and that while he is atoning for his sins his penance is actively therapeutic and reintegrates his personality. This concept is familiar to us from the Celtic penitentials and their descendants:

Diversity of guilt occasions diversity of penalty; for even the physicians of bodies prepare their medicines in various sorts ... so therefore spiritual physicians ought also to heal with various sorts of treatment the wounds, fevers, transgressions, sorrows, sicknesses and infirmities of souls.[62]

It also provides a convincing example of the standard view that the only completeness of life is to be found in the soul's union with God; and certainly the closer Gowther moves towards God, the more he becomes affectionate, loyal, grateful, generous, and noble, and the less cold, unfeeling, animal-like, and savage, as he was when dominated by the Devil.

A moral tale like *Sir Gowther* necessarily touches upon the knotty problem of divine justice, so feelingly and lucidly explored in *Pearl*. There were, towards the close of the Middle Ages particularly, many advocates of the view that it was almost impossibly difficult even for the righteous man to gain salvation, and that God's mercy was by no means to be relied upon by sinners.[63] If not even the righteous can be confident of salvation, how then can

---

[62] From the Penitential of Columbanus in J. T. MacNeill and H. M. Gamer, eds., *Medieval Handbooks of Penance* (New York, 1938), p. 251.

[63] See G. R. Owst, *Preaching in Medieval England* (Cambridge, 1926), pp. 334 ff.

someone like Gowther, whose sins could not very well be worse, ever hope to compensate for his wickedness? To some commentators the penance which Gowther performs seems scarcely adequate to atone for twenty years of godless depravity. He has caused large numbers of people, most of whom were nuns, priests, monks, or friars, to die cruel and agonizing deaths, and generally done his best to 'dystrye Holy Kyrke'. For this he endures a comparatively short penance at the court of an emperor. He suffers a certain amount of indignity and discomfort, but nothing like the indignity and discomfort suffered by Roberd of Cisyle in identical circumstances. Robert the Devil manages to make his penance relatively physically comfortable, but he has to endure it for twelve years; Gowther's, telescoped but intensified, seems to occupy only a few months at most. Dieter Mehl objects to having to consider Gowther's battles against the Saracens as directly expiatory, as is clearly implied by the colour symbolism of Gowther's armour.[64]

These objections are based on a literal interpretation of the text, of course. There is undoubtedly a non-literal dimension to the penance undertaken by Gowther, and the fighting of the Saracens, apart from balancing Gowther's earlier and less laudable martial exploits, probably relates on a symbolic level Gowther's conquest of his own sin, as suggested by Margaret Bradstock.[65] It is also possible to understand that the justification of Gowther's sins lies not in the length of penance endured but in the intensity of grief and repentance felt by him, and the strong sense created in the poem of Gowther's emotions being engaged in the fight for his soul. The influence of contritionism, though distanced from the poem by two centuries of increasingly rigid sacramentalism, is palpable here. Gowther could perform expiatory acts for many years, deprive himself of home, status, comfort, food, abase himself before the lowest beggar, and give himself up to be burned, but if he were not sorry, it would profit him nothing.

A recent series of articles has considerably advanced our appreciation of how medieval theologians understood the concept of divine justice[66] and the problem of reconciling that justice by

[64] Dieter Mehl, *The Middle English Romances of the Thirteenth and Fourteenth Centuries* (London, 1968), pp. 126–7.

[65] Bradstock, 'The Penitential Pattern in *Sir Gowther*', p. 5.

[66] Alistair E. McGrath, 'Divine Justice and Divine Equity in the Controversy between Augustine and Julian of Eclanum', *Downside Review*, 102 (1984), 312–19; id., 'Rectitude:

which God punishes the impious with that justice by which He
justifies the ungodly. The distinction between the justice of men,
defined by Cicero as 'rendering each man his due deserts', and the
justice of God in his dealings with men, which relates not to the
merit or deserts of the individual but to God's faith to Himself,
was understood in the first centuries after Christ, but obscured
later on. St Augustine, countering the arguments of Julian of
Eclanum (that, since God's justice is analogous to human justice, it
is impossible to accept the doctrine of original sin which is
obviously unfair), adduces the parable of the Labourers in the
Vineyard (like the Pearl maiden) to show that the ungodly, like the
labourers, 'have no strict claim to justification in terms of their
inherent worth, but do have a claim on the basis of the divine
promises of mercy made to them in Christ. In effect, Augustine
refers justice to God, rather than to man, seeing it as grounded in
the divine nature itself rather than in some aspect of human nature
which God is bound to respect on the basis of some *quid pro quo*
morality.'[67]

Alistair McGrath tells us that 'most theologians of the twelfth
century returned to the Ciceronian definition of *iustitia*, appar-
ently unaware of Augustine's explicit criticism of this concept. It is
probable that this is due to the influence of Abailard on the Pari-
sian schools of this period.'[68] He goes on to give a brief exposition
of how the concept of justice appeared in the writings of Abelard,
Stephen Langton, Godfrey of Poitiers, William of Auxerre, Simon
of Hinton, John of La Rochelle, and Bonaventure, of how the con-
cept was modified and developed by the introduction of the Aris-
totelian concept of *iustitia* (*esse ad alterum*) in the work of Duns
Scotus, and how this led to a 'hiatus between *iustitia* and *misericor-
dia* ... it points to the difficulty of rationalising the divine dispen-
sation of salvation in terms of justice, rather than mercy.'[69]

This is a distinction and a difficulty which continued to be felt at
all levels of religious discourse during the later Middle Ages, from
the complex disputes of the great theologians to the strategies

The Moral Foundation of Anselm of Canterbury's Soteriology', *Downside Review*, 99
(1981), 204–13; id., '*Nova et mira diffinitio iustitiae*: Luther and Scholastic Doctrines of
Justification', *Archiv für Reformationsgeschichte*, 74 (1983), 37–60; A. D. Horgan, 'Justice in
*The Pearl*', *Review of English Studies*, NS, 32 (1981), 174.

[67] McGrath, 'Divine Justice and Divine Equity', p. 316.
[68] McGrath, '*Nova et mira diffinitio iustitiae*', p. 49.
[69] McGrath, '*Nova et mira diffinitio iustitiae*', p. 51.

adopted in the pulpit for swaying the hearts of venal congrega-
tions. In medieval sermon-books there are clearly 'two great con-
trasted types of emotional appeal ... the threat of terror and
reproof and ... gentle references to the love and mercy of the
Crucified. ... Among the preachers themselves there seems to be
no small difference of opinion on their respective merits.'[70] These
two opposing strategies correspond to a view of salvation in which
God's justice is not compatible with God's mercy, and one in
which God's justice and mercy are interdependent. On the one
hand, sinners must be emphatically assured of the justice of God
which will result in the endless torments of Hell for the obdurate,
and terrified into repentance; on the other hand, they must be
assured of God's mercy so that they do not despair, and encour-
aged to repent in the trust that they will not be rejected. Advocates
of the latter course, Owst comments, 'are but rare oases in the
dreary desert of English Pre-Reformation preaching. The note of
gloom and repression easily predominates.'[71] Furthermore, a
strong opinion prevailed that 'this "presumpcion and over-
hopynge in the mercy of God" is one, if not the, most potent and
deadly of current popular heresies.'[72] Bromyard calls it a decep-
tion of the Devil; Myrc adds to his passage on how St Paul is a
great example of the wicked man who repents and is saved a stern
warning, lest sinners rely so much on God's mercy that they neg-
lect to repent of their sins.[73]

The concept of divine justice as 'a "making right", a restoring of
the relationship between God and man to what it should be', is a
key to the moral action of *Sir Gowther* and the expression of this in
the narrative. Gowther repents; but even this first impulse of tear-
ful penitence is, I think, the result of divine intervention, the equi-
valent act by God of the Devil's seduction of Gowther's mother.
Gowther is saved, we are told, by the aid of generous amounts of
God's grace, which he has in no way merited.

The author of *Sir Gowther* is not afraid that his message will
lead to dangerous complacency on the part of his audience. The
history of Gowther's progress from conception to the grave is one

[70] Owst, *Preaching*, p. 334.
[71] G. R. Owst, *Literature and Pulpit in Medieval England* (Oxford, 1961), p. 22.
[72] Owst, *Preaching*, p. 335.
[73] John Myrc, *Festial*, ed. Theodore Erbe, EETS, ES, 96 (London, 1905), p. 55.

in which God's justice *requires* the restoration of the proper re-
lationship between man and God which has been violated by the
intervention of the Devil and the sin of man, no less than one in
which His mercy to the repentant sinner is always apparent.
Gowther's moment of repentance is sufficiently a 'conversion
bouleversante' to make him detest and want to change utterly his
past life, but it is during the course of his penance that he is
brought closer to God and learns to love Him as a Father. It is
more than just a tag when God or Christ are referred to as 'That
bought man on rode so dere' in lines 5, 245–6, and 405. The infer-
ence is that which Myrc thought so dangerous: 'Þer byn men and
woymen þat . . . woll noþer for loue of God, ne for drede of God
and þe paynes of hell leue hor synne; but sayn þat God wyll not
lese þat he haþe boght wyth hys hert-blod.'[74] In *Sir Gowther*,
even more than in the other penitential romances, this is not a
dangerous sentiment, but a note of strength and hope for a man-
kind beleaguered and beset by the wiles of the Devil.

[74] Myrc, *Festial*, p. 55.

# 6

## Roberd of Cisyle

*Roberd of Cisyle* was, to judge from the number of surviving manu-
scripts, as well known and loved as *Guy of Warwick* or *Sir Ysum-
bras*, and it shares with them a number of striking features of the
penitent sinner archetype. In particular, there are striking similari-
ties between Roberd's enforced penance and Gowther's. Yet this
poem, much more than the other three, stands at the borderline of
romance.[1] Dieter Mehl notes that 'there are hardly any of the
meaningless clichés we find so often in the shorter romances.'[2]
There are other features of romance style not exploited in *Roberd
of Cisyle*; but even more important, perhaps, is the fact that the
poem makes use of a narrative technique which is quite dissimilar
from that which distinguishes the other three romances. *Roberd of
Cisyle* is a tale well told in a straightforward manner; it lacks the
characteristic obliqueness of the other poems. Roberd's shortcom-
ings, sufferings, and spiritual regeneration are not externalized and
expressed through symbolic action, but are presented more dir-
ectly by description and in Roberd's dramatic monologue. Though

[1] The poem survives in ten manuscripts: Bodleian Library English Poetry A. 1
(Vernon), fos. 300a. 3–301a. 3, *c*.1390, 444 lines (V); Trinity College, Oxford D. 57, fos.
165a–167a, *c*.1375, 440 lines (T); Cambridge University Library Ff. 2. 38 (*olim* More 690),
fos. 254a–257b, *c*.1475–1500, 516 lines (F); Cambridge University Library Ii. 4. 9, fos. 87b–
93b, *c*.1450, 374 lines (I); Caius College, Cambridge 174, fos. 456–68, *c*.1475–1500, 470
lines (C); BL Harleian 525, fos. 35a–43b, *c*.1450–75, 472 lines (Ha); BL Harleian 1701 (*olim*
Harley Plutarch 1701), fos. 92–5, *c*.1425–50, 486 lines (H); BL Additional 22283 (Simeon),
fos. 90b. 3–91b. 2, *c*.1400, 454 lines (S); BL Additional 34801, fo. 2, fragment on one leaf,
early 15th cent., 46 lines; Trinity College, Dublin 432 B, fos. 60a–61b, fragment, *c*.1458–61,
72 lines.

It has been edited several times; all quotations here are from *Roberd of Cisyle*, ed. Richard
Nuck (Berlin, 1887), which is based on V as representing the best and least-corrupted ver-
sion of the poem. Most of the other MSS contain extra passages, which Nuck concludes are
later interpolations. These passages apart, the MSS are very similar to one another and can-
not be said to represent different versions of the poem. In most MSS, the poem is grouped
with legends or other devotional literature rather than with romances; see Appendix B.

[2] Dieter Mehl, *The Middle English Romances of the Thirteenth and Fourteenth Centuries*
(London, 1968), p. 125.

certain elements of the poem, such as the extended descriptions of the clothes given by the angel to the emperor Valemound's messengers, have symbolic overtones, for the most part the poem and its homiletic message are presented in a more simply didactic way, with the moral spelt out at the end. W. R. J. Barron, who does not hesitate to call the poem a romance, observes:

> The romance mode, by its projection of an ideal in defiance of reality, is inherently revolutionary and reformist, though comparatively oblique in its didactic means. The association, however diluted, gave the flexible conventions of the genre particular expressive value for didactic writers in an age when didacticism was the dominant mode. The result was romances like *Roberd of Cisyle* . . .[3]

But in fact it is the very directness of *Roberd of Cisyle* which sets it somewhat apart from the other three penitential romances.

The folk-tale on which it is based, the Proud King Humbled, is found in many forms all over Europe.[4] The story was performed as a drama in the Middle Ages and reappeared more recently in Longfellow's *Tales of a Wayside Inn*.[5] The European form is usually entitled *Der nackte König* or *König im Bade*. In these stories the proud king commits his offence against God and some time later is punished by having his clothes stolen and his place usurped by an angel look-alike while he is bathing. From this archetype, as L. H. Hornstein points out in her helpful article '*King Robert of Sicily*—Analogues and Origins',[6] the English version departs significantly in removing the scene of transformation from the bath or river. Typical of the numerous retellings of this form of the tale is the story of the emperor Jovinian in the *Gesta Romanorum*, which is often cited as a 'source' of *Roberd of Cisyle*.

---

[3] W. R. J. Barron, *English Medieval Romance* (London, 1987), p. 199.

[4] Stith Thompson, *Motif-Index of Folk Literature* (3 vols.; Copenhagen, 1955–8), L. 400, Pride brought low; L. 411, Proud King displaced by angel; D. 451. 1, Kings exchange forms; Q. 330, Overweening punished; Q. 331, Pride punished. See H. Varnagen, *Ein inisches Märchen auf seiner Wanderung durch die asiatischen und europäischen Litteraturen* (Berlin, 1882), genealogical table facing p. 122, and id., *Longfellow's* Tales of a Wayside Inn *und ihre Quellen* (Berlin, 1884), genealogical table facing p. 160, for lists of over fifty analogues.

[5] No actual play survives from the Middle Ages, but there are records of performances; see E. K. Chambers, *The Medieval Stage* (Oxford, 1903), 2. 151, 356, 378, and J. P. Collier, *History of English Dramatic Poetry* (2 vols.; London, 1831), 1. 113 and 2. 128 and 415. The story appears in Longfellow as 'The Sicilian Tale'.

[6] L. H. Hornstein, '*King Robert of Sicily*—Analogues and Origins', *PMLA* 73 (1964), 12–23.

What may be a reference to it appears in lines 435–7:

> Al þis is write wiþoute lyȝe,
> At Rome to ben in memorye,
> At seint Petres cherche, I knowe.[7]

However, it does not share any of the features which distinguish *Roberd of Cisyle* from other versions of the *König im Bade* form. The emperor is said to be rich, secure, and wise. One night in bed he wonders whether there is any other God but him and, next day, while he bathes in a pool, his clothes and place are taken by an angel. The naked and defenceless emperor then applies successively to a knight, an earl, and his own wife for recognition before asking himself what he has done to incur God's wrath and concluding that it was his foolish thought of some nights ago. He confesses to a hermit, who subsequently recognizes him, and returns to his court in the hermit's clothes to confront the angel. Before the assembled court the angel explains all that has happened and vanishes from sight.[8]

The exact source of *Roberd of Cisyle* is not known, but is clearly a version of this popular tale. A very close analogue is *Li Dis dou Magnificat* by Jean de Condé,[9] as a brief comparison will demonstrate:

| *ROBERD OF CISYLE* | *LI DIS DOU MAGNIFICAT* |
|---|---|
| 1. Opening | |
| The King of Sicily is young, noble, handsome; a strong and fearless warrior; his brothers are the Pope Urban and Valemound, the Emperor of Germany. | The King of Sicily is proud, arrogant, and fierce, but in spite of his *grant orguel* he has two great virtues: he is just, and charitable to the poor. His brothers are the Duke of Bavaria and the King of Aragon. |

---

[7] The *Gesta* was 'long thought to have been compiled from Roman records', as noted in W. H. French and C. B. Hale's *Middle English Metrical Romances* (2 vols.; New York, 1930), 2. 946. This anthology contains the most accessible edition of *Roberd of Cisyle*, also based on V.

[8] Gesta Romanorum, ed. S. J. H. Herttage, EETS, ES, 33 (London, 1879), pp. 75–87.

[9] *Dits et contes de Baudouin de Condé et de son fils Jean de Condé*, ed. A. Scheler (Brussels, 1866), 2. 355–70.

## 2. Sin

However, Roberd is proud. One day at Evensong he hears the verse 'deposuit potentes de sede et exaltavit humiles.' Learning the meaning of the words, Roberd denies that anyone is powerful enough to bring him low.

One evening at Vespers the king hears the same verse from the Magnificat, and finds the idea displeasing. After the service he orders his priests never to utter the verse again, claiming that he is so powerful that God cannot harm him.

## 3. Transformation

Roberd falls asleep in the church, and when Evensong is over, an angel in his likeness leaves with his retinue. Roberd wakes up alone in the dark and shouts loudly for his men, but no one answers. A sexton comes, accuses him of being a thief, and then, fearing him to be a madman, lets him out.

On the third day after, the king takes a bath in his chamber. An angel sent by God takes on his likeness and clothes and departs with the attendants. The bath-water grows cold and the king shouts for attention, but no one answers. A chamberlain arrives, calls him 'sire ribaus', and has him violently ejected.

## 4. Sufferings

Roberd rushes to the palace and demands to be let in. The porter reports to the angel-king, who instructs him to let Roberd in. A fight ensues, and Roberd is put in a puddle by the porter's men. In the palace everyone is astonished at the 'fool' who claims to be king. The angel orders his head shaven, that he be given the costume of a fool, and an ape for his 'fere', and that he must eat with the dogs. At first Roberd is too proud to do this, but hunger drives him to

The king is severely beaten and chased by the dogs. He wanders about for three days, asking for alms, but no one will give him anything. He marvels at the strange adversity of fortune and decides to go to his brother in Bavaria for help. The journey is hard and he suffers much from hunger, thirst, and cold. In Bavaria he tells his story to his brother but is not believed and is again thrown out of town. He sets off to his other brother in Aragon, but after another painful journey the same thing

debase himself in the end. He bemoans his humiliation. After three years the angel-king is invited by Valemound to visit him and the Pope in Rome. Roberd goes too in the hope that his two brothers will recognize him and avenge him; but they do not, believing the angel to be their brother.

happens. Everyone to whom he tells his tale treats him harshly; all comfort and hope is gone. He weeps piteously, and asks God what he has done to deserve such suffering. He decides to return to his own land, seven years after his *grant ahan*.

## 5. Repentance

Roberd gives way to his grief, and then considers his past sin. He compares himself with Nebuchadnezzar and asks God to have mercy on him.

In the course of his complaint to God, the king regrets his former *hauteur*; however he does not appear to realize that this was a sin for which he is being punished.

## 6. Forgiveness

At intervals the angel would ask Roberd 'What art thou?', to which he would answer that he was the king, and the court would laugh at him. On their return to Sicily, the angel asks him once again, and this time Roberd replies that he is a fool, and worse than a fool. At this the angel takes him into a chamber and dismisses all the courtiers. He tells Roberd that God has forgiven him, and he is now returning to the joys of heaven. In an instant Roberd is king once more as the angel vanishes.

The king lines up with other poor beggars outside his palace to receive alms. The angel sees him and instructs his *aumonnier* not to give him anything but to bring him in, so that the angel can give him alms with his own hands. The king is at the limit of his physical strength, and he breaks down in tears. In reply to the angel's 'Qui es tu?' he stammers that he is not sure. The angel takes him alone into a chamber and explains to him that the reason for his reversal of fortune was his pride, but he has been reprieved because of his former virtues.

## 7. Conclusion

For the remaining two years of his life Roberd is pious and devout. The angel warns him of his impending death, and he has his story written down and sent to his brothers after his death. (In MSS C, H, Ha, and F the Pope then preaches a sermon on Pride, using Roberd as an example.)

The king, restored to his former position, gives thanks to God, and ensures that he continues to be just, charitable, and devout for the rest of his life. The poem ends with a *moralite* on pride and faith by the narrator.

It can be seen that *Roberd of Cisyle* is very similar to the French poem. Roberd's transformation however does not follow the bath pattern (a modification of the story unique to the English poem[10]) and the king in the *Dis* does not repent in the same manner, spontaneously from a consciousness of having deserved his adversity. This is because the moral point in the *Dis* is not that one's sins are forgiven and penance lifted on true repentance and prayer to God for grace, but that God is relenting towards the sinner as a result of his earlier good deeds, even though the sinner is still in ignorance of his sin.

*Li Dis dou Magnificat* and *Roberd of Cisyle* are not directly related to one another, but may possibly be derived from an identical version of the legend, since they share important features not universally present in other forms. The most significant of these is the hearing of the verse of the Magnificat at Evensong being the occasion for the king's outburst of blasphemous pride, and the fact that the angel uses the words 'What art thou?' to the king, and exchanges places with him in private. The two poems agree in other details too, such as that both heroes are the King of Sicily, both have two powerful brothers to whom they appeal for help (the earl and the knight to whom Jovinian appeals may reflect this element of the story), both shout angrily when they find themselves deserted by their retinue, and both are beaten when their attendants appear.[11] The two poems are also of almost equal length: *Li Dis* has 470 lines; complete manuscript copies of *Roberd*

[10] Hornstein, '*King Robert of Sicily*', p. 14.

[11] See Hornstein, '*King Robert of Sicily*', pp. 15–17 for a useful account of all the similarities and differences between the two poems, and an argument for the superiority of the English version over the French.

vary from 374 to 516 lines, and Nuck's edition, which is based on V, has 444.

Different versions of the story contain varying amounts of comic business, with the displaced king getting knocked about and insulted by servants. Possibly the amusing spectacle of the outraged monarch dunked by disbelieving menials in a 'podel'— an episode related with eloquent economy in ll. 129–30—contributed to the evident popularity of the poem, but the comic aspects of the tale are not over-exploited in *Roberd*. The poet's treatment of his narrative is masterful, ranging from lively comedy to the dramatic and moving scenes of Roberd's repentance and forgiveness. The scene of Roberd's awakening in the church, for example, shows great sureness of touch and depth of feeling:

> Þe kyng wakede, þat lay in cherche,
> His men he pouȝte wo to werche,
> For he was laft þer alon,
> And derk niȝt him fel uppon.          (ll. 69–72)

This comes just before a long comic interlude, beginning with the cowardly sexton, and is preceded by two lines describing the angel in the hall at supper, and how 'alle men of him were glade'. The effect is starkly to foreshadow Roberd's coming loneliness and misery, at the same time conveying unmistakable symbolic overtones of the 'derk niȝt' which is his state of sin. It is a subtle moment—stern towards the king, yet with great poignancy.

The structure of the poem is symmetrical and strictly controlled, like that of *Sir Ysumbras*. It shows the organic unity of plot and theme necessary in so short a work, and each detail is carefully worked out. MS V is 444 lines long. The first part of the poem, up to line 220, deals with Roberd's sin and punishment, while from 221 onwards there is a new phase of action: the visit to Rome which precipitates Roberd's crisis of conscience, and causes him to repent and be restored. These two simple, sweeping movements, each containing individual scenes with their own climactic moments, dominate the narrative, and are in harmony with the underlying 'real' structure of the romance, in which Roberd discovers the answer to the angel's repeated formulaic question, 'What art thou?'[12]

---

[12] MS V, ll. 145, 389. In other MSS the angel repeats the question every day.

All the heroes of these penitential romances can be said to be to some extent in ignorance of their sin up to the moment of repentance. In Roberd's case this ignorance is the result of continuous, deliberate sin, and is dramatically demonstrated in his foolish boast at Evensong. More clearly than in any of the other romances (with the exception, perhaps, of *Sir Gowther*) Roberd is a man who has a mistaken idea of his own identity, of his role in the created world and in relation to its creator. The extent of his profound misconception is shown in his speech in the church:

> 'Al ȝour song is fals and fable!
> What man haþ such pouwer,
> Me to bringe lowe in daunger?
> I am flour of chivalrye,
> Min enemys I may distrye;
> Noman liveþ in no londe,
> Þat me may wiþ strengþ wiþstonde.
> Þen is þis a song of nouȝt!'          (ll. 50–7)

Roberd thinks of God as merely one more powerful man such as himself. He has a high opinion of his own power and reputation; but even more, he sees himself as part of a confederacy of potentates; even if someone could compare with Roberd himself in might, he could not possibly hope to compete with the power and splendour of one whose brothers are the Emperor of Germany and the Pope. Roberd's sense of himself has grown so overwhelming that he has no sense of his littleness in the face of Divine power; no sense of reverence for Godhead at all, in fact. By his own reasoning his claim is quite serious and rational; but in reality it is the worst kind of folly.

However, it is a kind of folly which was recognized and had been extensively defined in theological discussion, particularly by St Bernard of Clairvaux. Chapter 21 of his influential book *De gradibus humilitatis*[13] explores the twelfth step of Pride: habitual sin. A man has come a long way in the path of Pride before he reaches this hardened and unregenerate state. Bernard explains that when God does not punish a man's first essays into sin, he becomes bolder, is drawn into the depths of sin, and forgets

---

[13] St Bernard of Clairvaux, *De gradibus humilitatis*, PL 182. 941–71; see also the excellent introduction to *The Steps of Humility*, ed. and trans. G. Bosworth Burch (New York, 1963).

reason. He quotes Psalm 13, verse 1:

> The fool hath said in his heart: there is no God

and says that only the highest and the lowest fly to their goals without let or hindrance; in the former perfect love, in the latter consummate wickedness, casts out fear. Truth makes one secure, blindness the other; for on this twelfth step fear of God is lost, and contempt of God acquired.

This is clearly applicable to Roberd, but he is not simply *self-reliant* in his contempt for God. Roberd's is a peculiar blindness, for his pride is not centred just on himself, but is dependent also on the exalted positions of his brothers. When he finds that his authority is denied, his first words in confrontation with the angel are:

> '. . . þou shalt wite wel,
> Þat i am kyng and kyng wil be;
> Wiþ wronge þou hast mi dignite.
> Þe pope of Rome is mi broþer,
> And þe emperour min oþer;
> Þei wil me wreke, for soþe to telle,
> I wot, þei nylle nouȝt longe to dwelle.'    (ll. 146–52)

A man who believes he has been wrongly treated might call on God to witness the justice of his case and avenge his wrongs; but Roberd calls on his brothers. His experience on the journey to Rome is thus doubly shattering; for he is rejected and denied by precisely those brothers in whom he had mistakenly placed his utmost trust. Only God, Roberd finds, is utterly reliable. His brothers, just like everyone else, are fooled by the angel. Instead of knowing his true state and asking God for mercy on his weakness, Roberd says, I am great, and my brothers support my greatness. The distance between these two states of mind is the ground covered by Roberd—most convincingly—during the course of the poem. He does not set himself up alone against God, but relates himself in the wrong way to the wrong authority. The author of the poem puts that authority in perspective when he writes:

> Þe angel was broþer mad bi sort;
> Wel was þe pope and þe emperour
> Þat hadde a broþer of such honour!    (ll. 278–80)

This mistaken confidence in the temporal power and infallible wisdom of his brothers is the reason why the angel gives Roberd an ape as his companion:

> Þi counseyler schal ben an ape,
> And o cloþyng ȝou worþ yschape.
> I schal him cloþen as þi broþer,
> Of o cloþyng; hit is non oþer.     (ll. 157–60)

in the hope that 'Sum wit of him þou miȝt lere' (l. 162).

The ape is not merely an accessory of Roberd's Fool costume, however; it has a symbolic and allusive value of its own. H. W. Janson shows that by the later Middle Ages the ape was more frequently associated with fools and madmen for its antics than, as earlier, with the Devil and sin for its ugliness, its distorted image of humanity; but the earlier connotations were not quite lost.[14]

The connection of apes with madmen is particularly interesting. Apes provided an image of man reduced to the level of a beast, deprived of his reason. Since madness itself could be and often was regarded as 'monitory and purgative, at once a visible token of sin, a punishment for sin, and a means of expiation',[15] they retained their emblematic value as the sinner himself, the outward image of the inner being degraded by sin. In addition, apes were particularly associated with the very sin for which Roberd is made to suffer—overweening pride, especially in temporal power, and especially if it causes the sinner to deny the power of God. Two examples of this association are particularly appropriate in the context of *Roberd of Cisyle*. In a copy of Nicholas de Lyra's *Postilla to Daniel*[16] is a crude depiction of Nebuchadnezzar during his seven years' madness, walking on all fours, covered with long shaggy hair, with a crown on his head. Behind him are two stags; beneath his feet what look like two bear cubs. On his left sits a grinning ape, looking out of the picture at the reader, and pointing to Nebuchadnezzar with its right hand.

The second example comes again from St Bernard:

---

[14] Horst W. Janson, *Apes and Ape-lore in the Middle Ages and the Renaissance* (London, 1952), chaps. 1 and 2.

[15] Penelope R. Doob, *Nebuchadnezzar's Children: Conventions of Madness in Middle English Literature* (London, 1974), p. 6.

[16] Nicholas de Lyra, *Postilla to Daniel*, in University of Basle Library MS A. II. 5, fo. 86b.

*De consideratione*, addressed to Pope Eugene III, contains passages fore-shadowing the literature of folly of the later Middle Ages. Here too we find what may well be the earliest proverbial phrase associating the ape with folly: *Simia in tecto, rex fatuus in solio sedens*, apparently a reference to the fable of the vain king of the apes and the two travellers. The context of this passage is of particular interest; it occurs in a chapter *dealing with the question 'What art thou?'* in the course of which the Pope is warned not to be like 'the ape on the roof, the king with fools enthroned'.[17]

Roberd of course compares himself with Nebuchadnezzar when he repents, in a passage which begins with Roberd close to despair:

> 'Allas,' quaþ he, 'now am i lowe!'
> For he hoped bi eny þing
> His breþeren wolde ha mad him kyng;
> And whan his hope was al ago,
> He seide allas and wellawo.        (ll. 296–300)

For some time he indulges in a frenzy of grief, tearing his hair and wringing his hands, and lamenting aloud. Then 'he þouȝte on his trespas'; and then 'He þouȝte on Nabugodonosore' (ll. 308–9). This 'noble kyng' too was said to have no peer, and when his general 'Sire Olyferne' claimed that 'þer nas no God in londe/ But Nabugodonosor' the king was pleased. He was punished by spending fifteen years in the desert (but Roberd does not mention that he was afflicted by madness), eating grass and roots and clad in 'mos', but when he repented, crying 'merci wiþ delful chere' (l. 331), God restored him to his former eminence. Roberd recognizes himself in this (ll. 333–4).

Roberd's version of Nebuchadnezzar's fall comes partly from the apocryphal Book of Judith, and partly from the biblical Book of Daniel. He has selected elements of the story which make Nebuchadnezzar appear to conform to the pattern of humbled pride; his own pattern. In the Book of Judith, Holofernes says:

Who art thou, Achior, and the hirelings of Ephraim, that thou hast prophesied among us today, and hast said, that we should not make war with the race of Israel, because their God will defend them? And who is God but Nebuchadnezzar? He shall send forth his might, and shall destroy them from the face of the earth, and their God shall not deliver them.[18]

---

[17] Janson, *Apes and Ape-lore*, p. 200 (my italics).

[18] *The Apocrypha and Pseudepigrapha of the Old Testament*, ed. R. H. Charles (2 vols.; Oxford, 1913), 1. 253, Book of Judith, 6. 1–4.

It is in Daniel, however, that Nebuchadnezzar is punished with his seven seasons' sojourn in the wilderness. In the commentaries, even more explicitly than in the scriptural text, it is made clear that his fault is pride,[19] and this in turn led to numerous literary versions in which the fault was specified as emulation of God (not, as in Daniel, pride in his achievement of the greatness of Babylon[20]). Chaucer's monk includes Nebuchadnezzar in his tale, but describes him exactly as if he were Roberd himself:

> This kyng of kynges proud was and elaat;
> He wende that God, that sit in magestee,
> Ne myghte hym nat bireve of his estaat.[21]

In *Cleanness* Nebuchadnezzar is mentioned by Daniel to Belshazzar as an example of one whom God punished for his sins when he ceased to honour God:

> Þenne blynnes he not of blasfemy on to blame þe dryȝtyn,
> His myȝt mete to Goddes he made wyth his wordes:
> 'I am god of þe grounde, to gye as my lykes,
> As he þat hyȝe is in heuen his aungeles þat weldes.'[22]

The story as Daniel tells it resembles that of *Roberd of Cisyle*, because he omits the prophetic dream with which he warned the king in the biblical version, and makes the punishment follow immediately on the sin.

Gower, by contrast, exploits the pathetic aspects of the story, and dwells on the sad contrast between Nebuchadnezzar's former royal state and present miserable dejection. In the *Confessio amantis* the king not only lives like a beast, but is actually transformed into one.[23]

Roberd is brought closer to these stories of Nebuchadnezzar in that he is compelled far more than Jovinian or the king of *Li Dis dou Magnificat* to live like a beast. Not only is he provided with an ape for his brother and self-image, but he must also eat with the dogs (an element of the penance which links him with *Sir Gowther*

[19] e.g. Jerome, *Commentaria in Danielem*, PL 25. 514–15; Albertus Magnus, *Commentaria in librum Danielis*, in *Opera*, 18 (Paris, 1893), 512–16.

[20] Dan. 4: 27.

[21] *The Riverside Chaucer*, ed. L. D. Benson (Boston, 1987), p. 244 (Fragment VII, Group B2, ll. 2167–9).

[22] *Cleanness*, ed. I. Gollancz (repr. London, 1974), ll. 1661–4.

[23] John Gower, *Confessio amantis*, in *John Gower's English Works*, ed. G. C. Macaulay, EETS, ES, 81 (London, 1900), pp. 111–19 (1. 2785–3042, esp. 2970–5).

and *Robert le Diable*). Roberd is degraded by having to live like this at his own court; his sense of self-esteem is broken down by sheer physical necessity. At first he is too proud to compete with the hounds for food, but extreme hunger drives him to submit to this.

P. R. Doob makes an interesting point when she remarks that the words used of Nebuchadnezzar in the *Ecloga Theoduli*,[24] *inscius esse Deum nisi se*,

... should probably be read as indicating the *cause* of Nebuchadnezzar's transformation—his false pride; but it can also be read as describing his state in the wilderness—a madman, ignorant of God, cured only by the eventual knowledge that there *is* a god beyond himself. This fruitful ambiguity emphasizes that Nebuchadnezzar's punishment is symbolic of his sin: voluntary denial of God becomes involuntary inability to acknowledge him, and metaphorical folly becomes literal madness ... men must learn that they are only men, lest they become irrational beasts.[25]

It is perhaps significant that line 330 of *Roberd of Cisyle* comments of Nebuchadnezzar's long sufferings in the desert, 'Al com þat bi Godes gras!' This does not refer to God's restoration and forgiveness of Nebuchadnezzar, but to the afflictions which ultimately made him conscious of the truth and caused him to ask for forgiveness. Roberd's awareness of the similarity between his case and that of Nebuchadnezzar both makes him aware of his own state of sin and makes him want to beg for God's forgiveness, and also teaches him to hope that he might receive it. The culmination of this spiritual regeneration occurs when the Angel asks him once more 'What artow?':

> 'Sire, a fol, þat wot i wel,
> And more þan fol, ȝif hit may be;
> Keep i non oþer dignite.'  (ll. 390–2)

This is a confirmation of the humble and grateful acceptance of his punishment which Roberd has achieved. The key word in the author's presentation of Roberd's change of heart is 'fol'. The events of the narrative illustrate in a lively and vivid style the theme of the king's folly; first, his general, unknowing folly, then his particular outrageous folly, then the divinely inflicted punishment which makes him appear in the eyes of men (and ultimately

---

[24] *Ecloga Theoduli*, ed. Joannes Osternacher (Urfahr Linz, 1902), ll. 237–44.
[25] Doob, *Nebuchadnezzar's Children*, p. 77.

in his own eyes) the fool he has always been, and finally his own acceptance that this is so.

The long soliloquy in which Roberd comes to terms with what has happened to him is an extraordinary piece of writing. Dieter Mehl comments:

[Roberd] breaks out in a devoutly humble prayer which, with its almost liturgical form (cf. the refrain), reminds one of some of the Middle English penitential lyrics and seems to be the moral centre of the poem.[26]

The action comes to a halt, as for an operatic aria. After his meditation on the career of Nebuchadnezzar and his conclusion that he himself is 'in such a cas', Roberd first formulates the history of his ingratitude and pride. Like Guy of Warwick, he sees that he owed God special thanks and respect for the blessings of his high estate and worldly success; but like Guy, he has been corrupted by pride and has neglected God. Roberd compares himself with the fallen angels, who had, like himself, been deprived of their 'maystrye' 'in twynklyng of an eiȝe' (l. 343). For the first time, he concedes that this is just and right:

> '... for mi gylt,
> Now am I wel lowe ypylt.
> And þat is riȝt þat I so be:
> Lord, on þi fol þou have pite.'     (ll. 345–8)

The refrain 'Lord, on þi fol þou have pite' is repeated every four lines for the next twenty-four, to the end of Roberd's speech, so that it appears as seven verses, and is indeed strongly reminiscent both of the 'Lord, have mercy' refrains in the liturgy and of penitential lyrics.[27] In these verses Roberd successively admits his fault (' "I hadde an errour in myn herte ... Lord, I leved nouȝt on þe" ', ll. 349, 351, and ' "Holy writ I hadde in dispyt" ', l. 353), accepts that he is under God's authority and that his punishment is just (' "Lord, I am þi creature,/ Þis wo is riȝt þat I endure" ', ll. 357–8), promises to amend in future (' "Lord, I have igylt þe sore,/ Merci, lord, I nyl no more" ', ll. 361–2), and asks Mary to intercede on his behalf for mercy (ll. 365–7, 369–71).

---

[26] Mehl, *Romances*, p. 125.

[27] A number of these appear in MS V, with refrains. See Carleton Brown, ed., *Religious Lyrics of the Fourteenth Century* (2nd edn., Oxford, 1957), pp. 196–200 'Make Amands', and pp. 208–16 'The Bird with Four Feathers', which has a verse on 'Nabugodonosor' and whose refrain is 'Parce michi domine'.

His earlier rebellious fury, when he cried and tore his hair, is now transformed into perfect acceptance of God's will:

> He seide no more allas, allas,
> But þanked Crist of his gras;
> And þus he gan himself stille
> And þanked Crist mid goode wille.   (ll. 373–6)

The soliloquy with its crescendo of repeated lines forms a dramatic climax in the action, paradoxically, by stopping the action and giving in this space for penitential meditation a convincing portrayal of Roberd's *conversion bouleversante* and spiritual rebirth. His admission to the angel that he now knows he is a fool, and worse than a fool, is necessary to bring about the completion of the action and the restoration of Roberd to his former position. The poet is at pains to point out to his audience, through the angel, that not even the exalted position of the King of Sicily can compare with the joys of heaven. The angel's three-year regency has been for him an irksome interruption of that bliss of which Roberd and we can have no comprehension:

> 'More ioye me schal falle
> In hevene among mi feren alle,
> In an houre on a day
> Þan in erþe, i þe say,
> In an hundred þousend ȝer,
> Þei al þe world, fer and ner,
> Were min at mi likyng'        (ll. 407–13)

Roberd, like Sir Ysumbras and Sir Gowther, when his worldly fortunes have been restored, is a changed man. The knowledge he has been given grace to achieve, of his own littleness, of God's immense power and infinite concern for men, causes Roberd to love God, 'holicherche', and God's lore (ll. 421, 424). He attains a kind of special relationship with God, and, like a saint, is warned by the angel when he is about to die.

It is clear that the treatment of penance in this poem is rather different from that in the other three penitential romances. The afflictions imposed on Roberd cannot, strictly speaking, be considered as a penance until after he has repented. Though they should certainly be seen in part as expiatory, the real narrative function of the sufferings which Roberd undergoes is to break down his misplaced pride and bring him to the point at which he acknowledges both that he has been at fault and that the infliction of this 'wo' is just and right.

The extreme nature of the penalties, in part derived from a pre-existent archetype as expressed in the other poems, is also a measure of the hardness of Roberd's heart. His obduracy is extreme, and extreme measures must be taken to prepare his heart for the sorrow necessary to true penitence. Once this has been attained, and the new Roberd, humble and sorry for having offended God, has accepted his punishment whole-heartedly, then he actively embraces the afflictions with a purposeful resignation to God's will, and only now can they be described as a penance. They last a further five weeks (ll. 377–80) before the angel returns to Sicily and, having satisfied himself that Roberd has learned his lesson, exchanges places with him again.

The sequence of events in the other poems is to a certain extent repeated: the hero sins, God intervenes, the hero endures a period of poverty, hardship, and loss of his former identity and position in the world, the sin is eventually atoned for, and the hero's fortunes are restored in token of divine forgiveness. But it is also to a certain extent turned upside-down. The losses and deprivations suffered by the heroes of the other three poems are undertaken voluntarily as penance by the sinners with the intention of making amends for their sins; only in *Roberd of Cisyle* are they inflicted on the sinner before he is repentant and before he is even aware that he has sinned.

In addition, we should note that the perfect humility and proper relationship with God which is achieved as a result of the penitence of the other heroes is here presented as a desirable moral goal in isolation, and is not, as in the other poems, related specifically to the hero's role and identity as a knight. Roberd is not referred to as a knight in the poem, only as 'þe kyng' or 'þe fol'. We do not see much of him as a king in action. Though we are told that the angel is such a good king that during his reign there was no treachery, strife, or guile among his subjects (and, by implication, this was not the case during the reign of the doughty but imperfect Roberd), and that the post-penitence Roberd is a much more devout person than he was before, nothing specifically relates his private lesson in humility to his public role as a ruler. We only see Roberd as king at the beginning of the poem, when he utters the blasphemous boast which occasions his chastisement, and he certainly appears to be a very stubborn, autocratic, and violent sort of king. But his identity as a monarch is not enlarged upon. It is the private man whose salvation we are called on to witness; Roberd's royal position serves only as a causal factor in his grotesque pride, and does not provide a medium for demonstrating the improvement which penitence has made in the state of his soul.

In this *Roberd* differs from the other three penitential romances, where it is crucial both to the action and meaning of the work that the hero should be a knight, and should be seen to perform the tasks required of a knight, well but imperfectly. The hero's embodiment of the ideal of knighthood is flawed by his sin, and is improved by his achieving a restoration of his relationship with God, which is mirrored by his own restoration of fortune.

# 7

# Conclusion

The evidence of sermons, instruction manuals for parish priests, and penitential handbooks for the layman shows us that from the second half of the thirteenth century onwards, the sacrament of penance consisted, for every member of medieval English society, of enforced regular confession to the parish priest. This was one of several ways in which thirteenth-century church reforms, designed initially to provide improved pastoral care, exercised increasing control over people's daily lives. The rule which obliged every layman to confess his intimate misdeeds regularly and in minute detail to his parish priest was a considerable intrusion of the institutional church into a relationship which had hitherto been largely a private matter between God and the individual. There was resistance to the enforcement of this rule, but the Church was powerful and in the end it succeeded.

The orthodox penitential literature issued by the Church is clear and consistent on the subject of penance. Contrition is highly desirable in a penitent; but confession to your parish priest, and faithful performance of the penance he enjoins is essential for the forgiveness of sin. In the view of works such as *Pricke of Conscience* or *Handlyng Synne*, the penitent must cultivate regular, conscientious habits of meditation designed to make available every detail of his sins, and he must be careful not to forget anything when submitting himself for examination in the confessional.

The penitential romances we have discussed consistently depict an experience of penitence which is far removed from this in both form and feeling. The penances endured by the heroes of *Guy of Warwick*, *Sir Ysumbras*, *Sir Gowther*, and *Roberd of Cisyle* are remarkably similar. Each hero must give up his position of worldly eminence for a period of poverty, physical hardship, and insignificance in which he (usually) wanders the world in a penitential pilgrimage and spends some time at a court (sometimes his own court) incognito, suffering humiliations and receiving alms. Specific prohibitions relate in the cases of *Sir Gowther* and *Roberd of Cisyle* to the food the penitent must eat; all penitents must be poorly clad.

The penitence experienced by the heroes similarly exhibits certain features in common. A distinct psychological progression, characterized by initial ignorance of sin, followed by a sudden revelation (usually stimulated by a third party) leads to a consciousness of guilt, accompanied by deep sorrow and contrition, and a profound desire to amend. A complete change of life follows, either imposed (by divine intervention or by the Pope) or voluntarily undertaken, with a view to expiating past sins through the patient endurance of poverty and tribulation, and to achieving a closer spiritual knowledge of and relationship to God. Typically when the penance has been completed the penitent returns to his former eminence and prosperity, and embarks on a new life of piety and good works.

The lack of formal procedures and the emotional crisis leading to penance are not typical of the sacrament of penance or the preparation for it recommended by the Church and featured in the penitential poems, tracts, and manuals which frequently appear side by side in the same manuscripts as our four romances (see Appendix B). The romance penances reflect ideas and procedures from earlier centuries: the form of 'Solemn Penance' with its preservation of archaic features of the harsh public penance practised in the early Church, and in connection with this the feelings of extreme sorrow and disgust at sin and the single-minded determination to amend life recommended by St Bernard and other Contritionist theologians, who emphasized contrition as the active (and sometimes the only) component in the process by which sin was forgiven.

The romances depict penitence as overwhelming, as experienced once only, and as much more concerned with the individual's relationship to God than his recourse to the offices of the Church. There are occasional hints, as in *Guy of Warwick*, that the conventional means of expiation are inadequate to the spiritual needs of the penitent sinner, and disapproval of such late medieval practices as commutations and indulgences.

It is unlikely that these penitential romances (or any other religious romances) were composed by their authors or understood by their readers to constitute a fundamentally different kind of literature from other romances which do not deal with predominantly religious or didactic subject-matter. This view is supported by the appearance of the poems with other romances in medieval manuscripts, and in their figuring in the condemnations of romance by ecclesiastical writers along with more 'secular' products. Yet the harmonious co-existence of such romances in manuscripts with more conventional kinds of penitential literature suggests that the two types of composition were not seen as incompatible with each other, but instead answered different needs in their medieval readers.

The best analogues of the kind of religious experience treated in these poems are to be found in saints' lives; and indeed we often find that tales of saintly penance, such as *Mary Magdalen* or *Gregorius*, or of extreme asceticism and voluntary poverty, such as *St Alexis*, or of the patient endurance of appalling hardships, such as *St Eustace*, appear in the same manuscripts and enjoy the same popularity as our poems. Penitential romances, like other religious romances, have taken over material from these productions (notably from *St Alexis* and *St Eustace*), perhaps under pressure of competition from these popular forms. Saints' lives, however, are in the first instance presented in a straightforwardly didactic way, while the romances adopt more subtle and skilful strategies for making their stories morally educative; and ultimately, the values exemplified in the religious romances are related to secular ideals and achievements which are not compatible with the resignation of worldly interests and submission to God's will projected in hagiography.

Where the particular pattern of penitential experience found in these romances came from is not clear, and may never be so. We can only guess that these poems take up and reinforce a pre-existent popular archetype of the nobly born sinner who repents and, abandoning his wealth and power, wanders through the world in poverty and hardship until, cleansed of sin, he can return to his rightful position. To this basic story the penitential romances add the dimension of the hero's moral education: his initial ignorance of his sinful state, and his dramatic reaction to that knowledge when it is forced upon him.

The treatment of penitence in the four romances can be most fruitfully understood in relation to the nature of romance itself. It is not concerned with the forms and rituals, the compromises and commonplaces of real-life penance—though it is often conscious of them, as the romance readers must have been. Instead, it cuts through to the heart of the matter with a perception and a directness that is at once primitive and sophisticated. The poems explore the nature of remorse and rehabilitation, learning and growth, by focusing on the sinner's awareness of his guilt and his relationship with God. To achieve this they relate anachronistically severe penances which force the hero into years of isolation and suffering. He confronts his own sinful nature and rejects it, expressing his contrition through his physical sufferings and self-abasement, after which he can emerge purged and renewed to take his place in society once more.

# Appendix A.    Other Romances Containing Penitential Episodes: *Valentine and Orson, Melusine, Athelston, Sir Gawain and the Green Knight*

Numerous other romances contain episodes or sequences in which a character sins, confesses, does penance, and is absolved. Of these, the most relevant to the penitential romances are *Valentine and Orson, Melusine, Athelston*, and *Sir Gawain and the Green Knight*.

*Valentine and Orson* and *Melusine* are romances which came into the English language late in the fifteenth and early in the sixteenth centuries. The former, translated from the French poem of the same name by Henry Watson in 1502, is described by its editor as 'a sort of compendium of many of the most popular elements of chivalric fiction'.[1] One of these elements is the penance undertaken by Valentine towards the end of the poem, which shows the strong influence of *Robert le Diable, Guy of Warwick, Roberd of Cisyle*, and the *Life of St Alexis*. The sin committed by Valentine is of the accidental, Gregorius-type. He kills his own father in battle, not knowing who he is. On discovering what he has done he is overwhelmed with grief and shame and begs his brother Orson to cut off his head. Orson advises him:

Brother said Orson take comfort vnto you and kepe you from dyspayre, be thynke you well brother that god is puyssaunte ynought for to pardon a more greater thynge. retorne you towarde him & aske him pardon for youre synne and promise to do penaunce.[2]

Valentine departs for Rome to confess to the Pope, accompanied only by one squire. Like Robert the Devil (and Sir Gowther) he enters the great church where the Pope is saying Mass and afterwards requests the Pope on his knees to hear his confession. The Pope agrees and then sets his penance:

My chylde vnderstonde what thou must doo for to haue pardon of thy synne. Fyrst thou shalt chaunge thyne habyt, and go poorely clothed, and this seuen yere thou shalt li vnder the staires of thy palays with out speche, if god giue the life so

---

[1] *Valentine and Orson*, ed. Arthur Dickson, EETS, os, 204 (London, 1937; repr. 1971), p. x.

[2] *Valentine and Orson*, chap. 109.

longe, and thou shalt neyther eate nor drinke but of the relefe of the table, and yf thou do this penuance thy sinnes are pardoned the, and not eles. (chap. 111)

Valentine agrees to do this. He changes his appearance by cutting his hair and living on roots in the forest for a time, then returns to Constantinople incognito. In his palace he is beaten by his own servants, and would have been thrown out but for the charity of his wife and brother, who for his sake will turn away no poor man from their door. When he is given food he rejects it, and will eat only from the basket of scraps intended for the relief of the poor. He lives under the stairs on a bed of straw. Orson commands the best meat to be put into the scrap baskets (chap. 112), but because the food in the baskets is now too fine, Valentine begins to eat the scraps tossed to the dogs (chap. 113). Other efforts to alleviate his misery are fruitless:

Clerimond had made a quilte to be broughte vnto him, but he lay vpon the erthe, & so he did his penaunce among the dogges. (chap. 115)

Valentine, like the earlier versions of Robert the Devil and Guy of Warwick, does not return to the world but spends the rest of his life in penance (though he is allowed to take time out to foil a plot against his wife). Like Robert the Devil, Guy, and Roberd of Cisyle, he foreknows his own end; and this part is clearly influenced by *Roberd of Cisyle*. At the end of his seven years' penance, he falls sick; an angel appears to tell him that he will die in four days. Valentine signals for pen and paper and writes an account of all that has happened to him; he then confesses to a priest and dies. With the story of his penance is a token he had made with Clarimond before setting off for Rome: half a ring. At the moment of his death all the bells of the city ring of their own accord. He is buried in the great church of Constantinople:

And it was not longe after but that the body was canonysed and put in shrine. Soo God shewed wel that he was wel worthy to be called saynt, for the daye that he dyed all sycke men were healed of theyr maladyes that vysyted his tombe.

Clarimond becomes abbess of an abbey founded in Valentine's honour (chap. 117).

Valentine's repentance, confession to the Pope, and subsequent penance are clearly derived from the story of Robert the Devil; the token he exchanges with his wife, her giving alms to the poor for his sake, and the tenor of the ending come from *Guy of Warwick*; the angelic warning of his death and the writing down of his story from *Roberd of Cisyle*. The miracles after death and sainthood could be derived from any number of saints' lives, but do bear a strong resemblance to *Sir Gowther* which may be owing to the (now lost) version of *Robert le Diable* which inspired it.

The penances of Raymondin and Geoffrey Great-Tooth from

*Melusine*[3] are not so well handled or so clearly derived, but once again show the influence of Robert the Devil. Geoffrey, the son of Raymondin and the fairy Melusine, commits the spectacular and Robert-like crime of burning down the abbey of Mailleses with all the monks inside it. Afterwards he feels remorse, but his knights tell him that it is too late to repent (chap. 41). Eventually Geoffrey is persuaded by his father to repent, and vows to rebuild the abbey. Raymondin decides to go on pilgrimage to Rome to confess his own sins; however, far from setting out alone or even attended by only one squire, he 'made his apparayll and with hym mounted on horseback many lordes & knightes, and toke with hym grete fynuance & hauoir and so departed' (chap. 56). At Rome Raymondin confesses his sins to Pope Benedict 'as touching this that he was forsworne ayenst god and Melusyne hys wyf', but the author is less interested in the actual penance; the Pope 'gaf hym therfor such penaunce as it playsed hym'. Raymondin becomes a hermit at Montserrat and spends the rest of his life in poverty and prayer. Geoffrey decides to go to Rome and confess to the Pope as well (chap. 57). Geoffrey confesses his sins 'and the Pope charged hym to make thabbaye of Maylleses to be edyfyed agayn & therto ordeyne six score monkes, & many other penitences the pope charged hym doo, the which as now present I shall not shewe' (chap. 58).

Geoffrey's life is not fundamentally and permanently changed by the penances imposed on him. Some time passes before he gets around to rebuilding the abbey, and his life continues much as before. While visiting his father he observes that the buildings of Montserrat are small and poor and wonders how anyone can bear to live there (chap. 59).

The author of *Valentine and Orson* was inclined to emphasize the psychological and pathetic aspects of the penance itself and succeeds in generating sympathy for the hero, who though forced to live incognito in his own home, and not allowed to reveal his identity under any circumstances, is permitted to intervene in the lives of those who remain in the world. The author of *Melusine*, on the other hand, and particularly its translator, were much more interested in the bizarre character of Geoffrey, who is viewed with slightly horrified admiration for his almost inhuman appearance, strength, ferocity, and exploits, rather like the hero of *Richard Coer de Lion*.

The next example is less straightforward. *Athelston* is a short tail-rhymed romance in which the author's attention is directed almost exclusively towards the intertwining themes of sworn brotherhood, loyalty and treachery to that bond, and the championing and triumphant vindication of the innocent in a trial by ordeal. Although not particularly early in composition its close relation to certain *chansons de geste* treating these

---

[3] *Melusine*, ed. A. K. Donald, EETS, ES, 68 (London, 1895; repr. 1973).

themes lends it the archaic 'epic' tone of *Havelok the Dane*.[4] Its char-
acters feel and behave in extremes, and it contains scenes of violence
which seem the more shocking because of the blunt language in which
they are presented.

The poem shows how an act of treachery such as Wymound's is a
powerfully disruptive force, both personally and socially. Once the har-
mony of the sworn brothers' right-dealings with each other has been
broken by Wymound's false accusation, the king is so disturbed by this as
to be wrenched awry from his true nature. In his unreasoning anger he
kicks his pregnant wife in the stomach, killing his unborn child, and the
author makes it clear that the unnatural state of affairs is a direct con-
sequence of the first unnatural act of treachery:

> Þus may a traytour baret rayse,
> And make manye men ful euele at ayse,
> Hymselff nouȝt afftyr it lowȝ.          (ll. 294–6)

For this brutal deed, and for the closely related angry threats towards
Alryke and disobedience to his ecclesiastical authority, Athelston repents
and is absolved by the archbishop:

> Vpon hys knees he knelyd adoun,
> And prayde þe bysschop of benysoun;
> And he gaff hym þat tyde.
> Wiþ holy watyr and orysoun
> He assoylyd þe kyng þat weryd þe coroun,
> And Yngelond long and wyde.          (ll. 549–54)

This is however an act of submission to Alryke's authority on the part of
the king; by it he stops the consequences of Wymound's treason from
spreading beyond himself and his family to the whole realm; for Alryke
had been on the point of putting England under an interdict if Athelston
continued to be unreasonable. Alryke is clearly prepared to use the grant-
ing or withholding of absolution as a weapon in his power struggles;
when Athelston refuses to reveal the name of the traitor, Alryke
responds:

> Þenne swoor þe bysschop: 'So moot I the,
> Now I haue power and dignyte
> For to asoyle the as clene
> As þou were houen off þe fount-ston;
> Trustly trowe þou þervpon,
> And holde it for no wene:

---

[4] *Athelston*, ed. A. McI. Trounce, EETS, os, 224 (London, 1951; repr. 1984). The poem
was probably written in the final quarter of the 14th cent., and Trounce demonstrates its
close affinities with the *chansons de geste Parise la Duchesse, Gaydon, Daurel et Beton*, and
*Aye d'Avignon* (pp. 4–25).

> I swere boþe be book and belle,
> But 3iff þou me his name telle,
> Þe ry3t doom schal I deme:
> Þyselff schalt goo þe ry3te way
> Þat þy broþer wente today,
> Þou3 it þe euele beseme.'     (ll. 675–86)

Alryke here threatens to make Athelston walk through the fire as a penance on which the absolution he has just granted him is conditional, unless he reveals the name of Egeland's detractor.

Similarly, when Wymound has been summoned to London to account for himself:

> My3te he neuere with crafft ne gynne,
> Gare hym schryuen off hys synne,
> For nou3t þat my3te befalle.     (ll. 771–3)

If Wymound is the subject of this sentence, it means that by no trick or stratagem could he get Alryke to hear his confession and absolve his sin; if Alryke is the subject, it means that he could not get Wymound to confess (because he denies having told the lie). The latter is the more likely sense, but the former is not impossible.

At any rate, it is clear that the introduction of penance into this poem is entirely unconnected with the kind of penance which is the subject of *Guy of Warwick*, *Sir Ysumbras*, *Sir Gowther*, and *Roberd of Cisyle*. It is too much subordinated to the other conflicts which are being explored to be concerned with the penitent's grief at having offended God and his spiritual regeneration through a morally educative penance, and is more concerned with political and legal realities.


### SIR GAWAIN AND THE GREEN KNIGHT

*Sir Gawain and the Green Knight* is a very different piece of work from any of the poems we have so far discussed. The others range from really quite good, to good in parts; but this poem is a masterpiece, infinitely rich, complex, and subtle. It takes up the forms and conventions of medieval romance, but is not bound by them; it transcends generic definition. While its surface is as brilliant and scintillating as Gawain's embroidered and bejewelled 'vrysoun', its ironies and ambiguities, its drama and directness evoke a wealth of cultural associations and grant us the rare pleasure of passage through a complete fictional world into which we step as strangers and from which we emerge with new insight into the human condition.

The poem is being discussed here in this appendix rather than in the main argument of the book, because it is not 'about' sin and penance in the same way that *Sir Ysumbras* or *Sir Gowther* is. *Sir Gawain and the Green Knight* is the story of a man whose virtues are being tested; but the author trebled the tests imposed on his hero, and vastly expanded what could in other hands have been simply a straightforward adventure story.[5] The author was clearly not interested in the straightforward; for while Gawain is, in the words of Sir Bertilak, 'on þe fautlest freke þat euer on fote 3ede',[6] he ultimately fails the test of his 'trawþe' by accepting, and keeping, the magic girdle offered to him by the Lady. It is in the treatment of the commission of this fault and Gawain's subsequent repentance of it, that we can draw some interesting comparisons with the penitential romances. The pattern of penitence is there, in Gawain's initial ignorance of his fault, in his being made aware of it by the revelation of a third party, in this revelation leading to great grief and shame on the part of Gawain, in his acknowledgement of being at fault, and in his voluntarily undertaking the penitential exercises of public confession and the wearing of the girdle as a permanent reminder of his transgression. But there are also telling differences: Gawain's fault is not treated as a sin (i.e. an offence against God), and he does not formally undertake penance with a view to being reconciled with God.

Confession and repentance are without doubt present in the poem, but there is much disagreement as to the meaning and importance of these elements. A great debate has been in progress on the subject of Gawain's Fault for more than thirty years and is still unresolved. This debate concerns the nature of the poem and the intentions of its author in the most fundamental way. Is it a serious, moral, religious poem or not? Does Gawain commit a mortal sin or a social *faux pas*? Is his acceptance and retention of the girdle more than a slight blot on his reputation as a peerless knight, or is it something we should laugh at good-naturedly, along with King Arthur and his court?

The debate was set in motion by this remark on Gawain's awkward predicament during the last day of his stay at Hautdesert:

Gawain had wilfully placed himself in a new dilemma; he could not fulfil one compact without breaking the other. This, however, was a dilemma that Gawain chose not to face; he repressed it. Despite this full intention of committing sin, Gawain went to confession and sought absolution. He endeavoured to safeguard his body by magic and his soul by a false confession. Thus, incongruously, the exemplar of piety took refuge in superstition and a false confession.[7]

[5] As e.g. in *The Grene Knight*, which tells the same story in 500 lines; ed. F. J. Furnivall and J. W. Hales, *Bishop Percy's Folio Manuscript: Ballads and Romances* (4 vols.; London, 1867–8; repr. Detroit, 1968), 2.

[6] *Sir Gawain and the Green Knight*, ed. J. R. R. Tolkien and E. V. Gordon (2nd edn. rev. N. Davis, Oxford, 1967), 2363.

[7] G. J. Englehardt, 'The Predicament of Gawain', *Modern Language Quarterly*, 16 (1955), 218–25; quotation from p. 222.

This seminal suggestion was later elaborated by J. A. Burrow, who argued with unimpeachable logic that Gawain, prior to leaving Hautdesert in the pursuit of his quest, commits a mortal sin by deliberately making a false confession.[8] Since then much ingenuity and erudition have been employed in the attempt to define exactly what was Gawain's fault, what were his motives, and the precise extent of his culpability. It is clear that during the third encounter with the Lady of Hautdesert in his bedroom, Gawain appears to put himself into an impossible position. He has entered into an agreement with his host Sir Bertilak (in which, even if it is nothing more serious than a game, his honour is involved[9] to exchange at night whatever each wins during the day—Sir Bertilak at hunting, Sir Gawain resting in the castle. So far he has fulfilled his bond honourably, giving Bertilak the kisses which were all he would allow the importuning Lady to give him, and receiving in exchange the venison and boar killed by Bertilak.

On the third day, having almost weakened in the face of the continued temptations of the Lady, and finally succeeded in rebuffing her without offence, Gawain accepts from her the gift of her green silk girdle, because she tells him that the man who wears it ' "my3t not be slayn for sly3t vpon erþe" ' (l. 1854). Gawain accepts the gift, and then promises the Lady not to reveal it to her husband, or anyone else:

> And ho bere on hym þe belt and bede hit hym swyþe—
> And he granted, and hym gafe with a goud wylle—
> And biso3t him, for hir sake, disceuer hit neuer,
> Bot to lelly layne fro hir lorde; þe leude hym acorde3
> Þat neuer wy3e schulde hit wyt, iwysse, bot þay twayne for no3te
>
> (ll. 1860–5)

At this point it is clear that Gawain must break his word either to the Lady or to Sir Bertilak; and it is more probable that the latter will be the case. Though a number of ingenious suggestions have been put forward to explain Gawain's conduct in this scene, involving his intention to restore the girdle to Bertilak secretly and tactfully, without implicating the Lady,[10] the narrative clearly implies that the only reason Gawain accepts the girdle is so that he can use it on the following day to protect himself

---

[8] John A. Burrow, *A Reading of 'Sir Gawain and the Green Knight'* (London, 1965), pp. 104–12, 127–59.

[9] Burrow had argued that the medieval reader would have understood the Exchange of Winnings agreement as a legally binding contract (*Reading*, p. 68); W. O. Evans, 'The Case for Gawain Re-opened', *Modern Language Review*, 68 (1973), 721–33 countered that the agreement, however quasi-legal in formulation, is only a game made in drink and play (p. 726).

[10] W. R. J. Barron, *'Trawþe' and Treason: The Sin of Gawain Reconsidered* (Manchester, 1980), pp. 94–5.

from the blow of the Green Knight's axe. He has just refused to accept the girdle, as emphatically as could possibly be consistent with perfect good breeding (ll. 1836–41), but when the Lady explains its magical properties, the idea of wearing it tomorrow comes to him:

> Þen kest þe kny3t, and hit come to his hert
> Hit were a juel for þe joparde þat hym iugged were:
> When he acheued to þe chapel his chek for to fech,
> My3t he haf slypped to be vnslayn, þe sle3t were noble.
> Þenne he þulged with hir þrepe and þoled hir to speke,
> And ho bere on hym þe belt . . .

> (ll. 1855–60)

It has been argued that Gawain's subsequent behaviour at the Green Chapel shows conclusively that he does not think the girdle will protect him from the blow,[11] but this by no means invalidates the point that at the moment of his accepting it he thought it would, and that that was his reason for doing so.

It is only after Gawain has decided that he wants the girdle and has given in to the Lady ('hym gafe with a goud wylle', l. 1861) that she 'biso3t hym, for hir sake, disceuer hit neuer./ Bot to lelly layne fro hir lorde' (ll. 1862–3), and Gawain agrees at once. He thanks the Lady profusely ('Ful þro with hert and þo3t', l. 1867); she kisses him for the third time that day and leaves him, the narrator remarks ominously, 'For more myrþe of þat mon mo3t ho not gete' (l. 1871).

Gawain gets up, dresses, then 'Lays vp þe luf-lace þe lady hym ra3t,/ Hid hit ful holdely þer he hit eft fonde' (ll. 1874–5). On the previous two days Gawain has gone to Mass in the chapel after getting up. This time he chooses to go to confession. What Barron describes as 'the impenetrably candid narrative'[12] gives no clue to Gawain's inner state at this point:

> Syþen cheuely to þe chapel choses he þe waye,
> Preuély aproched to a prest, and prayed hym þere
> Þat he wolde lyste his lyf and lern hym better
> How his sawle schulde be saued when he schuld seye heþen.
> Þere he schrof hym schyrly and schewed his mysdedez,
> Of þe more and þe mynne, and merci besechez,
> And of absolucioun he on þe segge calles;
> And he asoyled hym surely and sette hym so clene
> As domezday schulde haf ben dizt on þe morn.

> (ll. 1876–84)

[11] Tony Hunt, 'Gawain's Fault and the Moral Perspectives of *Sir Gawain and the Green Knight*', *Trivium*, 10 (1975), 1–18; quotation from p. 7.

[12] Barron, '*Trawþe*', p. 94.

But afterwards, Gawain spends the remainder of the day making merry among the ladies with such joyous spirits that the members of Bertilak's household comment: ' "Þus myry he watz neuer are,/ Syn he com hider, er þis" ' (ll. 1891–2).

This sequence of events has been the focus of attention for most of the contributors to the debate on the nature of Gawain's fault. A surprising number of possible interpretations have emerged, some more and some less consistent with the rest of the poem, but some not at all consistent with each other. Most resolve themselves into two camps: those who agree with Burrow that Gawain commits a sin by accepting and keeping for his own use the magic green girdle, and subsequently a much more serious sin by making a false confession, and that, since he does not during the remainder of the poem take himself to confession again, he remains in a state of mortal sin and, so far as we can judge from the text's evidence of his feelings and behaviour, uncontrite;[13] and those who disagree with Burrow and have elaborated the original arguments of P. J. C. Field against this view. These claim that Gawain either does not commit a sin at all, or that he commits only a venial sin which it was not necessary to mention in confession, and that after his own realization of his fault, Bertilak's forgiveness of it, his own admission of his failure to the court at Camelot, and the court's delighted adoption of the green girdle as a badge of honour, all matters relating to Gawain's fault are happily resolved.[14]

The moral significance of Gawain's actions in the last part of the poem can only be properly understood in the context of the rest. The wholeness implied by 'trawþe' and the perfect interlocking of the pentangle extend beyond the symbolic dimension of the poem to govern its structure and thematic development. We can easily see how 'the bedroom scenes are set within the hunting scenes and linked to them by the Exchange of Winnings agreement. The Exchange of Winnings agreement in its turn is set within the Beheading Game, and these two are linked, for the outcome of the Beheading Game is dependent on the outcome of the Exchange of Winnings agreement.'[15] It is impossible to detach one bit of

[13] Englehardt, 'Predicament'; Burrow, *Reading*; Barron, '*Trawþe*'; Nicolas Jacobs, 'Gawain's False Confession', *English Studies*, 51 (1970), 433–5; Hermione J. van Nuis, 'Gawain's Excesses: The Tension between his Real and Apparent Self', *Concerning Poetry*, 17 (1984), 13–25.

[14] P. J. C. Field, 'A Re-reading of *Sir Gawain and the Green Knight*', *Studies in Philology*, 68 (1971), 255–69; Hunt, 'Gawain's Fault'; Evans, 'Case for Gawain'; Michael Foley, 'Gawain's Two Confessions Reconsidered', *Chaucer Review*, 9 (1974–5), 73–9; G. M. Shedd, 'Knight in Tarnished Armour: The Meaning of *Sir Gawain and the Green Knight*', *Modern Language Review*, 62 (1967), 3–13; A. Francis Soucy, 'Gawain's Fault: "Angardez Pride"', *Chaucer Review*, 13 (1978), 166–76; Hubert E. Morgan, ' "To Be Her Seruant Soþly": Gawain's Service', *English Studies in Canada*, 11 (1985), 273–81; A. D. Horgan, 'Gawain's *Pure Pentaungle* and the Virtue of Faith', *Medium Ævum*, 56 (1987), 310–16.

[15] Gerald Morgan, 'The Action of the Hunting and Bedroom Scenes in *Sir Gawain and the Green Knight*', *Medium Ævum*, 56 (1987), 200–16; quotation from p. 206.

the poem from the preceding and succeeding sequences and interpret its meaning by reference to concepts not elaborated within the poem itself. Sin and penance are brought into the narrative, in vocabulary, symbols, and actions, but they do not have over-riding dominance in the thematic scheme of the poem, and a comparison with real penitential romances will quickly make this clear.

If we examine the poet's treatment of the religious aspects of Gawain's chivalric ideal, and the ways in which God, Christ, and the Virgin Mary are brought into the narrative, we will find that the opportunity for the hero to repent, in the sense that we understand repentance in *Sir Gowther*, for example, is denied; or rather, the opportunity is set up and expected, and then that expectation is disappointed. Gawain does not at any point acknowledge that his failure in 'trawþe' is a sin; he does not express any sorrow at having offended God, and he does not ask God for forgiveness. Bertilak says the offence was against him, that Gawain has done penance for it 'apert of þe poynt of myn egge', and he jokingly absolves Gawain:

> 'I halde þe polysed of þat plyȝt, and pured as clene
> As þou hadez neuer forfeted syþen þou watz fyrst borne'
>
> (ll. 2393–4)

Gawain himself is not eased by this absolution; he seems to feel that the offence goes deeper and he cannot forgive himself. But the one direction in which the unfolding events of the final fitt of the poem never turns is towards God. It is inconceivable that if the poet had wished us to understand Gawain had committed a mortal sin by abusing the sacrament of penance, he would not have had Gawain realize and repent of this before the end of the poem.

So what is the purpose of the introduction of this motif? What does the poem mean? The poet has created an engaging surface. Many witty tricks are played with the audience's expectations, and fun is poked at romances; but this glittering curtain can be whisked aside in an instant to reveal the more serious concerns of the poem. The audience's response is never allowed to be clear-cut and simple; the mood of the narrative is changeable, full of disturbing ambiguities which keep the reader divided between delight and unease.

In the very opening lines of the poem, when the poet is referring to the legendary descent of the ancient kings of Britain from the Trojan hero Aeneas, the nationalistic pride that usually accompanies such a genealogy is undercut by reference to the fact that Aeneas, though 'þe trewest on erthe' (l. 4),[16] was also 'þe tulk þat þe trammes of tresoun þer wroȝt'

---

[16] 'Þe trewest on erthe' may refer to the 'tricherie' committed by Aeneas, rather than to himself; A. C. Cawley glosses the words 'the most certain on earth' in this way in his edition (London, 1962), but I think the line makes better sense if the words refer to Aeneas.

(l. 3) and 'Watz tried for his tricherie' (l. 4). The descendants of this equivocal paragon afterwards conquered most of Western Europe, and included 'Felix Brutus', the famous founder of Britain. But Britain, even in those ancient days, did not enjoy a golden age of unmixed prosperity; 'wonder' has always been accompanied by 'werre and wrake', and a period of 'blysse' is inevitably followed by one of 'blunder' (ll. 16–19).

This ambivalence is of course entirely appropriate to a story in which the hero, and through him perhaps the whole edifice of Western chivalry, is going to be tested and found slightly less than perfect, and it at once alerts the reader to a characteristically ironic turn of phrase which will be encountered often in the course of the poem.

It is also worth noticing at this point that the poet does not make the standard invocation to God, to bless him and his audience, or help them to make a good end. Most Middle English romancers do make such an appeal at the openings of their productions, and it is very unusual indeed for a poem with a serious moral or religious dimension not to do so. The Gawain poet tends not to use the standard formulae of romance, so we cannot be surprised at not finding the expressions, but I think we should expect to find the sentiments, and their absence is not without significance.

The fact is that God rather takes a back seat in this romance. For a poem in which there is a considerable amount of religious observance on the part of the characters—people praying, attending Mass, making confession—God as a character is surprisingly, and conspicuously, absent from the text. Religious feast-days are often mentioned,[17] characters often swear by God, or by Christ, or Mary, or a Saint,[18] and they often commend one another to God, or utter other similar formulae,[19] and at Hautdesert they go to Mass every day;[20] but independent mentions of God by the narrator are quite rare.[21] When they do occur, it is noticeable that the poet avoids stating that God (or Mary, or whoever) has actually done something. This may be implied at first reading, but closer examination reveals the ultimate retirement of God from active intervention. For instance, at line 696, the narrator tells us that Gawain had no one but God to talk to on his journey. In the first place, we notice that it is Gawain who is doing the talking, and then we realize that this is actually a de-

---

[17] e.g. ll. 37, 51, 63, 65, 734, 750–62, 805, 907, 922, 932, 985, 996, 1022, 1036, 1049, 1135, 1311, 1414, 1558, 1655, 1690, 1878–84.

[18] e.g. ll. 256, 323, 390, 549, 674, 813, 1055, 1064, 1110, 1268, 1644, 1776, 1788, 1938, 1942, 1949, 2119, 2122–3, 2140, 2156, 2185, 2205, 2250. Most of these are uttered by Gawain himself.

[19] e.g. ll. 370, 596, 762, 839, 920, 1038, 1063, 1256, 1263, 1279, 1292, 1307, 1535, 1963, 1967, 1982, 2057, 2067, 2073, 2120, 2239, 2410, 2429, 2441–2, 2472–3.

[20] e.g. ll. 1135, 1311, 1414, 1558, 1690.

[21] e.g. ll. 642–3, 646–7, 692, 696, 702, 724–5, 736–9, 776, 1768–9, 1837, 1999, 2529–30.

scription of Gawain's loneliness on his quest; the clear implication is that God is not very good company. The people Gawain comes across 'in þe wyldrenesse of Wyrale' are described as not loving either God or man 'wyth goud hert' (ll. 701–2), but this is an indication that they are rough and uncivilized rather than that they are wicked. A little later on, in line 724, Gawain would have been killed if he had not been brave and served God—which is not quite the same as saying that God protected him.

Similarly, when Gawain makes his prayer to God and the Virgin on Christmas Eve, the castle appears as if in answer to the prayer; but the poet does not say that it did do so, or that God answered Gawain's prayer by making the castle appear, or by making Gawain aware of it. Again, during the third temptation scene, Gawain is feeling the power of the Lady's marvellous beauty, and 'Gret perile bitwene hem stod/ Nif Mare of hir knyȝt mynne' (ll. 1768–9). This is the closest the poet ever comes to saying that Gawain has been saved from danger by divine intervention; but that is not what he actually does say. What he does is to remind the reader of Gawain's special devotion to Mary, and how we were told earlier in the poem that Gawain 'alle his forsnes feng at þe fyue joyez/ Þat þe hende heuen-quene had of hir chylde', and that when he looked at her picture on the inside of his shield 'his belde neuer payred' (ll. 646–50). Gawain ought by rights to be thinking of Mary, not Mary of Gawain.

The ultimate effect is quite the reverse of the reassurance which the romance reader expects to receive from such remarks. The poet deliberately introduces the potential for divine approval, or divine interaction, but then slides away from fulfilling it. The effect is that the scene of the moral action, as it were, is firmly placed within the characters themselves. Even God's role as the prime mover of events is usurped by Morgan le Faye; ' "Morgne þe goddes" ', as Bertilak calls her (l. 2452), turns out to have planned the whole business. What, then, is the real nature of Gawain's much-emphasized piety? Expectation is set up and disappointed from early on in the poem. The description of Gawain's arming is magnificent and solemn; Gawain himself becomes a kind of icon of perfect knighthood. He faces his ordeal bravely; he looks and behaves as a hero of romance should.

The discourse on the meaning of the pentangle is of crucial importance for understanding what is going on later in the poem—a fact which has been curiously overlooked by several commentators who try to explain Gawain's fault without reference to it. The pentangle is a symbol of Gawain's chivalric ideal, his personal aspiration; it is somehow made up of a continuous association of five sets of five things, four of which have been explicitly and firmly set in the context of Christian doctrine:

> Fyrst he watz funden fautlez in his fyue wyttez,
> And efte fayled neuer þe freke in his fyue fyngres,

And alle his afyaunce vpon folde watz in þe fyue woundez
Þat Cryst kaȝt on þe croys, as þe crede tellez;
And quere-so-euer þys mon in melly watz stad,
His þro þoȝt watz in þat, þurȝ alle oþer þynges,
Þat alle his forsnes he feng at þe fyue joyez
Þat þe hende heuen-quene had of hir chylde

(ll. 640–7)

Medieval readers would have been familiar with the discourses in many vernacular penitential handbooks on how the penitent should prepare himself for confession by examining the ways in which he has sinned. Typically he would begin by asking himself if he had committed any of the seven deadly sins; then he should discover whether he has sinned in any of his five senses, which covers a whole range of offences.[22] Gawain, we are informed, does not sin in any of these ways. The fact that he has never failed in his five fingers may mean that his hands have never led him into sin; or it may mean that he was good at fighting.[23] The five wounds of Christ are a familiar subject of devotional literature: here Gawain has total faith in the redemptive power of Christ's sacrifice for his salvation; and he derives all his fortitude from contemplation of the Five Joys of Mary. Gawain's special personal devotion to Mary has led him to have her image painted on the inside of his shield; when he looks at this his courage never fails (ll. 648–50).

Gawain is by this account unusually devout. His pre-eminence in knightly virtue has not caused him, like Guy of Warwick, to forget God. Far from being proud, he appears to be especially conscious of the fact that without the help of God's grace he can achieve nothing. The poet is emphatic: Gawain puts *all* his trust in the Five Wounds, and derives *all* his fortitude from the Five Joys. Correspondingly, he is at present 'as gold pured,/ Voyded of vche vylany' (ll. 633–4). It is important that we remember this later in the poem, and in fact the poet reminds us of it several times.

Meanwhile, the fifth set of five is a special collection of interrelated social virtues:

Þe fyft fyue þat I finde þat þe frek vsed
Watz fraunchyse and felaȝschyp forbe al þyng,
His clannes and his cortaysye croked were neuer,
And pite, þat passez alle poyntez, þyse pure fyue
Were harder happed on þat haþel þen on any oþer.

(ll. 651–5)

---

[22] See R. W. Ackerman, 'Gawain's Shield: Penitential Doctrine in *Sir Gawain and the Green Knight*', *Anglia*, 76 (1958), 254–65.
[23] As suggested by Horgan, 'Gawain's *Pure Pentaungle*', p. 313.

We are not told that he is brave, or strong, or that no man could stand against him in battle; these things go without saying. Instead we are presented with a faultless hero, whose personal piety is counterbalanced by his exemplary practice of virtues which are principally concerned with his behaviour towards other men and women. In case we feel that there might be some implicit conflict in the demands of these private and public values, the poet carefully assures us that they are all perfectly interrelated with one another, and the integrity of the whole is without flaw (ll. 656–65). The effect of this statement is not altogether reassuring, however, for it implies that a failure in any one component of the whole will break the 'endeles knot' and the complex of 'trawþe' will be vitiated.

This is the ideal which Gawain has chosen for himself, and which he now has to live up to. It is indeed a testing one. Gawain does not want merely to be better than other knights (which does not sound too difficult, judging by the behaviour of the knights at Camelot), he wants to be perfect. But in spite of all his caution, he fails; where did he go wrong? The great strength of Gawain's aspiration to perfection, to embody the ideal of Christian knightly virtue, is his reliance on the grace of God to achieve it, and his acknowledgement of the necessity of that reliance. Perfection, or even goodness, is something which one cannot achieve on one's own. This is a point which is made time and again by the Gawain poet in his other poems. Your own merit is never going to be adequate for your justification, as is shown by the Pearl Maiden's account of the Parable of the Labourers in the Vineyard; God's justice is not the same as the human concept of fairness, it refers back to His own divine nature. The copious abundance of God's grace is necessary to supplement merit and supply the deficiencies of human frailty in order to achieve salvation, and it is always available to those who truly desire it. Ask, and it will be given unto you; knock, and the door will be opened.

Gawain, when it comes to the point, does not ask. Instead, he seizes the opportunity provided by the Lady to protect himself from the Green Knight with a magic girdle. If this is a sin, it is a sin of omission; he omits to have perfect faith in the gift of love of our Saviour, in God's redeeming grace. But Gawain himself does not think he has sinned, and does not appear to be conscious that his trust in the magic girdle constitutes an impairment of his trust in God; he 'seems quite unaware that in relying on this pagan talisman to deliver him from the death he fears, he is falling short in that fortitude which ought to spring from his devotion to the Blessed Virgin'.[24]

One problem that has to be faced by the proponents of the Mortal Sin by False Confession theory is that Gawain's subsequent behaviour appears to be disgustingly deceitful. Barron comments:

[24] Horgan, 'Gawain's *Pure Pentaungle*', p. 314.

If Gawain's *ioye* is heartfelt, it implies moral blindness; if feigned, at best social tact, at worst cynical hypocrisy covering conscious wrongdoing.[25]

And it is hard to escape the conviction that Gawain's behaviour towards Bertilak when he returns from the third day's hunt does show some consciousness of wrongdoing. Gawain feels uneasy because he knows he should be giving the girdle to Bertilak with the kisses. But he simply has not confronted in his own mind the full implications of what he has done. The evidence of what follows tends to support this view; and it is perhaps the clear-sighted penetration and thoroughness of Barron's own mind, coupled with his great familiarity with the text, which makes it so difficult for him to credit the kind of wilful stupidity with which Gawain succeeds in blinding himself to his own motivations. It is all very well for us to criticize Gawain's inconsistency and woolly-mindedness from the leisure of our armchairs; who can say what we would have done in the same testing circumstances, in fear of death, and without the benefit of hindsight?

Gawain's reactions when the Green Knight reveals to him the extent of his folly and self-deceit make it clear that he had previously thought himself blameless, or at least, had not fully realized the moral implications of his failure in 'trawþe':

> Þat oþer stif mon in study stod a gret whyle,
> So agreued for greme he gryed withinne;
> Alle þe blode of his brest blende in his face,
> Þat al he schrank for schome þat þe schalk talked.

(ll. 2369–72)

This is also, I would suggest, the moment at which the reader (if we can imagine to ourselves what it was like to read this poem for the first time) becomes fully aware of these things. The technique which we have observed in the other poems, of making the reader identify with the hero, is here developed to a fine art. Since the brightly coloured picture of the Good Knight arming himself and setting off on his quest, at the beginning of the second fitt, we have become much more intimate with Gawain, have become privy to his thoughts and fears and feelings. He has emerged from that image of heroic splendour to become very real, very human. The impenetrable candour of the narrative at those crucial points of Gawain's acceptance of the girdle, his subsequent confession and absolution, and his behaviour for the rest of his time at the castle, are designed specifically to prevent the premature realization of those moral implications of his conduct which cause such anxiety to Barron. The revelation at the Green Chapel would lose half its force if the reader has not been able to share Gawain's blindness.

[25] Barron, *'Trawþe'*, p. 104.

Although we must be careful not to let our instinctive reactions to a medieval text blind us to matters which would have been clear to a fully informed medieval reader, it is also true that we must not use special historical or theological knowledge to do violence to those instinctive reactions. Most people who read the poem accept Bertilak's account of the three blows at Gawain and their correspondence to the results of the Exchange of Winnings agreement on the three preceding days at the castle. They know that this is the right explanation. No one has yet adduced evidence of the widespread efficacy of magic charms to prove that the reason why the Green Knight does not succeed in cutting off Gawain's head is that he was wearing the girdle.[26]

The fact is that the reader is led to identify with Gawain in all the twists and turns, the blindness and inconsistency fostered by his predicament; and it is a moving experience. One cannot read the poem without going under the axe with Gawain, without understanding how he forgets the hoped-for qualities of the green girdle, without feeling his joy at finding himself still alive, and without sharing the shattering disappointment and shame produced by the Green Knight's explanation of events. It is a bitter realization that, if Gawain had only followed the straight path indicated by ' "Trwe mon trwe restore" '—and had lived up to the ideal of the pentangle—he would have been better protected than by a thousand magic girdles.

The confession which Gawain makes to Bertilak at the Green Chapel is clearly intended to cover all those faults which were not confessed to the priest at Hautdesert. The language and formulae of real confession are *almost* used; but Gawain's fault is not referred to as a sin,[27] the Green Knight does not use the word 'absolve' when he forgives Gawain, and most telling of all, God is not mentioned once. It is very unlikely that we are intended to deduce from this that Gawain's fault was a mortal sin and

---

[26] But see the interesting article by Helen Cooper, 'Magic that Does Not Work', *Medievalia et Humanistica*, NS, 7 (1976), 131–46, about other supposedly magical objects in medieval romance which either do not function or whose function is made irrelevant by subsequent events.

[27] The word 'sin' is used in *Sir Gawain and the Green Knight* only once, at l. 1774, where it refers to the mortal sin of adultery which Gawain does not commit. Elsewhere the poet uses the word 'misdeed' (ll. 760, 1880) to mean sin; however, then as now this word had other meanings (*MED* 1*a*), an offence, a transgression, misdeed; sin, crime) which tended to give it the implication of a less serious offence than the word 'sin' itself. This sense of 'less serious sin' for 'misdeed' as opposed to 'really serious sin' for 'sin' is shown by the lines in *Speculum Gy de Warewyke*: 'Many on wepeþ for his misdede,/ Ac to do sinne noht hij ne drede' (ll. 829–30). The words used of Gawain's fault—faut, fals, fylþe, feintise, forfet, surfet—almost all have other meanings besides that of sinfulness. Why do almost all of them begin with F? Perhaps because they remind us of the five fives of the pentangle, and the numerous virtues listed there which also begin with F—faythful, fautles, afyaunce, forsnes, fraunchyse, felazschyp.

that God was very offended by it. Once again, the possibility of doing so was created, and the poet has deliberately passed it by. Gawain himself does not confess either directly or by implication that his 'fawty fare' consisted of abusing the sacrament, or of theft, or of pride, or any of the other things people have suggested. He does specifically acknowledge his faults:

> 'For care of þy knokke cowardyse me taȝt
> To acorde me with couetyse, my kynde to forsake,
> Þat is larges and lewté þat longez to knyȝtez.
> Now am I fawty and falce, and ferde haf ben euer
> Of trecherye and vntrawþe: boþe bityde sorȝe and care!
> I biknowe yow, knyȝt, here stylle,
> Al fawty is my fare;
> Letez me ouertake your wylle
> And efte I schal be ware.'

(ll. 2379–88)

The faults of which he accuses himself, 'cowardyse' and 'couetyse',[28] are here seen in opposition to the virtues of 'larges' and 'lewté' which ought to have governed his behaviour. Fear of death made him cowardly, which led him to the 'couetyse' of hanging on to the girdle when 'larges', the open-handedness of the noble knight, and 'lewté', the loyalty and fidelity to one's word and to the general obligations of knightly conduct, both dictated that he should give it to Bertilak. In this way he has 'forsaken his kynde'—not behaved like a knight—and been 'fawty and falce', guilty of 'trecherye and vntrawþe'. This refers back to the pentangle; Gawain has been false to his ideal and, more specifically, has been guilty of treachery to God, in trusting to the magic girdle instead of His grace.

The pattern we have observed in the penitential romances has been sustained—even deliberately evoked—in *Sir Gawain and the Green Knight* up to a point. Gawain is in ignorance of his fault, then is made aware of it by the Green Knight's revelation. The realization of his wrongdoing, as in *Guy of Warwick*, *Sir Gowther*, *Sir Ysumbras*, and *Roberd of Cisyle*, is a deeply traumatic experience for the hero. He is ashamed, and disgusted with himself; the pattern there stops short of full penitential force. At this point in a penitential romance the hero's soul is prepared by disgust with self and detestation of the sin to be softened by the love of God and sorrow at having offended Him into true contrition and amendment of life. The Gawain poet could very easily have proceeded in this way, but the fact is that he chose not to. He is much more interested in getting Gawain to the point of being humbled, of realizing where he went wrong, of being educated, than in directing the reader's attention to sin and its consequences. Once Gawain has recognized the

---

[28] Gawain repeats this charge three times, in ll. 2374, 2379–80, 2508.

error of his ways, he imposes on himself the penance of wearing the girdle always as a check to his pride:

> 'Bot in syngne of my surfet I schal se hit ofte,
> When I ride in renoun, remorde to myseluen
> Þe faut and þe fayntyse of þe flesche crabbed.
> How tender hit is to entyse teches of fylþe;
> And þus, quen pryde schal me pryk for prowes of armes,
> Þe loke to þis luf-lace schal lepe my hert.'

(ll. 2433–8)

This reaction has been seen by some critics as excessive, and has led them to search for more serious crimes committed by Gawain than those provided in the text. But all Gawain is saying here is that the girdle will remind him that he is not infallible, not perfect, not unsusceptible to temptation; he managed to escape the 'teches of fylþe' this time,[29] but that ought not to make him complacent for the future.

The story of Gawain as we have it is the story of a young man who had grown rather too accustomed to his reputation as peerless and faultless, and is taken down a peg or two. Again, there are clear parallels with the less subtle treatment of a similar story in *Guy of Warwick*, *Sir Ysumbras*, and *Roberd of Cisyle*, where the heroes think too much of themselves and are then humbled in repenting of the sin of Pride; but even more importantly, there are parallels with *Pearl* and *Patience*:

for it is then the case that in all three poems we have a central character of high moral pretensions who falls short of an ideal of behaviour and is suitably rebuked by a figure of authority and made to seem foolish.[30]

Gawain has a tendency to take himself rather too seriously, with which we can all sympathize, and which is counteracted by the judgement of Bertilak and the reaction of the court at Camelot, who laugh at him and adopt the green girdle as a badge of honour. But it is better to take yourself too seriously in matters of moral conduct than too lightly (like the knights at Camelot), and at the end of *Sir Gawain and the Green Knight* the reader feels sure that Gawain, whose shame and suffering at his own shortcomings has not grown less during his return journey, will not make the mistake of relying too heavily on his own judgement again.

At the same time he need not I think be anxious that Gawain must go to confession as soon as possible because his soul is in danger of eternal damnation.[31] There can be no doubt that, at the end of the poem as elsewhere, the poet likes to play games with his readers; one last game is Bertilak's attribution of the whole elaborate plot to Morgan le Faye as a

---

[29] 'Fylþe' has unmistakable overtones of sexual sin, see *MED* 3a a, b, and 3b.
[30] Horgan, 'Gawain's *Pure Pentaungle*', p. 314.
[31] Burrow, *Reading*, p. 156; Barron, '*Trawþe*', pp. 139–42.

product of devilish cunning and very hostile intent (ll. 2446–62), followed by his invitation to Gawain to ' "com to þyn aunt" ' (l. 2467). But the reader's instinctive reaction is to agree with Bertilak that Gawain is to be loved ' "as wel . . . As any gome vnder God for þy grete trauþe" ', and to feel that such offence as he committed has been atoned for, both under the Green Knight's axe and in his own shame and sorrow, and in his intention not to commit it again. He will wear the girdle for the rest of his life to remind him of his frailty and his need to rely on God's grace. The poem ends, as it did not begin, with a characteristically romance-like appeal to that grace:

> Now þat bere þe croun of þorne,
> He bryng vus to his blysse! AMEN.

# Appendix B.   The Manuscripts

A total of twenty-five manuscripts contain one or more of the four romances which are the subject of this book. Of these, five are 'fragments': single leaves or pieces of leaves from lost manuscripts, which have survived by being used as part of the binding or as fly-leaves in other manuscripts:

1. BL MS Additional 14408, eight folios with contemporary numeration 74–81 of what must originally have been a large manuscript, containing a section of *Guy of Warwick*.
2. BL MS Sloane 1044, one leaf of much-trimmed vellum containing lines from *Guy of Warwick*.
3. National Library of Wales MS 572, parts of four leaves, remnants of an old binding, containing lines from *Guy of Warwick*.
4. Gray's Inn MS 20, an early single leaf from a manuscript, containing lines from *Sir Ysumbras*, used as a fly-leaf at the end of a volume of Latin homilies.
5. BL MS Additional 34801, a single leaf used as a fly-leaf in an early fifteenth-century collection of tracts concerning the offices of the Earl Marshal and the Admiralty, containing twenty-three lines of *Roberd of Cisyle* written as prose.[1]

It is hard to deduce anything from these fragments, since they contain no clue as to what else the lost portions of manuscript might once have contained. It is certainly extraordinary that half the surviving manuscripts of *Guy of Warwick* are fragments from old bindings or fly-leaves, and it suggests that manuscripts of *Guy* were once very common indeed.

In addition, two further manuscripts of *Sir Ysumbras* are incomplete for other reasons: Biblioteca Nazionale MS XIII. B. 29 was left unfinished by the scribe, with space for the rest of the poem to be filled in later. University College, Oxford MS 142 originally contained only the text of *Pricke of Conscience*, but other items, including a passage from *Sir Ysumbras*, were added to its blank final leaves.

*Guy of Warwick* is the only one of the four to occupy a whole manuscript on its own (Caius College, Cambridge MS 107), though both the surviving texts of *Sir Gowther* were originally in separate 'booklets'

---

[1] For much of the information on manuscripts not kept in the Bodleian Library or the British Library, this Appendix draws heavily on Gisela Guddat-Figge, *Catalogue of Manuscripts Containing Middle English Romances* (Munich, 1976).

before being bound up with their current companions.[2] *Sir Gowther* (once) and *Roberd of Cisyle* (six times) occur in religious miscellanies which do not contain any other romances. In all other cases, our poems appear in manuscripts in the company of two or more other romances, usually in manuscripts of the 'compendium' type described by Harriet Hudson:

[Such manuscripts] were compilations of certain types of materials, literary and non-literary, including secular and religious works. A combination of works on important elements of the Christian faith, instruction in Christian living and edifying examples of the same, along with stories of exemplary chivalry and treatises on manners and morals is typical.[3]

In fact it is remarkable how regularly the same items crop up again and again in these compendia. Of the thirteen most important compendia listed by Ms Hudson,[4] two contain *Guy of Warwick*, and seven *Sir Ysumbras*. As is shown in Figure 1, *Libeus Desconus* occurs three times in the same manuscripts as our poems, as do *The Erle of Toulous*, *Octovian*, and *Sir Degarre*; *Sir Eglamour of Artois* and *Beues of Hamtoun* coincide with our poems in four manuscripts. Not only the same, popular romances appear over and over again, but also the same religious and devotional material.

*The Compleynt of God* appears in three of the manuscripts which contain our four romances; poems on the Ten Commandments in five; on the seven deadly sins in four. The *Lamentacio peccatoris* prologue of the Adulterous Falmouth Squire appears four times (twice with the rest of the piece), *Pricke of Conscience* four times, *Handlyng Synne* (or parts of it) three, Tundale's *Vision* three, the *Trentall of St Gregory* three, the *Charter of Christ* four, and many other pious or devotional works, including *Speculum Gy de Warewyke*, the English Form of Confession, the *Castle of Love*, and *Speculum Vitae* two or three times.

A very large proportion of this material is on the subject of sin and penance, after a practical style—it is not concerned with theological refinements, but with questions of how to prepare yourself for confession, what sins to avoid, what virtues to practise, what prayers to say. Many manuscripts contain poems on the seven penitential psalms, the five wits, the seven virtues, the seven sacraments, the five joys and five sorrows, etc. These are largely derived from the traditional methods of instructing

---

[2] See Philippa Hardman, 'A Medieval Library *in parvo*', *Medium Ævum*, 47 (1978), 262–73 for a detailed account of National Library of Scotland, Advocates 19. 3. 1, and M. C. Seymour, 'The English Manuscripts of *Mandeville's Travels*', *Transactions of the Edinburgh Bibliographical Society*, 4 (1966), 185–6 for BL MS Royal 17. B. 43.

[3] Harriet Hudson, 'Middle English Popular Romances: The Manuscript Evidence', *Manuscripta*, 28 (1984), 67–78; p. 73.

[4] Hudson, 'Middle English Popular Romances', pp. 69–70.

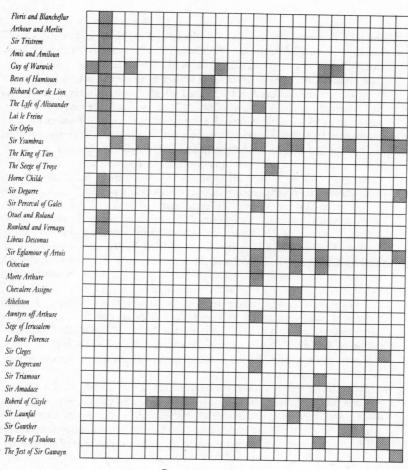

Romances (in approximate order of composition)

Manuscripts (in approximate order of date)

FIG. 1.  Romances occurring in the same manuscripts as *Guy of Warwick*, *Sir Ysumbras*, *Sir Gowther*, and *Roberd of Cisyle*.

the laity developed in manuals for clergy and for literate laymen, following the decree of Archbishop Peckham in 1281 that parish priests must instruct their flocks in essential articles of faith at least four times a year.

Romances are usually grouped together in these manuscripts, discrete from devotional material. Other items which frequently recur are versified instructions on polite conduct (*Stans puer ad mensam*, *Vrbanitas*), saints' lives (*Mary Magdalene*, *Katherine*, *Margaret*, and *Eustace* are well represented), miracle stories, treatises on hunting and carving, medical receipts, and a certain amount of historical, chronicle material. Only one manuscript (Douce 261) contains nothing but romances.

*Roberd of Cisyle* is unusual in appearing much more often in religious miscellanies unaccompanied by other romances, where it clearly owes its presence to its moral and didactic nature. It is placed with other romances in Cambridge University Library Ff. 2. 38; in six other manuscripts it is surrounded by exclusively religious material, and in Trinity College, Oxford MS D. 57 it is even entitled *Sancti Cicilie vita Roberti*. Trinity College, Dublin MS 432 B contains mostly secular items, though no other romances, and in BL MS Harleian 525 it appears sandwiched between *The Seege of Troye* and *Speculum Gy de Warewyke*.[5]

The content and arrangement of manuscripts of Middle English romances offer interesting evidence that three of our four poems were considered to be romances in the late Middle Ages. The doubtful classification of *Roberd of Cisyle* in critical terms is reflected in the way in which it is sometimes grouped with romances, more often with religious material, in the manuscripts.

In addition the manuscripts have much to tell us about the kind of reading material medieval people liked to own, and therefore saw as valuable: a combination of devotional, recreational, and practical texts, in which radically different approaches to the same perennially fascinating subject—penance—coexisted in harmony and complemented each other, answering different emotional and imaginative needs.

---

[5] The version of the poem contained in the Simeon MS (BL Additional 22283) was not discussed by Nuck in his edition (based on the Vernon MS) and has not since been collated. Simeon scribe 2, who wrote this item, is the same person as the Vernon scribe; this may be the only example we have of a romance existing in two manuscripts written by the same scribe. However, the result is, as might be expected, that the Simeon version is identical in substance to that in the Vernon MS (Bodleian Library English Poetry A. 1), except for one or two words and some interesting variations in spelling.

# Appendix C.    The Two Manuscripts of
## *Sir Gowther*

The following is an account of the most important differences between
the two MSS of *Sir Gowther*, to explain my preference of A over B in my
interpretation of the poem.

MS A has 737 lines, B has 691 (not counting the Explicits); seventy-
two lines are identical in both, a large number similar. A contains
seventy-seven lines which do not appear even in a modified form in B,
while B has thirty-six which do not appear in A. Careful comparison of
the texts shows that A's omissions are for the most part due to loss or
damage to the manuscript.[1] A further six lines appear to have been lost
through eye-slip on the part of the scribe.[2]

B's 'missing' lines are more difficult to account for. Apart from five
single lines omitted through simple scribal error, all the lines which
appear in A and not in B have disappeared in half-stanzas and whole
stanzas, and result in no loss of sense. Did A expand the archetype, or did
B abridge it? Where B has lost a half-stanza present in A it invariably fails
to complete the standard rhyme scheme *aabccbddbeeb*, but instead rhymes
*aabccbddeffe*. This occurs in stanzas 12, 21, 42, 61, and 62. It seems likely
in these places that B has lost lines which were once part of the poem and
were similar to those remaining in A. These losses, particularly those
from stanza 12, result in important thematic developments not being
made available to the audience. However, this is not always the case
where A has more lines than B.[3]

---

[1] Breul suggests (*Sir Gowther*, ed. K. Breul (Oppeln, 1886), p. 1) that a leaf containing a
decoration, title, and the first 14 lines has been removed from A at some stage. Ll. 34 and 35
have also been damaged and only the first 3 words of each remain.

[2] Stanzas 4 and 39 in A have each lost 3 lines from the middle. In both cases the nearest
remaining rhyme word in A and the remaining one in B are almost identical and this, to-
gether with the fact that A, fo. 21ᵛ begins at l. 462, makes eye-slip the most likely explana-
tion.

[3] Three stanzas, nos. 44, 50, and 52 of Breul's edition, have in my opinion been added to
A. These stanzas contain descriptions of the second and third battles against the Saracens,
much expanded from what we read in B. This fondness for lengthy accounts of combat
seems to be a peculiarity of MS A. There is a version of *Sir Ysumbras* in A as well, which
has had (by comparison with 5 other complete MSS) battle sequences expanded in a similar
way.

It seems to me that all other lines occurring in A and not in B have been lost from B, but
if stanzas 44, 50, and 52 must be discounted, it is no longer possible to agree with Breul that

An interesting discrepancy occurs at line 378. In the middle of stanza 32, B has six extra lines which anticipate the growing love between Gowther and the Emperor's daughter. Here, while the twelve lines of the stanza in A conform to the rhyme sequence *aabccbddbeeb*, it is the extra, supposedly interpolated lines in B which complete the sequence, while the lines which in B correspond to the last half of A's stanza have a different rhyme for the short third lines.[4]

There is also the question of alliteration and metre, though it is less safe to identify textual corruption by failures in these since they may not have been perfectly regular in the original. However, an overall comparison shows that B alliterates less often and less confidently than A, and frequently spoils the metre of lines by having too many syllables in them.

In addition, it has frequently been acknowledged that the various different readings of A and B result in an important divergence in tone and style. Breul comments:

überhaupt bietet B eine etwas feinere fassung, und fast hat es den anschein, als hätten wir es hier mit einer version zu tun, welche die ursprüngliche, oft reichlich derbe romanze für ein besseres publikum gelegentlich leise überarbeitete . . . der ton in A ist frischer und volkstümlicher.[5]

This contrast between the robustness of A and the comparative refinement of B can be seen particularly in lines 55–60 and 187–9, where B's version has been visibly softened and A's reflects the tone and details of the source. During this refinement, it seems to me that B has tended to blur the importance of such motifs as Gowther's sword and the gradual revelation of the princess's love, of which A has a clearer grasp.

It is demonstrable in at least one place that losses to the text had occurred before B was written. Line 448 had disappeared from B's exemplar; there is an attempt to rationalize the resulting discontinuity in sense:

> A. Þo mayden toke too gruhowndus fyn
> And waschyd hor mowþus cleyn with wyn
>   And putte a lofe in þo ton,
>   And in þo todur flesch full gud;
>   He raft boþe owt with eyggur mode

'mancher dieser kurzungen in B sind nicht unpassend und ungeschickt gemacht' (*Sir Gowther*, ed. Breul, p. 5), and indeed the whole question of whether B's omissions were the result, as Breul claims, of deliberate editing must be re-examined.

[4] Breul discusses the possibility that B's extra lines are all that remains of a lost stanza, so that A has actually lost the last 6 lines of stanza 32 and the first 6 of 33, while B has only lost the latter (*Sir Gowther*, ed. Breul, p. 4). Breul rejects this theory in favour of there being a later addition and, since they throw the stanzas out of sequence, leaves them out of his text. It should be noted that B is marked in the margin for stanza division every 6 lines, but the variation *aabccbddeffe* occurs only 8 times, *aabccbddbeeb* being retained elsewhere throughout the poem.

[5] Breul, p. 5.

B.  The lady toke twey greyhoundos fyn
    And wyssh here mouthes clene with wyne
    And put a lofe in that one

    He rawght it fro him with eger mode

Presumably the B scribe did not know about the flesh which Gowther took from the second greyhound, since he now snatches 'it' from 'him' instead of 'both' bread and meat. It is clear that line 448 was once there and has been lost.

B's line losses, some of which disrupt the rhyme scheme and 12-line stanza form which was clearly the form of the original composition, incline me to believe that it represents a corrupt and inferior manuscript tradition, and that the important themes which it weakens but which are given prominence in A are close to the intentions of *Sir Gowther*'s author.

# Bibliography

## 1. PRIMARY TEXTS

ABELARD, PETER, *Epitome theologiae christianae*, PL 178.

—— *Ethics*, PL 178.

AILRED OF RIEVAULX, *Speculum caritatis*, PL 195.

ALAN OF LILLE, *Liber poenitentialis*, PL 210.

ALBERTUS MAGNUS, *Commentaria in librum Danielis*, in *Opera*, 18 (Paris, 1893).

ALEXANDER OF HALES, *Glossa in quattuor libros sententiarum Petri Lombardi*, Bibliotheca Franciscana scholastica medii aevi, 15 (Florence, 1957).

*St Alexius*, ed. F. J. Furnivall, from Bodleian MS Laud Misc. 622, EETS OS 69 (London, 1878; repr. 1973).

AMBROSE OF MILAN, *De poenitentia*, PL 16.

—— *Epistola XX*, PL 16.

*Amis and Amiloun*, ed. MacEdward Leach, EETS OS 203 (London, 1937).

*The English Text of Ancrene Riwle*, ed. M. Day, EETS OS 225 (London, 1952).

*Ancrene Wisse*, ed. J. R. R. Tolkien, EETS OS 249 (London, 1962).

ANSELM OF CANTERBURY, *Cur Deus homo*, ed. F. S. Schmitt (Bonn, 1929).

*Apocrypha and Pseudepigrapha of the Old Testament*, ed. R. H. Charles (2 vols.; Oxford, 1913).

*Apollonius of Tyre*, ed. J. Raith, *Die alt- und mittelenglischen Apollonius Bruchstücke* (Munich, 1956).

AQUINAS, THOMAS, *Quaestiones de potentia Dei*, in *Opera omnia*, 8 (Antwerp, 1612).

—— *Summa theologiae* (Rome, 1962).

*Arthour and Merlin*, ed. O. D. Macrae-Gibson, EETS OS 268 and 279 (London, 1973, 1979).

*Athelston*, ed. A. McI. Trounce, EETS OS 224 (London, 1951; repr. 1984).

*The Auchinleck Manuscript* (facsimile), ed. D. Pearsall and I. C. Cunningham (London, 1979).

AUGUSTINE OF HIPPO, *De civitate Dei*, PL 41.

—— *De poenitentia*, 1, PL 17.

—— *Enchiridion*, 66, *PL* 15.

—— *Epistola LI, CLIII ad Macedonio, CCXXVIII, PL* 33.

—— *In Psalmo CXVIII expositio sermo X, PL* 15.

—— *Sermo XCIX, PL* 38.

—— *Sermo CCCLII, PL* 39.

BASIL THE GREAT, *Epistola*, trans. Sr. Agnes Clare Way, *Fathers of the Church*, 28 (New York, 1955).

BERNARD OF CLAIRVAUX, *De conversione*, *PL* 182.

—— *De gradibus humilitatis, PL* 182.

—— *De modo bene vivendi, PL* 184.

—— *Epistola CXIII, PL* 182.

—— *Sermo in vigilia nativitatis domini, PL* 183.

—— *The Steps of Humility*, trans. G. Bosworth Burch (New York, 1963).

*Beues of Hamtoun*, ed. E. Kölbing, EETS ES 46, 48, 65 (London, 1885, 1886, 1894; repr. as 1 vol., 1973).

*Le Bone Florence of Rome*, ed. C. Heffernan (Manchester, 1976).

ROBERT DE BORON, *Merlin*, ed. W. A. Nitze in *Le Roman de l'Estoire dou Graal* (Paris, 1927), Appendix, pp. 126–30.

BROMYARD, JOHN, *Summa praedicantium* (Venice, 1586).

BROWN, CARLETON, ed., *Religious Lyrics of the Fourteenth Century* (2nd edn. rev. G. Smithers, Oxford, 1957).

BURCHARD OF WORMS, *Decretals, PL* 140.

CAESARIUS OF ARLES, *Homilia XIII, PL* 67.

—— *Sermones CIV, CCXLIX, CCLVI, CCLVIII, CCLXII de poenitentia, PL* 39.

*Cambridge University Library MS Ff. 2. 38* (facsimile), ed. F. MacSparran and P. R. Robinson (London, 1979).

CELESTIN I, *Epistola IV, PL* 50.

CHAUCER, GEOFFREY, *The Riverside Chaucer*, ed. L. D. Benson (Boston, 1987).

CHRÉTIEN DE TROYES, *Erec et Énide*, ed. Mario Roques (Paris, 1952; new edn. Paris, 1978).

CHRYSOSTOM, JOHN, *Ad Theodorum lapsum*, trans. Paul W. Harkins, *Fathers of the Church*, 72 (Washington, 1984).

—— *De beato Philogonio*, trans. Paul W. Harkins, *Fathers of the Church*, 72 (Washington, 1984).

—— *De incomprehensibili Dei natura*, trans. Paul W. Harkins, *Fathers of the Church*, 72 (Washington, 1984).

*Cleanness*, ed. A. C. Cawley (London, 1962).

CLEMENT OF ALEXANDRIA, *Stromateis*, trans. Revd William Wilson, *Ante-Nicene Christian Library*, 12 (Edinburgh, 1869).

*The Clensyng of Mannes Sowle*, MS Bodleian Library 923.

CONDÉ, JEAN DE, *Dits et contes de Baudouin de Condé et de son fils Jean de Condé*, ed. A. Scheler (Brussels, 1866).

*Cursor Mundi*, ed. R. Morris, EETS os 68 (London, 1878; repr. 1966).

CYPRIAN, *De lapsis*, trans. Roy J. Deferrari, *Fathers of the Church*, 36 (New York, 1958).

—— *Epistola* 12, 13, 14, *PL* 4.

DAMIAN, PETER, *Opuscula V*, *PL* 145.

DE BURGO, J., *Pupilla Oculi* (Paris, 1518).

*De vera et falsa poenitentia*, *PL* 40.

ECGBERT, *Dialogus de institutione catholica*, *PL* 89.

*Ecloga Theoduli*, ed. Joannes Osternacher (Urfahr Linz, 1902).

*Sir Eglamour of Artois*, ed. F. E. Richardson, EETS os 256 (London, 1965).

ELIGIUS OF NOYON, *Homilia II* and *Homilia XV*, *PL* 87.

*Emaré*, ed. E. Rickert, EETS es 99 (London, 1908; repr. 1958).

EPIPHANIUS, *Adversus haereses*, trans. O. D. Watkins, *A History of Penance* (London, 1920), 1. 75.

EUCHERIUS, *Homilia V*, *Homilia IX*, *PL* 50.

EUSEBIUS, *Historia ecclesiastica*, trans. Roy J. Deferrari, *Fathers of The Church*, 19 (Washington, 1953).

*Floris and Blancheflur*, ed. A. B. Taylor (Oxford, 1927).

FRENCH, W. H. and HALE, C. B., ed., *Middle English Metrical Romances* (2 vols.; New York, 1930).

FULGENTIUS, *De remissione peccatorum*, *PL* 65.

*Sir Gawain and the Green Knight*, ed. A. C. Cawley (London, 1962).

—— ed. J. R. R. Tolkien and E. V. Gordon (2nd edn. rev. N. Davis; Oxford, 1967).

—— ed. and trans. W. R. J. Barron (Manchester, 1974).

GAYTRIGE, DAN, *Lay Folks' Catechism*, ed. T. F. Simmons and H. E. Nolloth, EETS os 118 (London, 1901; repr. 1973).

*Gesta Romanorum: The Early English Version of the Gesta Romanorum*, ed. S. J. H. Herrtage, EETS es 33 (London, 1879; repr. 1962).

GOWER, JOHN, *Confessio amantis*, in *John Gower's English Works*, ed. G. C. Macaulay, EETS es 81 (London, 1900; repr. 1978).

*Sir Gowther: Eine englische Romanze aus dem XV Jahrhundert*, ed. K. Breul (Oppeln, 1886).

GRATIAN, *Decretals*, *PL* 187.

GREGORY THE GREAT, *Homiliarum in evangelia*, *PL* 76.

*The Grene Knight*, ed. F. J. Furnivall and J. W. Hales, *Bishop Percy's Folio Manuscript: Ballads and Romances* (4 vols.; London, 1867–8; repr. Detroit, 1968), 2.

*Guillaume d'Angleterre*, ed. Maurice Wilmotte (Paris, 1927).

*Gui de Warewic*, ed. A. Ewert, 2 vols. (Paris, 1932, 1933).

*The Romances of Guy of Warwick*, from the Auchinleck MS. and the Caius MS., ed. J. Zupitza, EETS e.s. 42, 49, 59 (London, 1883, 1887, 1891; repr. as 1 vol., 1966).

*The Romance of Guy of Warwick, the 2nd or 15th-cent. version*, ed. Julius Zupitza (London, 1875, 1876; repr. as 1 vol., 1966).

HALITGAR, *Poenitentiale romanum*, *PL* 105.

HALLIWELL, J. O., ed., *The Thornton Romances*, Camden Society, 30 (London, 1884).

HARDYNG, JOHN, *The Chronicle of John Hardyng*, ed. H. Ellis (London, 1812).

HARTMANN VON AUE, *Gregorius*, ed. and trans. S. Z. Buehne (New York, 1966).

HERMAS, *Pastor*, trans. Joseph M. F. Marique, *The Fathers of the Church*, 1 (Washington, 1947).

HIGDEN, RANULPH, *Polychronicon*, trans. John of Trevisa, ed. Churchill Babington (2 vols.; London, 1865).

HORSTMANN, C., ed., *Altenglische Legenden* (Heilbronn, 1881).

HUGH OF ST VICTOIRE, *De sacramentis christianae fidei*, *PL* 176.

—— *Summa sententiarum*, *PL* 176.

INNOCENT I, *Epistola XXV*, *PL* 20.

*Ipomadon*, ed. E. Kölbing (Breslau, 1889).

IRENAEUS, *Contra haereses*, trans. Revd John Keble, *Library of the Fathers*, 42 (London, 1872).

ISIDORE OF SEVILLE, *Etymologiarum libri XX*, *PL* 82.

IVO OF CHARTRES, *Decretals*, *PL* 161.

—— *Epistola CCXXVIII*, *PL* 162.

*Jacob's Well: an English Treatise on the Cleansing of Man's Conscience*, ed. A. Brandeis, EETS OS 115 (London, 1900; repr. 1973).

JEROME, *Commentaria in Danielem*, *PL* 25.

—— *Commentarium in evangelium Matthaei*, *PL* 26.

—— *Dialogus contra Luciferianos*, *PL* 23.

—— *Vita S. Pauli primi eremitae*, *PL* 23.

JOHN OF SALISBURY, *Policraticus*, *PL* 212.

JUSTIN MARTYR, *Apology*, in *The Ante-Nicene Fathers*, 1, trans. A. Roberts and J. Donaldson (New York, 1980).

*The King of Tars*, ed. J. Perryman, Middle English Texts, 12 (Heidelberg, 1980).

LACTANTIUS, *Divinarum institutionum*, *PL* 6.

*Laud Troy Book*, ed. J. E. Wülfing, EETS OS 121, 122 (London, 1902, 1903; repr. as 1 vol., 1973).

LEO I, *Epistola CVIII ad Theodorum* and *Epistola CLXVII ad Rusticum*, *PL* 54.

*Libeaus Desconus*, ed. M. Mills, EETS os 261 (London, 1969).

LOMBARD, PETER, *Sententiae*, 4, *PL* 192.

MANNYNG, ROBERT OF BRUNNE, *Robert of Brunne's 'Handlyng Synne' and its French Original*, ed. F. J. Furnivall, EETS os 119, 123 (London, 1901, 1903; repr. as 1 vol., 1973).

—— *Handlyng Synne*, ed. Idelle Sullens (New York, 1983).

MANSI, GIOVANNI DOMENICO, ed., *Sacrorum consiliorum*, 1–13 (Florence, 1759–67); 14 (Venice, 1769).

MARMOUTIER, JEAN DE, *Gesta consulum andegavorum*, ed. Louis Halphen and René Poupardin, in *Chroniques des comtes d'Anjou et des seigneurs d'Amboise* (Paris, 1913).

*Melusine*, ed. A. K. Donald, EETS es 68 (London, 1895; repr. 1973).

MICHEL, DAN, *Dan Michel's Ayenbite of Inwyt*, ed. R. Morris, EETS os 23 (London, 1866; rev. P. Gradon, repr. 1965).

MIGNE, J. P., ed., *Patrologiae cursus completus series graeca* (Paris, 1857–66).

—— *Patrologiae cursus completus series latinus* (Paris, 1844–65).

MILLS, MALDWYN, ed., *Six Middle English Romances* (London, 1973).

*Morte Arthure*, ed. V. Krishna (New York, 1976).

MOUSKES, PHILIPPE, *Chronique rimée*, ed. J. Reifenberg (2 vols.; Brussels, 1838).

MYRC, JOHN, *Festial*, ed. Theodore Erbe, EETS es 96 (London, 1905; repr. 1973).

—— *Instructions for Parish Priests*, ed. E. Peacock, EETS os 31 (London, 1868; repr. 1973).

*Octovian*, ed. Frances McSparran, EETS os 289 (London, 1986).

*Sir Orfeo*, ed. A. J. Bliss (2nd edn. Oxford, 1966).

ORIGEN, *Commentaria in evangelium secundum Matthaeum*, trans. Revd John Patrick, *The Ante-Nicene Christian Library*, 25 (Edinburgh, 1897).

—— *Homilia in Leviticum*, *PG* (in Latin), 12.

PACIAN, *Paraenesis*, *PL* 13.

PENAFORT, RAYMUND, *Summa casibus* (Rome, 1603; republ. in facsimile, Farnborough, 1967).

PETER OF ALEXANDRIA, *Epistola Canonica*, canons 1, 2, 3, trans. Revd James B. H. Hawkins, *The Ante-Nicene Christian Library*, 14 (Edinburgh, 1873).

PETER OF BLOIS, *De confessione sacramentis*, *PL* 207.

PHILO OF ALEXANDRIA, *On Giants*, in *Works*, trans. C. D. Yonge (4 vols.; London, 1854–5), 1.

—— *Questions and Answers of Genesis*, in *Works*, trans. C. D. Yonge (4 vols.; London, 1854–5), 4.

*The Vision of Piers Plowman*: B text, ed. A. V. C. Schmidt (London, 1978); C text, ed. D. Pearsall (London, 1978).

PLATO, *Meno*, trans. W. C. K. Guthrie (London, 1956; repr. 1982).

POMERIUS, JULIANUS, *De vita contemplativa*, PL 59.

POWICKE, F. M., and CHENEY, C. R., eds., *Councils and Synods with Other Documents Relating to the English Church*, 2 vols. (Oxford, 1964).

*Pricke of Conscience (Stimulus Conscientiae) a Northumbrian Poem by Richard Rolle de Hampole*, ed. R. Morris, Philological Society (Berlin, 1863).

*The Prymer or Lay Folks' Prayer Book*, ed. H. Littlehales, EETS os 105, 109 (London, 1895, 1897; repr. as 1 vol., 1973).

RALPH OF DICETO, *Ymagines historiarum*, ed. W. Stubbs in *The Historical Works of Master Ralph of Diceto*, Rolls Series, 68a (London, 1876).

REGINO OF PRÜM, *Disciplinis ecclesiasticis*, PL 132.

RICHARD OF ST VICTOIRE, *De potestate ligandi et solvendi*, PL 196.

*Richard Coer de Lion*, ed. K. Brunner (Leipzig, 1913).

*Roberd of Cisyle*, ed. Richard Nuck (Berlin, 1887).

*Le Dit de Robert le Diable*, ed. Karl Breul in *Abhandlungen Herrn Professor Dr Adolf Tobler* (Halle, 1895).

*Robert le Diable*, ed. E. Loseth, SATF (Paris, 1903).

*Roberte the Deuyll*, ed. W. E. Hazlitt, *The Remains of the Early Popular Poetry of England*, 1 (London, 1864).

RUMBLE, THOMAS C., ed., *The Breton Lays in Middle English* (Detroit, 1965).

SANDS, D. B., ed., *Middle English Verse Romances* (New York, 1966).

SCHMIDT, A. V. C., and JACOBS, N., eds., *Medieval English Romances* (2 vols.; London, 1980).

SIRICIUS, *Epistola I ad Himerium*, PL 13.

*Speculum Christiani*, ed. G. Holmstedt, EETS os 182 (London, 1933; repr. 1971).

*Speculum Gy de Warewyke*, ed. G. L. Morrill, EETS es 75 (London, 1898; repr. 1973).

*Speculum religiosorum and speculum ecclesie*, ed. H. P. Forshaw, *Auctores Britannici medii aevi*, 3 (London, 1973).

*The Squyr of Lowe Degre*, ed. W. E. Mead (Boston, 1904).

TERTULLIAN, *De poenitentia*, PL 1.

—— *De pudicitia*, PL 2.

THEODULF, *Capitularia*, PL 105.

THOMAS OF CHOBHAM, *Summas confessorum*, ed. F. M. Bromfield, *Analecta medievalia namurcensia*, 25 (Louvain, 1968).

*The Thornton Manuscript*, Lincoln Cathedral MS 91 (facsimile), ed. D. S. Brewer and A. E. B. Owen (London, 1977).

*Torrent of Portyngale*, ed. E. Adam, EETS es 51 (London, 1887; repr. 1973).

*Sir Triamour*, ed. A. J. Erdmann-Schmiat (Utrecht, 1937).

*Tydorel*, ed. G. Paris, 'Lais inédits', *Romania*, 5 (1979), 32–74.

UTTERSON, E. V., *Select Pieces of Early English Popular Poetry* (London, 1817).

*Valentine and Orson*, ed. Arthur Dickson, EETS os 204 (London, 1937; repr. 1971).

*Vices and Virtues*, ed. F. Holthausen, EETS os 89, 159 (London, 1888, 1920; repr. 1967).

*The Book of Vices and Virtues: A Fourteenth Century English Translation of the* Somme Le Roi *of Lorens D'Orleans*, ed. W. Nelson Francis, EETS os 217 (London, 1942; repr. 1984).

WILLIAM OF AUVERGNE, *De sacramento penitentiae*, in *Opera omnia* (Paris, 1674; republ. in facsimile, Frankfurt, 1963).

WULFSTAN, *The Homilies of Wulfstan*, ed. Dorothy Bethurum (Oxford, 1957).

*Sir Ysumbras*, ed. J. Zupitza and G. Schleich, *Palaestra*, 15 (1901).

## 2. SECONDARY TEXTS

AARNE, A., *The Types of the Folk-Tale*, ed. and trans. Stith Thompson (Helsinki, 1928).

ACKERMAN, R. W., 'Gawain's Shield: Penitential Doctrine in *Sir Gawain and the Green Knight*', *Anglia*, 76 (1958), 254–65.

ALLEN, HOPE EMILY, 'Mystical Lyrics of the *Manuel de Pechiez*', *Romanic Review* 9 (1912).

—— *The English Writings of Richard Rolle, Hermit of Hampole* (Oxford, 1931).

ANCIAUX, P., 'Le Sacrément de Pénitence chez Guillaume d'Auvergne', *Ephemerides theologicae lovaniensis*, 24 (1948), 98–107.

—— *La théologie du sacrement de Pénitence au XIIe siècle* (Louvain, 1949).

ARNOULD, E. J., *Le Manuel des péchés: Étude de la littérature religieuse anglo-normande* (Paris, 1940).

ASHDOWN, M., 'Single Combat in Romance', *Modern Language Review*, 17 (1922), 113–30.

AUERBACH, ERICH, *Mimesis*, trans. Willard R. Trask (Princeton, 1953).

BALDWIN, DEAN R., '*Amis and Amiloun*: The Testing of Treuþe', *Papers on Language and Literature*, 16 (1980), 353–63.

BARRON, W. R. J., *English Medieval Romance* (London, 1987).

—— 'Trawpe' and Treason: The Sin of Gawain Reconsidered (Manchester, 1980).

BARROW, S. F., The Medieval Society Romances (New York, 1924).

BAYLEY, JOHN, 'The "Irresponsibility" of Jane Austen', in Critical Essays on Jane Austen, ed. B. C. Southam (London, 1968).

BEDIER, J., Les Légendes épiques (2nd edn. Paris, 1917).

BENNETT, J. A. W., Middle English Literature, ed. and compl. D. Gray (Oxford, 1986).

BERNHEIMER, R., Wild Men in the Middle Ages: A Study in Art, Sentiment and Demonology (Cambridge, Mass., 1952).

BLAICHER, GÜNTHER, 'Zur Interpretation der Mittelenglischen Romanze Sir Ysumbras', Germanische Romanische Monatschrift, NS 21 (1971), 136–43.

BLOOMFIELD, MORTON W., The Seven Deadly Sins (Michigan, 1952).

BOSSUAT, R., Histoire de la littérature française, 1, Le Moyen Age, ed. J. Calvet (2nd edn. Paris, 1955).

BOYD, BEVERLEY, The Middle English Miracles of the Virgin (San Marino, 1964).

BRADSTOCK, MARGARET, 'The Penitential Pattern in Sir Gowther', Parergon, 20 (1974), 3–10.

—— 'Sir Gowther: Secular Hagiography or Hagiographical Romance or Neither?', AUMLA 59 (1983), 26–47.

BRASWELL, LAUREL, 'Sir Isumbras and the Legend of St Eustace', Medieval Studies, 27 (1965), 128–51.

BRASWELL, MARY FLOWERS, 'Confession and Characterisation in the Literature of the Late Middle Ages', unpublished doctoral thesis (Emory University, 1978).

BREWER, D., 'The Nature of Romance', Poetica, 10 (1978), 9–48.

BRODY, SAUL N., Disease of the Soul (London, 1974).

BROWN, CARLETON, and ROBBINS, RUSSELL HOPE, Index of Middle English Verse (New York, 1943).

BRUNNER, KARL, 'Middle English Romances and their Audiences', in Studies in Middle English Literature in Honour of Professor A. C. Baugh, ed. MacEdward Leach (Philadelphia, 1962), pp. 219–27.

BRYAN, W. F., and DEMPSTER, G., eds., Sources and Analogues of Chaucer's Canterbury Tales (Chicago, 1941).

BURROW, JOHN A., Medieval Writers and their Work: Middle English Literature and its Background, 1100–1500 (Oxford, 1982).

—— A Reading of 'Sir Gawain and the Green Knight' (London, 1965).

CALLUS, DANIEL A., Robert Grosseteste (Oxford, 1955).

CHAMBERS, E. K., The Medieval Stage (2 vols.; Oxford, 1903).

CHANDLER, J., 'Some Aspects of the Legend of Merlin as Represented by Celtic Sources and in the Work of Early Chroniclers', M.Litt. thesis (Oxford, 1978).

CHENEY, C. R., *English Synodalia of the Thirteenth Century* (Oxford, 1968).

—— 'Legislation of the Medieval Church', *English Historical Review*, 50 (1935), 193–224, 385–417.

CHILDRESS, DIANA T., 'Between Romance and Legend: "Secular Hagiography" in Middle English Literature', *Philological Quarterly*, 57 (1978), 311–22.

CLIFTON-EVEREST, J. M., *The Tragedy of Knighthood* (Oxford, 1979).

COHN, NORMAN, *Europe's Inner Demons* (London, 1975).

—— *The Pursuit of the Millennium* (London, 1970).

COLEMAN, JANET, *Medieval Readers and Writers* (London, 1981).

COLLIER, J. P., *History of English Dramatic Poetry* (2 vols.; London, 1831).

COOPER, HELEN, 'Magic that Does Not Work', *Medievalia et Humanistica*, NS 7 (1976), 131–46.

CRANE, R. S., 'An Irish Analogue of the Legend of Robert the Devil', *Romanic Review*, 5 (1914), 55–70.

—— 'The Vogue of *Guy of Warwick*', *PMLA* 30 (1915), 125–94.

CRANE, SUSAN, '*Guy of Warwick* and the Question of Exemplary Romance', *Genre*, 17 (1984), 351–74 (as Susan Crane Dannenbaum).

—— *Insular Romance* (London, 1986).

—— 'Insular Tradition in the Story of *Amis and Amiloun*', *Neophilologus*, 67 (1983), 611–22.

DELEHAYE, FR. HIPPOLYTE, *The Legends of the Saints*, trans. V. M. Crawford, ed. R. J. Schoeck (London, 1961).

DICKERSON, ARTHUR INSKIP, 'The Sub-plot of the Messenger in *Athelston*', *Papers on Language and Literature*, 12 (1976), 115–24.

DONALDSON, E. TALBOT, 'Malory and the Stanzaic *Morte Arthure*', *Studies in Philology*, 47 (1950), 460–72.

—— *Speaking of Chaucer* (London, 1977).

DOOB, PENELOPE R., *Nebuchadnezzar's Children: Conventions of Madness in Middle English Literature* (London, 1974).

ENGLEHARDT, G. J., 'The Predicament of Gawain', *Modern Language Quarterly*, 16 (1955), 218–25.

EVANS, W. O., 'The Case for Gawain Re-opened', *Modern Language Review*, 68 (1973), 721–33.

EVERETT, DOROTHY, 'The Characterization of the English Metrical Romances', in *Essays on Middle English Literature* (Oxford, 1955).

FIELD, P. J. C., 'A Re-reading of *Sir Gawain and the Green Knight*', *Studies in Philology*, 68 (1971), 255–69.

FINLAYSON, JOHN, 'Definitions of Middle English Romance', *Chaucer Review*, 15 (1980/1), 44–63 and 168–81.

FOLEY, MICHAEL M., 'Gawain's Two Confessions Reconsidered', *Chaucer Review*, 9 (1974/5), 73–9.

FORD, B., *The Age of Chaucer* (London, 1954).

FOWLER, ALISTAIR, *Kinds of Literature* (Oxford, 1982).

FRIEDMAN, JOHN BLOCH, 'Orfeo, Heurodis and the Noon-day Demon', *Speculum*, 41 (1966), 22–9.

FRYE, NORTHROP, *Anatomy of Criticism* (Princeton, 1957).

—— *The Secular Scripture: A Study of the Structure of Romance* (London, 1976).

GAIDOZ, H., 'L'Amitié d'Amis et Amiles', *Revue Celtique*, 4 (1874), 201–4.

GEROULD, GORDON HALL, 'Forerunners, Congeners and Derivatives of the Eustace Legend', *PMLA* 19 (1904), 335–448.

—— *The Grateful Dead* (London, 1908).

—— 'The Hermit and the Saint', *PMLA* 20 (1905), 529–43.

—— *Saints Legends* (Boston, 1916).

GILLESPIE, VINCENT A., 'The Literary Form of the Middle English Pastoral Manual with Particular Reference to the *Speculum Christiani* and some Related Texts', D.Phil. thesis (Oxford, 1981).

GILSON, ÉTIENNE, *The Mystical Theology of St Bernard*, trans. A. C. Downes (London, 1940).

GOUGAUD, L., *Devotional and Ascetic Practices in the Middle Ages*, trans. G. C. Bateman (London, 1927).

GRAY, DOUGLAS, *Themes and Images in the Middle English Religious Lyric* (London, 1972).

GUDDAT-FIGGE, GISELA, *Catalogue of Manuscripts Containing Middle English Romances* (Munich, 1976).

HARDMAN, PHILIPPA, 'A Medieval Library *in parvo*', *Medium Ævum*, 47 (1978), 262–73.

HIBBARD, LAURA A., *Medieval Romance in England* (rev. edn. New York, 1960).

HILLS, D. F., 'Gawain's Fault in *Sir Gawain and the Green Knight*', *Review of English Studies*, NS 14 (1963), 124–31.

HOOPS, REINALD, 'Der Begriff Romance in der mittelenglischen und fruhnen-englischen Literatur', *Anglistische Forschungen*, 68 (Heidelberg, 1929), 34–7.

HORGAN, A. D., 'Gawain's *Pure Pentaungle* and the Virtue of Faith', *Medium Ævum*, 56 (1987), 310–16.

—— 'Justice in *The Pearl*', *Review of English Studies*, NS 32 (1981), 173–80.

HORNSTEIN, L. H., '*King Robert of Sicily*—Analogues and Origins', *PMLA* 79 (1964), 12–23.

HORNSTEIN, L. H., '*King Robert of Sicily*: A New Manuscript', *PMLA* 78 (1963), 451–8.

HUDSON, HARRIET, 'Middle English Popular Romances: The Manuscript Evidence', *Manuscripta*, 28 (1984), 67–78.

HUME, KATHRYN, '*Amis and Amiloun* and the Aesthetics of Middle English Romance', *Studies in Philology*, 70 (1973), 19–41.

—— 'The Formal Nature of Middle English Romance', *Philological Quarterly*, 53 (1974), 158–80.

—— 'Structure and Perspective: Romance and Hagiographic Features in the Amicus and Amelius story', *JEGP* 69 (1970), 89–107.

HUNT, TONY, 'Gawain's Fault and the Moral Perspectives of *Sir Gawain and the Green Knight*', *Trivium*, 10 (1975), 1–18.

HURLEY, MARGARET, 'Saints' Lives and Romance Again: Secularization of Structure and Motif', *Genre*, 8 (1975), 60–73.

JACOBS, NICOLAS, 'Gawain's False Confession', *English Studies*, 51 (1970), 433–5.

JANSON, HORST W., *Apes and Ape-lore in the Middle Ages and the Renaissance* (London, 1952).

KANE, GEORGE, *The Liberating Truth: The Concept of Integrity in Chaucer's Writings*, John Coffin Memorial Lecture (London, 1979).

—— *Middle English Literature* (London, 1951).

KEEN, MAURICE, *Chivalry* (New Haven and London, 1984).

—— *The Outlaws of Medieval Legend* (London, 1977).

KEMP, E., *Canonization and Authority in the Western Church* (Oxford, 1948).

KER, N. R., *Medieval Libraries of Great Britain* (2nd edn. London, 1964).

KER, W. P., *Epic and Romance* (2nd edn. London, 1908).

KIERNAN, K. S., '*Athelston* and the Rhyme of the English Romances', *Modern Language Queries*, 36 (1975), 339–53.

KIESSLING, NICHOLAS, *The Incubus in English Literature* (Washington, 1977).

KITTREDGE, GEORGE, *Witchcraft in Old and New England* (London, 1927).

KLAUSNER, DAVID N., 'Didacticism and Drama in *Guy of Warwick*', *Medievalia et Humanistica*, NS 6 (1975), 103–19.

KRAMER, D., 'Structural Artistry in *Amis and Amiloun*', *Annuale Medievale*, 9 (1968), 103–22.

KRAPPE, A. H., 'The Legend of Amicus and Amelius', *Modern Language Review*, 18 (1923), 152–61.

—— 'La leggenda di S. Eustachio', *Nuovi studi medievali*, 3 (1928), 223–58.

—— 'An Oriental Theme in *Sir Ysumbras*', *Englische Studien*, 67 (1932), 175–86.

KRATINS, OJARS, 'The Middle English *Amis and Amiloun*: Chivalric Romance or Secular Hagiography?', *PMLA* 81 (1966), 347–54.

LANCASTER, C. M., *Saints and Sinners in Old Romance* (Nashville, 1942).

LEA, HENRY C., *History of Auricular Confession and Indulgences* (3 vols.; London, 1896).

—— *Materials Toward a History of Witchcraft*, arranged and ed. A. C. Howland, 3 vols. (Philadelphia, 1939).

LEACH, H. G., *Angevin Britain and Scandinavia* (Cambridge, Mass., 1921).

LECLERQ, JEAN, *The Love of Learning and the Desire for God*, trans. C. Misrahi (New York, 1961).

LEFF, GORDON, *Bradwardine and the Pelagians* (Cambridge, 1957).

—— *William of Ockham: The Metamorphosis of Scholastic Discourse* (Manchester, 1975).

LEGGE, MARY DOMINICA, *Anglo-Norman Literature and its Background* (Oxford, 1963).

LOOMIS, LAURA HIBBARD, 'The *Athelston* Gift Story', *PMLA* 67 (1952), 521–37.

—— 'The Auchinleck Manuscript and a Possible London Bookshop of 1330–1340', *PMLA* 57 (1942), 595–627.

—— 'Chaucer and the Auchinleck Manuscript: *Sir Thopas* and *Guy of Warwick*', in *Essays and Studies in Honour of Carleton Brown* (New York, 1940), 111–28.

—— 'Chaucer and the Breton Lays of the Auchinleck Manuscript', *Studies in Philology*, 38 (1941), 14–32.

LYNCH, KILIAN F., 'The Doctrine of Alexander of Hales on the Nature of Sacramental Grace', *Franciscan Studies*, 19 (1959), 334–83.

McGRATH, ALISTAIR E., 'Divine Justice and Divine Equity in the Controversy between Augustine and Julian of Eclanum', *Downside Review*, 102 (1984), 312–19.

—— '*Nova et mira diffinitio iustitiae*: Luther and Scholastic Doctrines of Justification', *Archiv für Reformations Geschichte*, 74 (1983), 37–60.

—— 'Rectitude: The Moral Foundation of Anselm of Canterbury's Soteriology', *Downside Review*, 99 (1981), 204–13.

McNEILL, J. T., *The Celtic Penitentials and their Influence* (Paris, 1923).

—— and GAMER, H. M., eds., *Medieval Handbooks of Penance* (New York, 1938).

MAHONEY, E. J., *Sin and Repentance* (New York, 1928).

MARCHALONIS, SHIRLEY L., '*Sir Gowther*: The Process of a Romance', *Chaucer Review*, 6 (1971/2), 14–29.

MEHL, DIETER, *The Middle English Romances of the Thirteenth and Fourteenth Centuries* (London, 1968).

MELITSKY, D., *The Matter of Araby in Medieval England* (New Haven, 1977).

MEYER, P., 'L'Enfant voué au diable', *Romania*, 33 (1904), 163–78.

MICHAUD-QUANTIN, P., *Sommes de casuistique et manuals de confession du moyen âge (XII–XVI siècles)*, Analecta medievalia namurcensia, 13 (Louvain, 1962).

MOORE, A. K., '*Sir Thopas* as a Criticism of 14th Century Minstrelsy', *JEGP* 53 (1954), 532–45.

MORGAN, GERALD, 'The Action of the Hunting and Bedroom Scenes in *Sir Gawain and the Green Knight*', *Medium Ævum*, 56 (1987), 200–16.

MORGAN, HUBERT E., ' "To Be Her Seruant Soþly": Gawain's Service', *English Studies in Canada*, 11 (1985), 273–81.

MORTIMER, R. C., *The Origins of Private Penance in the Western Church* (Oxford, 1939).

MURRAY, J., 'The Eustace Legend in Medieval England', *Modern Humanities Research Association*, 1 (1927), 35–46.

NUIS, HERMIONE J. VAN, 'Gawain's Excesses: The Tension between his Real and Apparent Self', *Concerning Poetry*, 17 (1984), 13–25.

OAKDEN, J. P., *Alliterative Poetry in Middle English* (Manchester, 1935).

OAKLEY, T. P., *English Penitential Discipline and Anglo-Saxon Law in their Joint Influence* (New York, 1923).

O'DONNELL, M. J., *Penance in the Early Church* (Dublin, 1907).

OGLE, M. B., 'The Orchard Scene in *Tydorel* and *Sir Gowther*', *Romanic Review*, 13 (1922), 37–43.

OWST, G. R., *Literature and Pulpit in Medieval England* (Oxford, 1961).

—— *Preaching in Medieval England* (Cambridge, 1926).

PANTIN, W. A., *The English Church in the Fourteenth Century* (Oxford, 1955).

PATTERSON, F. A., *The Medieval Penitential Lyric* (New York, 1911).

PAYEN, J. C., *Le Motif du repentir dans la littérature française médiévale* (Geneva, 1967).

PEARSALL, DEREK, 'The Development of Middle English Romance', *Medieval Studies*, 27 (1965), 91–116.

—— 'John Capgrave's *Life of St Katharine* and Popular Romance Style', *Medievalia et humanistica*, NS 6 (1975), 121–37.

—— 'Middle English Romance and its Audiences', in *Historical and Editorial Studies in Medieval and Early Modern English for Johan Gerritsen*, ed. Mary-Jo Arn and Hanneke Wirtjes (Groningen, 1985), pp. 37–47.

PFANDER, H. G., 'Some Medieval Manuals of Religious Instruction in England and Observations on Chaucer's *Parson's Tale*', *JEGP* 35 (1936), 243–58.

POTTS, T. C., *Conscience in Medieval Philosophy* (Cambridge, 1980).

PROSSER, E., *Drama and Religion in the English Mystery Plays* (Stanford, 1961).

RAMSEY, LEE C., *Chivalric Romances: Popular Literature in Medieval England* (Bloomington, 1983).

RAVENEL, FLORENCE LEFTWICH, '*Tydorel* and *Sir Gowther*', *PMLA* 20 (1905), 152–77.

REEVES, M., *The Influence of Prophecies in the Late Middle Ages* (Oxford, 1969).

REMY, P., 'La Lèpre: Theme littéraire au moyen âge', *Moyen Age*, 52 (1946), 195–227.

RICHMOND, V. B., 'Chaucer's *Book of the Duchess* and *Guy of Warwick*', *Papers on Language and Literature*, 11 (1975), 404–7.

—— '*Guy of Warwick*: A Medieval Thriller', *South Atlantic Quarterly*, 73 (1974), 554–63.

—— *The Popularity of Middle English Romance* (Bowling Green, Ohio, 1975).

ROBERTSON, D. W., 'Certain Theological Conventions in Mannyng's Treatment of the Commandments', *Modern Language Notes*, 61 (1946), 505–19.

—— 'The Cultural Tradition of *Handlyng Synne*', *Speculum*, 22 (1947), 162–85.

—— 'The *Manual de péchés*', *Modern Language Notes*, 61 (1946), 505–19.

—— 'The *Manual de péchés* and an English Episcopal Decree', *Modern Language Notes*, 60 (1945), 439–47.

ROBBINS, ROSSELL HOPE, *Encyclopaedia of Witchcraft and Demonology* (London, 1959).

RONDET, H., *The Theology of Sin*, trans. R. W. Hughes (Notre Dame, Ind., 1960).

ROWLAND, BERYL, *Animals with Human Faces* (Knoxville, 1973).

RUBEL, H. F., 'Chobham's *Penitential* and its Influence in the Thirteenth Century', *PMLA* 40 (1955), 225–39.

RUSSELL, G. H., 'Vernacular Instruction of the Laity in the Later Middle Ages: Some Texts and Notes', *Journal of Religious History*, 2 (1962–3), 98–119.

RUSSELL, J. B., *Religious Dissent in the Middle Ages* (New York, 1971).

SACHS, A., 'Religious Despair in Medieval Literature and Art', *Medieval Studies*, 26 (1964), 231–56.

SAJAVAARA, K., 'The Relationship of the Vernon and Simeon Manuscripts', *Neuphilologische Mitteilungen*, 68 (1967), 428–39.

SANDOZ, E., 'Tourneys in the Arthurian Tradition', *Speculum*, 19 (1944), 389–420.

SAVAGE, E., *Old English Libraries* (London, 1911).

SCHELP, HANSPETER, *Exemplarische Romanzen im Mittelenglischen*, Palaestra 246 (Göttingen, 1967).

SCHLAUCH, MARGARET, 'Historical Precursors of Chaucer's Constance', *Philological Quarterly*, 29 (1950), 402–12.

SEVERS, J. BURKE, *A Manual of Writings in Middle English, 1050–1500*, 1, *Romances* (New Haven, 1967).

SHEDD, G. M., 'Knight in Tarnished Armour: The Meaning of *Sir Gawain and the Green Knight*', *Modern Language Review*, 62 (1967), 3–13.

SICILIANO, F. X., 'Narrative Technique in *Guy of Warwick*', Ph.D. thesis (University of Wisconsin, 1976).

SMITHERS, G. V., 'Story Patterns in Some Breton Lays', *Medium Ævum*, 22 (1953), 61–92.

—— 'What *Sir Gawain and the Green Knight* is About', *Medium Ævum*, 32 (1963), 171–89.

SOUCY, A. FRANCIS, 'Gawain's Fault: "Angardez Pride"', *Chaucer Review*, 13 (1978), 166–76.

SOUTHERN, R. W., *The Making of the Middle Ages* (London, 1953).

—— *Western Society and the Church in the Middle Ages* (London, 1970).

SPEARING, A. C., *The Gawain Poet: A Critical Study* (Cambridge, 1970).

SPEIRS, JOHN, *Medieval English Poetry: The Non-Chaucerian Tradition* (2nd edn. London, 1962).

STEVENS, JOHN, *Medieval Romance: Themes and Approaches* (London, 1973).

SUMPTION, JONATHAN, *Pilgrimage: An Image of Medieval Religion* (London, 1975).

TAYLOR, A. B., *An Introduction to Medieval Romance* (London, 1930).

TEETAERT, A., 'La *Summa de Poenitentia* de Saint Raymond de Penafort', *Ephemerides theologicae lovaniensis*, 5 (1928), 49–72.

TENTLER, T. N., *Sin and Confession on the Eve of the Reformation* (Princeton, 1977).

THOMPSON, STITH, *Motif-Index of Folk Literature* (3 vols.; Copenhagen, 1955–8).

TROUNCE, A. M., 'The English Tail-Rhyme Romances', *Medium Ævum*, 1 (1932), 87–108, 168–82; 2 (1933), 34–57, 189–98; 3 (1934), 30–50.

VARNAGEN, H., *Ein indisches Märchen auf seiner Wanderung durch die asiatischen und europäischen Litteraturen* (Berlin, 1882).

—— *Longfellow's* Tales of a Wayside Inn *und ihre Quellen* (Berlin, 1884).

WATKINS, O. D., *A History of Penance* (London, 1920).

# BIBLIOGRAPHY

WESTON, J. L., *The Three Days' Tournament* (London, 1902).

WIMBERLY, L. C., *Folk-lore in the English and Scottish Ballad* (New York, 1959).

WITTIG, SUSAN, *Stylistic and Narrative Structures in the Middle English Romances* (Austin, 1978).

# Index

Abelard, Peter 47 n., 50, 52, 176
absolution 200, 209
  private 40
  sacerdotal power 46
  sacramental 47, 50, 53, 54, 56
  in *Sir Gowther* 151
Ailred of Rievaulx, *Speculum caritatis* 75 n.
Alan of Lille 45 n., 53 n.
Albertus Magnus 190 n.
Alcuin 43
*Alexander* 5
Alexander of Hales 50, 54
Ambrose, St 39
*Amis and Amiloun* 16–19, 71
*Ancient Mariner, The* 154
*Ancrene Wisse* 24, 31
Andreas Capellanus 7, 76
Anglo-Norman romances 11
Anselm of Canterbury, St 49, 50, 52
Antichrist 167–9
apes, in *Roberd de Cisyle* 188–9
*Apocrypha and Pseudepigrapha of the Old Testament* 165 n.
*Apollonius of Tyre* 10 n.
*Arme Heinreich, Der* 22
*Arthour and Merlin* 4, 167, 168
Arthurian stories 9, 12 n., 165
*Athelston* 11, 12 n., 71, 200, 202–4
  editor A. McI. Trounce 203 n.
atonement 21, 118, 147, 150
  voluntary 35
attrition, introduced and defined by
  William of Auvergne 54–5
Aue, Hartmann von 22, 146 n.
Auerbach, Erich, *Mimesis* 6 n., 7 n.
Augustine of Hippo, St 39, 46 n., 52, 166, 176
Austen, Jane 25, 26, 99 n.
authors (of Romances) 33
*Aye d'Avignon* 203 n.
*Ayenbite of Inwyt* 60

Barron, W. R. J. 180, 206 n., 207, 213–14
  *Medieval English Romance* 3, 28 n., 31 n., 123

Basil the Great, St 39 n.
Bayley, John 25, 26
Beckett, St Thomas 45
Bede 44
Bennett, J. A. W., *Middle English Literature* 13 n.
Bernard of Clairvaux, St 10, 50, 51–2, 66, 186–9, 197
Bertrand of Ray 67
*Beues of Hamtoun* 4, 30 n., 70 n., 71, 73, 220
Blaicher, Günther 132 n., 134, 135, 137, 139, 140, 142
*Boeve de Hamstone* 120
Bonaventure 176
*Bone Florence of Rome, Le* 5, 12 n., 30 n., 121, 128
Boron, Robert de, *Merlin* 167
Bourbon, Étienne de 149
Bradstock, E. M. 144, 145, 175 n.
Braswell, Laurel 13 n., 120–1, 122, 124, 128
Breton lais 158–63
Breul, Karl, Editor of *Sir Gowther* 144 n., 148, 149, 158 n., 159 n., 160 n., 163, 223 n.
Brody, Saul N., *Disease of the Soul* 17 n.
Bromyard, John, *Summa praedicantium* 132, 177
*Bruce* 5
Burke Severs, J., *see* Severs, J. Burke
Burrow, John A. 206, 208, 217 n.
  *A Reading of 'Sir Gawain and the Green Knight'* 22 n.

*Caballero Cifar, El* 120, 135
Caesarius of Arles, St 40
Callistus, Bishop 37
*Canterbury Tales* 24, 74
Cassian 41
*Castle of Love* 220
Celestin I, Pope 47
Celtic Church 41
*Chanson de Roland* 96 n.
*chansons de gestes* 6, 7, 14, 202–3, 203 n.

Charlemagne 43
*Charter of Christ* 220
Chaucer 190 n.
  *Canterbury Tales* 24, 74
  *Sir Thopas* 5, 70 n., 71–4
*Chevalere Assigne* 12 n.
Childress, Diana T. 13 n., 70, 71 n., 121 n.
chivalry 19, 29
Chrétien de Troyes 3, 18, 86
christian morality 8
Cicero 176
*Cleanness* 24, 190
Columbanus, St 43
commutation
  of penance 34, 57–8
  *see also* commutations and indulgences
*Compleynt of God, The* 220
*Confessio amantis* 190
confession 21, 23, 40, 41, 48, 50, 56, 65, 66,
  196, 200, 212
  frequent 55
  second part of penance 60–3
  in *Sir Gawain and the Green Knight* 205
  contrition 36, 39, 53, 196, 197, 199, 216
  according to Hugh of Saint-Victoire 52–3
  according to St Bernard 51
  first part of penance 60–3
  *Guy of Warwick* 108, 116
  importance of 66
  opposed to attrition 54–5
  in romance 68
Contritionists, The 33, 50–5, 66, 68, 108,
  117, 174, 175, 197
corteisie 7
councils
  of Chalons (AD 813) 44
  of Clermont (AD 1095) 57
  Fourth Lateran (AD 1215) 45, 59
  of Nicaea (AD 325) 38
  of Paris (AD 829) 44
  of Tours (AD 813) 44
'Courtly Love' 27, 29
Crane, Susan 68, 76–9, 143
  *Insular Romance* 11 n., 17 n.
*culpa* and *poena* 51, 53, 54, 57–8
culpability 49, 52, 62, 146–7
  of Sir Gawain 206
*Cursor Mundi* 30 n., 60, 64–5, 119–20
*Cymbeline* 156
Cyprian, St 38

Damian, Peter, commutes penance 58
Daniel, Book of 189, 190

Dante 8
*Daurel et Beton* 203 n.
de Boron, Robert, *see* Boron, Robert de
deathbed repentance 40
Decian persecution 37
Delehaye, Fr. Hippolyte 12
*Desiré* 162
divine justice, in *Sir Gowther* 174–8
Donaldson, E. Talbot 76
Donatists 47
Doob, P. R. 191
Duns Scotus 176
Dylan, Bob 25
*Dyoclecyane* 5

Ecgbert 43 n.
*Ecloga Theoduli* 191
Eligius of Noyon 41 n.
*Emaré* 12 n., 121, 128
*Emma* 25, 26
Empire, conversion of 39
*Enfant voué au diable, L'* 163
Englehardt, G. J. 205 n.
Enoch, Book of 165
epic poetry 6, 7
Epiphanius, *Adversus haereses* 36 n.
*Erec et Enide* 85–6
*Erle of Toulous, The* 30 n., 128, 220
Eusebius 36
Eustace, St, *see* St Eustace, Life of
'Eustace-Constance-Florence-Griselda'
  legends 120, 121, 124
Everett, Dorothy 6 n.
exile 67

fasting 64, 137
Field, P. J. C. 208
Finlayson, John 5, 14–19, 75
*Floris and Blancheflur* 10 n.
forgiveness (of sin) 21–2, 34–5, 47, 54–5,
  117, 137, 146, 191–2, 196
  in *Roberd de Cisyle* 191–2
Franciscans 58, 59
free will 49

Gamer, H. M., *see* McNeill, J. T. and
  Gamer, H. M.
*Gaydon* 203 n.
Genesis 165
Gerould, G. H., 'Forerunners, Congeners
  and Derivatives of the Eustace
  Legend' 120, 122

*Gesta Romanorum* 123–4, 140, 180–1
Gilles de Saint-Michel, penance of 45
Godfrey of Poitiers 176
Gospels, of St Matthew and St
    John 34
grace 50, 53–6, 61, 171
    god-given 146–7
*Graf von Savoien, Der* 120
grail romances 15, 16, 19
Gratian 50
Gregorian reforms 50
*Gregorius* 22, 146–7, 198
Gregory the Great, Pope 48, 52
*Grene Knight, The* 205 n.
*Gui de Warewic* 67, 79, 102 n., 103, 112
Guido of Milan, Archbishop 58
*Guillaume d'Angleterre* 120, 135
*gute Frau, Die* 120
Guthrie, W. C. K. 26
*Guy of Warwick* 9, 12, 15, 21, 22, 31, 40,
    68, 131, 133, 142, 144, 179, 196, 197,
    200, 201, 204, 216
    commutation in 57–8
    indulgence in 58
    literary and historical context 72–6
    manuscripts 219–22; number of 30 n.
    Middle English versions of 78–80
    penance in 43, 78, 105–18
    popularity of 70, 119
    presentation and development of Guy's
        character 82–90, 95–101
    as religious romance 76–9
    repentance 102–5
    sin of 81, 103–5, 170
    structure 71–2, 72, 80–2, 90–4

hagiography, secular 12–20, 70
*Handlyng Synne* 31, 60, 63, 196, 220
*Havelok the Dane* 12 n., 203
Hebrews, Epistle to 34
Henry II of England 45
Hermas, *Pastor* 35
Hibbard, L. A. 132
Higden, Ranulf, *Polychronicon* 166
histriones 75 n., 132
homilectic romances 12, 15
Hoops, Reinald 4
Hornstein, L. H. 180, 184 n.
Hudson, Harriet 220
Hugh of Saint Victoire 50, 52–3
Hume, Kathryn 13 n., 17 n.
Hurley, Margaret 13 n.

incestuous Corinthian 34
incubi 162, 163–8
indulgences and commutations 34, 57, 142,
    197
Innocent I, Pope 39 n.
instruction manuals 196
*Ipomedon* 155 n.
Irenaeus, *Contra haereses* 36 n.
Isidore of Seville 165
Ivo of Chartres 51

Jacobs, Nicolas, *see* Schmidt, Carl and
    Jacobs, Nicolas
*Jacob's Well* 60–2, 64, 65
Janson, Horst W., *Apes and Apelore in the
    Middle Ages and the Renaissance* 89 n.,
    188 n.
Jean de Condé, *Li Dis dou Magnificat* 181–
    4, 190
Jedi Knights 4
Jerome, St 39, 47, 52, 165–6, 190 n.
John Chrysostom, St 39
John of La Rochelle 176
Judith, Book of 189
Julianus Pomerius 40
Justin Martyr 165

Kane, George 24, 124 n.
Katherine, St, life of 24, 222
Keen, Maurice, *Chivalry* 19 n.
Ker, W. P., *Epic and Romance* 6 n.
*King of Tars, The* 12 n., 121, 128
Klausner, David N., 'Didacticism and
    Drama in *Guy of Warwick*' 70, 71 n.,
    104
Krappe, A. H., 'La leggenda di S.
    Eustachio' 120
Kratins, Ojars 12, 17 n.

Lactantius 46 n.
*Lamentacio peccatoris* 220
Lancelot 9
*Lancelot* 28
*Lancelot of the Laik* 5
Langton, Stephen 176
*Laud Troy Book* 5, 73
*Lay Folk's Catechism* 60
*Lay Folk's Prayer Book* 60
*Lay le Freine* 158
Lea, H. C. 32 n.
Leach, MacEdward 17 n., 19
Leo I, Pope 40 n., 47

*Li Dis dou Magnificat*, Jean de Condé 181–4, 190
*Libeaus Desconus* 74, 220
Lombard, Peter 45 n., 50, 53

McGrath, Alistair E. 175 n., 176
McNeill, J. T. and Gamer, H. M., *Medieval Handbooks of Penance* 41 n.
Malory 9, 23
'Man tried by fate', story motif or tale type 120–1
Mannying of Brunne, Robert, *Handling Synne* 31, 60, 63, 196, 220
manuals
penitential 29, 34, 41, 69, 105, 174; Penitential of Columbanus 43, 174 n.; Penitential of Cummean 42; Penitential of Finnian 41, 43; Penitential of Theodore 44
vernacular: of confession 60, 62–6, 68–9; of religious instruction 59
Marchalonis, Shirley 144 n., 148 n., 155 n.
Margaret, St, life of 24, 222
Marmoutier, Jean de 45 n.
*Mary Magdalene* 198, 222
Matter of England (— of France, — of Troy) 6
medieval romance, definition of 4, 6, 13, 30
*Meditations on the Life and Passion of Christ* 5
Mehl, Dieter 72, 179, 192
*Middle English Romances of the Thirteenth and Fourteenth Centuries* 6, 12, 70, 71, 122–3, 125, 130–1, 175
*Melusine* 200, 202
*Merlin* 165, 167
Middle English romance, definition and central tradition 11, 12, 13, 30, 77
Mills, Maldwyn 12, 144 n.
Minot, *Poems* 5
miracles of the Virgin 11, 13, 146, 163
Montanist schism 37, 46
Morgan, Gerald 208 n.
*Mort Artu* 9
mortal sin 54, 64, 209
*Morte Arthur* 9
*Morte Arthure* 9, 12 n., 165
*Morte Darthur* 9
Myrc, John 177–8
*Instructions for Parish Priests* 60, 62–4, 65
*Myrour of Lewed Men* 5

Nebuchadnezzar 24, 188, 189–90, 191, 192
Nicaea, Council of 38
Novationist Schism 37–8, 46, 47
Nuck, Richard, editor *Roberd of Cisyle* 179 n., 185, 222 n.

*Octavian* 5, 11, 30, 121, 128, 220
'Ode to a Nightingale' 28–9
Ogle, M. B. 148, 169 n.
Origen 52
seven means to remit sin 37, 48
Orleans, Frère Lorens d', *Somme le Roi* 60
Owst, G. R.
*Literature and Pulpit in Medieval England* 132, 177
*Preaching in Medieval England* 174 n.

Pacian, *Paraenesis* 34 n.
*Parise la Duchesse* 203 n.
*Partenope of Blois* 5
Paul, St 34
Payen, J. C., *Le Motif du repentir dans la littérature française médiévale* 146 n., 171 n.
*Pearl* 174, 176, 213
Pearsall, Derek 6 n., 11
Peckham, Archbishop 59
penance 23, 65, 171, 197, 200, 204–5
alms-giving 132
in the Early Church 35–40
in the gospels 34–5
in *Guy of Warwick* 43, 78, 105–18
history of 32–69
poverty 107, 108, 116
prayer, fasting and almsgiving 64
public penance 32–41, 43, 44, 51, 64, 69, 137, 197
in *Roberd of Cisyle* 190–1, 194–5
in romance 21–3, 31, 35, 62, 66–9
sacrament of 29, 33, 45, 50, 52–6, 57, 69, 117, 196, 197, 209
in *Sir Gawain and the Green Knight* 209
in *Sir Gowther* 43, 54, 145–57, 152–7, 170–5, 178
in *Sir Ysumbras* 43, 125, 132–9, 142–3, 154–5
as social therapy 42
solemn penance 32, 45, 68, 69
three parts of 60–3
two types of 52
voluntary 35, 40, 62
penitential handbooks 196, 212

penitential pattern in romances 115–16,
121, 144–5, 179, 194, 198, 205, 216
penitential romances 20–3, 68, 196–7,
197–8, 205, 209
Peraldus, Guglielmus, *Summa virtutum ac
vitiorum* 60
*Pericles* 28
Peter of Blois, *De confessione sacramentali*
75 n.
Philo of Alexandria 165
pilgrimage 21, 116, 196–7
Plato, *Meno* 26
*poena see culpa* and *poena*
Power of the Keys 45, 47, 52
preaching 58
*Pricke of Conscience* 31, 60, 196, 219, 220
pride 65, 78, 81, 105, 116, 132–3, 186–7,
195
*Pride and Prejudice* 99 n.
'Proud King Humbled' 180–1
purgatory 51, 52

Radulphus Totarius 17 n.
Ralph of Diceto 45 n.
Ramsey, Lee C., *Chivalric Romances;
Popular Literature in Medieval
England* 13 n., 70 n.
Ravenel, Florence Leftwich 148–9
Raymund Penafort, St 53 n.
'recognition', literary technique 25–9
reconciliation 39, 41, 43, 46, 137
Regino of Prüm 41 n., 44
Reinbrun 78, 79
religious romances 12–20, 197–8
remission, of sin
*culpa* and *poena* 51, 53, 54, 57–8
two kinds of 52
repentance 23, 52–6, 171
in *Guy of Warwick* 102–5
in *Roberd of Cisyle* 189, 193
sign of divine pardon 50
in *Sir Gawain and the Green Knight* 205
repetition with variation, in *Guy of
Warwick* 82, 90–4
*Richard Coer de Lion* 5, 73, 155 n., 167, 202
Richard of Saint Victoire 50, 53–4
*Roberd of Cisyle* 12, 16, 22, 71, 121, 122,
123, 125, 133, 139, 144, 196–7, 197,
200, 201, 204, 216
apes in 188–9
comparison with *Li Dis dou Magnificat*
181–4
ending of 115

forgiveness in 191–2
sin in 182, 186–7, 192
manuscripts 219–22; number of 30 n.,
179 n.
penance in 43, 190–1, 194–5
popularity of 179
repentance in 189, 193
sources and analogues 180–5
structure 195; similar to *Sir
Ysumbras* 185
*Robert the Devil* 139, 147, 172, 201, 202
*Robert le Diable* 200
compared with *Sir Gowther* 145–57, 161
Robert of Normandy 45
*Roland and Otuel* 5
*roman courtois* 15
romance
definition 1
exemplary 11, 76
idea of 1–12
in literature 1, 30
medieval 4, 6, 13, 30
penitential romances 20–3, 196–7,
197–8, 205
religious romances 12–20, 77, 197–8
semantic history 4–5
typical storyline 7–8
*romanz* 4
*Romauns of Partenay, The* 5, 22, 67
*Romaunt of the Rose* 5
Round Table 9

sacraments
necessity of 54–5
seven 50
*St Alexis, Life of* 19, 70, 78, 105, 198, 200
*St Eustace, Life of* 21, 120, 121, 124, 198,
222
compared with *Sir Ysumbras* 125–8,
134–5, 139, 141
*St Gregory* 5
*St Katherine, Life of* 24
*St Margaret, Life of* 24
*St Paul the First Hermit, The Life of* 166
saints, lives of 11, 12, 13, 16, 19, 22, 24, 77,
115, 146, 198, 222
satisfaction, final part of penance 60–3
Schelp, Hanspeter 12, 70, 71 n., 72, 81
structure of *Guy of Warwick* 72
Schleich, Gustav, editor of *Sir
Ysumbras* 119 n., 133 n., 141 n.
Schmidt, Carl and Jacobs, Nicolas,
*Medieval English Romances* 6, 8–9

secular hagiography 12–20, 70
*Seege of Troye, The* 222
*Sege of Melayne, The* 12 n.
sermon exempla 13, 20, 60, 146
sermons 196
Severs, J. Burke, *A Manual of Writings in Middle English* 5 n., 6, 71 n., 120 n., 144 n.
*Siege of Thebes* 12 n.
Simon of Hinton 176
sin 171, 200, 204–5
　forgiven 197
　forgiveness of 21–2, 34–5, 47, 54–5, 117, 137, 146, 191–2, 196
　Gregorius-type 200
　in *Guy of Warwick* 81, 103–5, 170
　mortal 54, 64, 209
　nature of, according to Peter Abelard 52
　original 176
　post-baptismal, unforgivable 34
　in *Roberd of Cisyle* 186–7, 192
　in romances 20, 23, 31
　in *Sir Gawain and the Green Knight* 209
　in *Sir Gowther* 146–7, 150
　of *Sir Ysumbras* 131, 132, 139–42, 170
　three unforgivable 34
　two types of 52
　*see also* remission, of sin
*Sir Cleges* 12 n.
*Sir Degaré* 30 n., 220
*Sir Eglamour of Artois* 5, 11, 30 n., 121, 128, 220
*Sir Gawain and the Green Knight* 22, 23, 200, 204–18
*Sir Gowther* 5, 12, 20, 21, 22, 65, 67, 71, 121, 125, 139, 196–7, 197, 201, 204, 205, 209, 216
　as a Breton lai 158–63
　common elements with *Sir Ysumbras* 142–3
　comparison with *Robert le Diable* 145–57, 161
　divine justice in 174–8
　ending of 115
　incubi in 163–8
　indulgence in 57
　manuscripts 219–22, 223–5
　penance in 43, 54, 145–7, 152–7, 170–5, 178
　sin 146–7, 150
　sources and analogues 147–57
　structure 144–5, 150
*Sir Orfeo* 10, 11, 158, 159, 160–1

*Sir Perceval of Gales* 5
*Sir Thopas* 5, 70 n., 71–4
*Sir Torrent of Portyngale* 5, 11, 121, 128
*Sir Triamour* 11, 30 n., 121, 128
*Sir Ysumbras* 5, 10, 11, 12, 16, 20, 22, 40, 71, 144, 154, 196, 204, 205, 216, 223 n.
　common elements with *Sir Gowther* 142–3
　commutation in 57
　compared with Legend of St Eustace 125–8
　ending of 115
　manuscripts 219–22; number of 30 n., 119 n.
　penance in 43, 125, 132–9, 142–3, 154–5
　popularity of 70, 119–20
　as religious romance 75
　sin of 131, 132, 139–42, 170
　sources and analogues 120–8
　structure of 125, 129–30
Siricius, Pope 39
Skywalker, Luke 4
Smithers, G. V., 'Story Patterns in some Breton Lays' 161–2
Socrates 26
'Solemn Penance' 197
Southern, R. W., *The Making of the Middle Ages* 2–3, 49
*Sowdane of Babylone, The* 5
*Speculum Christiani* 60
*Speculum Gy de Warewyke* 215 n., 220, 222
*Speculum Vitae* 70 n., 73 n., 74–5, 119–20, 220
*Stans puer ad mensam* 222
Star Wars 1, 3–4
Stevens, John, *Medieval Romance: Themes and Approaches* 1–2

*Tales of a Wayside Inn*, H. W. Longfellow 180
*Tempest, The* 28
Tertullian 34 n., 36
Theodore of Tarsus, Archbishop 43, 44
theology, of sin and penance 46–56, 58
Thomas Aquinas, St 45 n., 56, 166
Thomas of Chester, *Lybeaus Desconus* 74
*Trentall of St Gregory* 220
*Tydorel* 148–9, 153, 161–2

Urban II, Pope 57
*Urbanitas* 222

*Valentine and Orson* 22, 67, 200–1, 202
vassalage 7
*Vices and Virtues* 60
*Vie des Pères* 170
*Vie du Pape Gregoire* 170
*Vie du saint Sauveur l'ermite, La* 163
*Vision of Tundale* 220

Watkins, O. D., *A History of Penance* 34
*Wilhelm von Wenden* 120, 135
William of Auvergne 54–5
William of Auxerre 176

William of Nassyngton, and *Speculum
    Vitae* 70 n., 73 n., 74–5, 119–20
Wulfstan, *Homilies* 169 n.
Wynkyn de Worde 148 n.

*Yonec* 161
*Ypotis* 73–4
*Yvain* 28

Zupitza, Julius
    editor of *Guy of Warwick* 79 n., 80, 94 n.
    joint editor *Sir Ysumbras* 119 n.